Dream Big, Aim High and Soar

Become a Rocket Scientist

Ignatious Antony

Dedication

To my family, whose unwavering support and encouragement have guided me every step of the way.

To my parents, whose love and sacrifices have been my constant source of strength and inspiration.

To my friends, whose belief in me has never wavered, even in the face of challenges.

To my mentors and teachers, who have inspired me to reach for the stars and believe in the power of perseverance and hard work.

To the dreamers and the doers, who remind us that everything is possible with a journey of clear purpose, resilience, perseverance and actions.

And to all who strive to create their own good future, may this book serve as a guide and a testament to the power within you.

With deepest appreciation and gratitude,

Ignatious Antony

Acknowledgements

I am deeply grateful to many people who have supported and inspired me throughout the journey of writing this book.

First and foremost, my heartfelt thanks go to my beloved wife, Annie. Your unwavering love, patience, and encouragement have been my greatest sources of strength. To my son, Anil, and my daughter, Aneena, thank you for your understanding and for always being a source of joy and inspiration.

I wish to pay special tribute to my late father and mother, Antony and Celine, whose wisdom and guidance continue to influence my life. Thank you for your endless love and support.

I express my gratitude to my elder sister, Ms. Baby Varghese, for her constant support and encouragement. My brothers, Dr. Paul Chakkalakkal and James C.A., have helped me immensely in my journey so far. I express my profound gratitude to them.

Finally, I extend my deepest gratitude to all my teachers who taught me to read and write. Your dedication and passion for teaching have shaped who I am today, and for that, I am eternally grateful.

Ignatious Antony

Published by: Ignatious Antony

First Edition: June 2024

Disclaimer:

This book is intended for informational purposes only. The views expressed in this book are the author's own and do not constitute professional advice. The author and publisher disclaim any liability for any direct, indirect, incidental, or consequential damages arising from the use of the information provided in this book. The reader is encouraged to seek professional guidance and conduct their own research before making any decisions based on the information contained herein.

Contact Us:

Please send all your suggestions and remarks in the following

email id: ignatious.luck@gmail.com

Table of Contents

1. INTRODUCTION 15

2. WHY YOU SHOULD BECOME A SCIENTIST: 17

3. A ROCKET-FUELLED EXPLORATION 17

4. UNDERSTANDING THE ROCKET AND ROLE OF A ROCKET SCIENTIST 37

5. ACADEMIC BACKGROUND OF ROCKET SCIENTISTS 85

6. SCIENCE: THE FOUNDATION OF ROCKET SCIENCE 85

7. HISTORY OF ROCKETRY AND EARLY EXPERIMENTS: 120

8. FROM FIREWORKS TO FIRST FLIGHTS 120

9. THE STORY OF ROCKETS IN INDIA 137

10. PRIVATELY OWNED LAUNCH VEHICLE STARTUPS 163

11. SKYROOT AEROSPACE 163

12. AGNIKUL COSMOS 171

13. WORLDWIDE ROCKET LAUNCHING AGENCIES, 179

14. WHERE ROCKET SCIENTISTS ARE BEING MADE. 179

15. HOW TO BECOME A ROCKET SCIENTIST 184

16. WHAT MAKES A ROCKET SCIENTIST 236

17. PLAN OF ACTION TO BECOME A ROCKET SCIENTIST 308

18. THE THINKING PROCESS OF ROCKET SCIENTISTS 321

19. ADVANCING AS A ROCKET SCIENTIST 358

20. CONCLUSION 369

21. TO A DREAMING ROCKET SCIENTIST 372

22. ANNEXURE: 374

23. ABOUT THE AUTHOR 389

24. BIBLIOGRAPHY 391

Dream Big, Aim High, and Soar

Dream big, young heart, let your visions unfurl,
Like a vibrant tapestry woven across the world.
The cosmos, a canvas, awaits your own hue,
Where your story, like a shooting star, streaks anew.

With eyes set on stardust, your feet firmly hold,
Like a mountain rooted, yet yearning for gold.
Aim high, dear girl, where galaxies gleam,
For wonders abound, a celestial dream.

Embrace each new challenge, a dragon you'll slay,
With courage that roars and grace that lights the way.
Resilience your armour, strength your guiding star,
Through trials you'll navigate, no matter how far.

Curiosity's lantern shall pierce the unknown,
Like a beacon that beckons, where secrets are sown.
With science, a scalpel, dissect every why,
Unravel the mysteries, reach for the sky.

In dreams, a compass, your true north defined,
With positive sails, catch the future's kind wind.
Soar high, young dreamer, let ambitions ignite,
A rocket scientist you'll be, bathed in starlight.

For within your grasp, the future takes flight,
A blazing phoenix, on wings of pure light.
Dreams, like constellations, map your own way,
Shine on, young explorer, illuminate the day!

Chapter 1

Introduction

Have you ever looked up at the night sky, captivated by the sparkling stars, and imagined yourself traveling beyond our atmosphere? Does the idea of designing rockets, exploring distant planets, and pushing the boundaries of space travel ignite a fire in your soul? If so, then "Dream Big, Aim High, and Soar - Become a Rocket Scientist" is your launchpad to a phenomenal journey!

This book is your one-stop guide to transforming that childhood dream into a tangible reality. We'll blast off by unveiling the secrets of this fascinating field, delving into the core principles of rocket science and the remarkable minds that have shaped its history.

But this isn't just a theoretical exploration. We'll equip you with the essential tools and strategies you need to take flight. From setting clear goals and igniting your passion to developing a structured plan and building unwavering resilience, this book will be your compass on your journey to the stars.

We'll explore the educational paths you can take, highlight the exciting career options that await, and share the invaluable wisdom of those who have already charted their course through the cosmos. Get ready to be inspired by the stories of pioneering rocket scientists, their triumphs and challenges, and the unwavering spirit of exploration that fuels their endeavours.

So, get ready, future space explorer! "Dream Big, Aim High and Soar: Become a Rocket Scientist" is your invitation to ignite your passion, unlock your potential, and become a part of the extraordinary legacy of those who dared to reach for the stars. It's time to turn your dreams into reality, one rocket launch at a time!

By implementing the strategies outlined in this book, you can forge a path towards your dream career. Stay dedicated, fuel your curiosity with every challenge, and never stop reaching for the stars. Your unwavering commitment and hard work will pave the way for a future, where humanity's footprint extends beyond our planet, a testament to the enduring human spirit of exploration. Remember, as Neil Armstrong eloquently stated as he stepped onto the moon, "That's one small step for a man, one giant leap for mankind." The future of space exploration rests in your hands. So, take that first step, and embark on your own incredible journey to the stars.

In the Annexure, you will find the names of several institutions that offer Graduate, Post Graduate, and Doctoral programs designed to equip aspiring young scientists to become professional rocket scientists and engineers. Additionally, a detailed plan of action for pursuing a career in rockets and space exploration is provided.

Chapter 2.

Why You Should Become a Scientist:

A Rocket-Fuelled Exploration

Have you ever gazed at the stars, a million tiny diamonds scattered across velvet darkness, and wondered what lies beyond? Have you ever gazed up at the night sky and felt a sense of wonder and curiosity about the universe? Have you ever been captivated by the mysteries of the cosmos and the potential for human exploration beyond our planet? Or, perhaps, you tinker with gadgets, take apart toasters just to see how they tick, and dream of one day building something that soars beyond the atmosphere? If this resonates with you, then my friend, you might be naturally inclined towards a career in Science and Engineering. You too can aspire to become a rocket scientist, might be your perfect launchpad. Becoming a scientist, especially a rocket scientist, offers a unique and fulfilling journey filled with intellectual challenges, the thrill of discovery, and the opportunity to make significant contributions to humanity's understanding of the universe.

At the same time, being a scientist isn't just about spaceships and distant galaxies (though, those are pretty awesome perks). It's a mindset, a way of approaching the world. *One of the fundamental qualities of a scientist is an insatiable curiosity*. As a scientist, you'll constantly ask questions and seek answers about how the world works. This mindset drives you to explore the unknown, challenge existing knowledge, and push the boundaries of what's possible. Whether you're investigating the properties of matter at the quantum level or developing new technologies for space exploration, your curiosity will be your guiding star. Imagine yourself as a detective, constantly curious, questioning everything. You see an anomaly, a bump in the data, a flickering light in the night sky, and your mind races with possibilities. Is it a new type of star? A quirk in the machine? This insatiable curiosity fuels your relentless pursuit of knowledge.

Scientific research is not just about finding answers but also about discovering new questions. This process of continual inquiry is both intellectually stimulating and deeply rewarding. It's a journey that requires patience, creativity, and a willingness to embrace uncertainty. In the words of Albert Einstein, *"The important thing is not to stop questioning. Curiosity has its own reason for existence."*

The life of a scientist is one of continuous learning and discovery. You'll work on the frontiers of knowledge, conducting experiments, analyzing data, and developing theories that advance our understanding of the natural world. Your daily routine might involve complex problem-solving, collaborative projects with other scientists, and the use of cutting-edge technology.

Rocket scientists, in particular, experience the unique thrill of contributing to space exploration. Imagine working on missions that send satellites into orbit, land rovers on Mars, or even plan future manned missions to other planets. The sense of achievement and pride that comes from being part of such groundbreaking projects is unparalleled.

Moreover, the scientific community is a global network of like-minded individuals who share your passion for discovery. You'll have the opportunity to attend conferences, publish your research, and collaborate with experts from around the world. This community not only supports your professional growth but also fosters a sense of belonging and purpose.

The life of a scientist isn't always glamorous. There are long nights hunched over microscopes, pages filled with complex equations, and experiments that fizzle more often than they fly (pun intended!). But there's a certain thrill in the chase, the slow burn of discovery. Every failed experiment brings you closer to the answer, every setback a stepping stone on the path to a breakthrough.

Then, there's the moment of revelation. It might be a sudden flash of insight, a eureka! echoing in the lab, or the quiet satisfaction of a perfectly executed experiment that confirms your hypothesis. This is the magic that keeps scientists going, the knowledge that their work has the potential to change the world.

Rocket science, in particular, pushes the boundaries of human achievement. You'll be part of a team of visionaries, engineers, and physicists, all working together to push the limits of what's possible. Imagine the impact: developing sustainable space travel, unraveling the mysteries of the cosmos, or even colonizing new worlds. The possibilities are as vast as the universe itself.

But here's the real kicker: becoming a scientist isn't about personal glory (though a Nobel Prize would be nice!). It's about contributing to the grand tapestry of human knowledge. Your discoveries could have a ripple effect, impacting fields you never even imagined.

It courses through your veins, doesn't it? That insatiable itch to unravel the universe's deepest secrets? You stare up at the night sky, a canvas ablaze with a million burning questions. What lies beyond those twinkling specks? Are we alone? This primal urge to understand, to pierce the veil of the unknown – that's the fire that burns within a scientist, and it burns brightest within a rocket scientist like you.

Here's the reality: pursuing science isn't merely a career choice; it's a bold defiance against the ordinary. You refuse to settle for the status quo. To you, the world is a puzzle filled with mysteries waiting to be unravelled. Each equation you solve, every experiment you perform, is a small triumph in the larger battle against ignorance. You are an innovator, a creator of dreams. Picture the exhilaration of building a machine that defies gravity, a vessel that carries humanity's hopes and dreams into the boundless unknown. That is the power you will hold as a rocket scientist.

But science isn't just about cold logic and sterile labs. It's about the primal human urge to explore and conquer new frontiers! Think about the explorers of old, braving uncharted oceans in search of new worlds. You, my friend, are an explorer of the cosmos. Every new planet you discover, every celestial body you analyze, is a fresh page in the story of existence. The spirit of Meriwether Lewis and William Clark, the daring American explorers, and Vasco da Gama, the intrepid Portuguese navigator, flows through your veins, urging you to push the boundaries of human knowledge.

And here's the most incredible part: it all matters. Your discoveries, your innovations, they ripple outwards, impacting fields you never even imagined. Your work will not only satisfy your intellectual curiosity but also contribute to the collective knowledge and progress of humanity.

In addition, science and technology play a crucial role in shaping the future. From developing sustainable energy solutions to advancing medical research and exploring space, scientists are at the forefront of addressing the world's most pressing challenges. As a scientist, you'll have the opportunity to make a meaningful impact on society and inspire future generations to follow in your footsteps. A new rocket propulsion system might lead to cleaner energy on Earth. Research on space radiation could revolutionize cancer treatment. The connections may not always be obvious, but they are there, waiting to be unearthed.

The Attractions of a Scientific Career: Launching Your Dreams

Embarking on a career in science, particularly rocket science, offers a multitude of compelling reasons to dive into this fascinating field. Here are some reasons why this path is so exciting:

1. Intellectual Challenge: A Never-Ending Puzzle

Science is an endless quest for knowledge, a thrilling puzzle waiting to be pieced together. Every discovery, every breakthrough, fuels your desire to learn more. Think of it as a lifelong adventure, where the next challenge is always just around the corner.

"Somewhere, something incredible is waiting to be known." – Carl Sagan

Imagine yourself like **Stephen Hawking**, delving into the mysteries of black holes. Despite his physical limitations, Hawking's intellectual curiosity led him to propose groundbreaking theories about the nature of black holes and the universe. Your journey in science could lead to similarly profound discoveries, constantly challenging and expanding your understanding of the cosmos.

Think yourself unraveling the mysteries of the cosmos like the legendary **Katherine Johnson** who was an extraordinary mathematician, whose calculations were instrumental in the success of several NASA space missions, including the Apollo moon landings. Working at NASA's Langley Research Center, she made critical contributions to the trajectory analysis for the first American in space, Alan Shepard, and the first human landing on the moon with Apollo 11. Her work with complex orbital mechanics and her ability to solve equations by hand were pivotal in ensuring the safety and success of these missions.

Or imagine yourself as **Jane Goodall**, who is a renowned primatologist and anthropologist who revolutionized our understanding of chimpanzees. Through her groundbreaking research in Gombe Stream National Park, Tanzania, she observed chimpanzees making and using tools, a behaviour previously thought to be unique to humans. Her detailed observations and documentation of chimpanzee social and familial behaviours revealed striking similarities between chimpanzees and humans, challenging long-held beliefs and reshaping our understanding of primate behaviour. Goodall's work has had a profound impact on the fields of ethology and anthropology, and she has been a tireless advocate for wildlife conservation and animal welfare. Her dedication and passion continue to inspire people around the world to appreciate and protect our closest animal relatives.

Science is a playground for curious minds, constantly challenging you to think critically and creatively.

2. Innovation and Creativity: Building the Impossible

Science isn't just about memorizing facts; it's about pushing the boundaries of what we know. As a scientist, you'll be an innovator, a sculptor of the future.

"Two things are infinite: the universe and human stupidity; and I'm not sure about the universe." – Albert Einstein

Think of yourself as **Wernher von Braun** who was a pioneering aerospace engineer and rocket scientist, who played a crucial role in the development of rocket technology in both Germany and the United States. After World War II, he was brought to the U.S. and became a key figure in the American space program. Von Braun was instrumental in developing the Saturn V rocket, which enabled the Apollo missions to reach the moon. His leadership and expertise as the director of NASA's Marshall Space Flight Center significantly advanced human space exploration. His work laid the foundation for modern rocketry and space travel, making him one of the most influential figures in the history of space exploration.

Picture yourself like **Elon Musk**, taking revolutionary ideas and turning them into reality. Musk's work on reusable rockets with SpaceX has transformed space travel, making it more sustainable and cost-effective. Your role as a scientist will involve similar feats of innovation, whether it's developing new technologies or finding creative solutions to complex problems.

As a scientist, you'll be a sculptor of the future, just like **Mae Jemison**. The first African-American woman in space, she didn't just break barriers; she also conducted valuable research on bone density loss during spaceflight, pushing the boundaries of medical science.

Channel your inner **Marie Curie**, whose pioneering work on radioactivity not only led to groundbreaking discoveries but also opened doors for women in science. Innovation is the lifeblood of scientific progress, and you'll be right at the forefront, crafting solutions and shaping the world of tomorrow.

As a rocket scientist, you will outperform **Kalpana Chawla** who was an Indian-American astronaut and aerospace engineer who made history as the first woman of Indian origin to go to space. Born in Karnal, India, she pursued her dreams of flight and space exploration, earning a doctorate in aerospace engineering. Chawla's first space mission was aboard the Space Shuttle Columbia in 1997, where she served as a mission specialist and primary robotic arm operator. She returned to space in 2003 on the ill-fated STS-107 mission, which tragically ended when the Columbia disintegrated upon re-entry into Earth's atmosphere. Despite this tragedy, Chawla's legacy continues to inspire millions. She is remembered for her passion, dedication, and the pioneering spirit that broke barriers for women and people of Indian descent in the field of space exploration.

3. Impact and Contribution: Leaving a Mark on Humanity

The work you do as a scientist has the potential to change the world. Maybe it's developing new sustainable energy sources like Sally Ride envisioned, or perhaps it's pioneering new medical treatments like **Mae Jemison**, the first African-American woman in space. Your discoveries could ripple outwards, impacting fields you never even imagined.

"The important thing is not to stop questioning. Curiosity has its own reason for existing." – Albert Einstein

Reflect on the contributions of **Rosalind Franklin**, whose work on X-ray diffraction was crucial to understanding the structure of DNA. Her meticulous research paved the way for significant advancements in genetics and medicine. Your work as a scientist could have a similar far-reaching impact, addressing some of the world's most pressing challenges.

4. Exploration and Adventure: Reaching for the Stars

Space is the ultimate frontier, and becoming a rocket scientist, puts you at the forefront of exploration. The thrill of pushing the limits of human knowledge, venturing into the unknown, is a powerful motivator.

"The sky calls to us. If we do not destroy ourselves, we will one day venture to the stars." – Carl Sagan

Imagine yourself like **Neil Armstrong,** taking humanity's first steps on the moon. Armstrong's historic achievement was the result of years of meticulous planning, innovation, and bravery. As a rocket scientist, you will be part of missions that explore new worlds, unravel the mysteries of the cosmos, and push humanity further into space. Space is the ultimate frontier, and becoming a rocket scientist puts you at the forefront of exploration.

Imagine yourself like **Sally Ride**, the first American woman in space, who conducted groundbreaking research on space physiology.

5. Collaboration and Community: A Network of Support

The scientific community thrives on collaboration. You'll work alongside brilliant minds from diverse backgrounds, sharing knowledge and building lasting connections. This camaraderie fosters a supportive and stimulating environment, where you can learn from your peers and push each other to achieve even greater things.

"Science is a beautiful thing and, like all beautiful things, it is difficult." – Marie Curie

Think about the collaboration that brought the International Space Station (ISS) to life. Scientists and engineers from around the world worked together to create a laboratory in orbit, fostering international cooperation and scientific advancement. Your career in science will involve similar collaborations, making new friends and colleagues while achieving extraordinary things together.

The scientific community thrives on collaboration. You'll work alongside brilliant minds from diverse backgrounds, just like the team behind the **James Webb Space Telescope**. This marvel of engineering is a testament to the power of international cooperation, with scientists from NASA, ESA, CSA, and JAXA coming together to create a revolutionary tool for astronomical exploration.

Think about the countless researchers who contributed to the **Human Genome Project**, a massive undertaking that mapped the entire human genetic code. Your career in science will be a collaborative journey, fostering friendships and achieving extraordinary things together.

6. Lifelong Learning: A Journey of Discovery Never Ends

Science is a dynamic field, constantly evolving with new discoveries. As a scientist, you'll be a lifelong learner, continually expanding your knowledge and adapting to new challenges.

"I do not know what I may appear to the world, but to myself, I seem to have been only like a boy playing on the seashore, and diverting myself in now and then finding a smoother pebble or a prettier shell than ordinary, whilst the great ocean of truth lay all undiscovered before me." – Isaac Newton

Consider first flight of the Wright brothers, Orville and Wilbur Wright, who were pioneering American inventors and aviation pioneers who are credited with inventing, building, and flying the world's first successful motor-operated airplane. On December 17, 1903, near Kitty Hawk, North Carolina, they achieved the first powered, controlled, and sustained flight of an airplane with their aircraft, the Wright Flyer. Their innovative design included a three-axis control system, which is still used in modern aircraft. The Wright brothers' groundbreaking work laid the foundation for the field of aviation and transformed the way people travel, connect, and understand the world. Their insatiable curiosity and dedication to learning, propelled them to achieve this incredible feat.

Science and Technology is a dynamic field, ever-evolving with new breakthroughs.

Picture yourself like **Galileo Galilei**, who revolutionized our understanding of the cosmos through his pioneering observations with the telescope. His relentless curiosity and willingness to challenge established ideas are hallmarks of the scientific spirit. As a scientist, you'll be a lifelong learner, forever on a quest to unravel the universe's mysteries.

7. Personal Growth and Problem-Solving Skills

Science demands a meticulous approach, honing your critical thinking and problem-solving abilities. You'll learn to analyze data, troubleshoot challenges, and develop innovative solutions.

"We cannot solve our problems with the same thinking we used when we created them." – Albert Einstein

Imagine you're faced with a malfunction in a critical component of your spacecraft, similar to the Apollo 13 mission. Your ability to think on your feet, analyze the situation, and develop a solution could save the mission. This problem-solving prowess is what sets scientists apart. Think about the ingenuity of the engineers who brought the Apollo 13 astronauts back home. Faced with a life-threatening situation, they used limited resources to devise a solution that saved lives. This example underscores the critical problem-solving skills you will develop and utilize in your scientific career.

8. Global Impact: Addressing Global Challenges

Scientific research plays a crucial role in tackling global challenges like climate change, food security, and resource management. As a scientist, you could contribute to developing sustainable solutions that benefit future generations.

"The Earth is the cradle of humanity, but mankind cannot stay in the cradle forever." – Konstantin Tsiolkovsky

Reflect on the collaborative effort behind the creation of the mRNA COVID-19 vaccines. Scientists from around the world pooled their knowledge and resources to develop a solution in record time, showcasing the global impact and importance of scientific research. Your work could help mitigate climate change, making a significant impact on the planet's future.

9. Communication and Advocacy: Sharing Your Passion

Science isn't just about research; it's also about communication. You'll learn to explain complex concepts in an engaging way, fostering public understanding of scientific advancements.

"The good thing about science is that it's true whether or not you believe in it." – Neil deGrasse Tyson

Picture yourself as **Carl Sagan,** whose TV series "Cosmos" brought the wonders of the universe into living rooms around the world. His ability to communicate complex scientific ideas in an engaging manner inspired countless individuals to pursue careers in science. Imagine yourself speaking at conferences, writing articles, or even hosting your own science podcast, making complex topics accessible and exciting for everyone.

Channel your inner **Neil deGrasse Tyson**, a renowned astrophysicist who captivates audiences with his engaging explanations of complex scientific concepts.

Imagine yourself like **Bill Nye the Science Guy**, who inspires a love of science in young minds through his engaging and informative shows. Your ability to translate complex ideas into clear and compelling messages will not only educate

10. Sense of Purpose: Contributing to Something Bigger

Science allows you to contribute to something bigger than yourself. You'll be part of a global community dedicated to unraveling the mysteries of the universe and improving the lives of others. This sense of purpose can be incredibly rewarding, fueling your passion and dedication.

"Somewhere, something incredible is waiting to be known." – Carl Sagan

Think about the legacy of **Hubble Space Telescope scientists** who have expanded our understanding of the universe. Their work has not only answered many questions but also opened up new realms of inquiry, illustrating the profound sense of purpose that comes from contributing to scientific advancement. Imagine working on a project that aims to find solutions for water scarcity in developing countries, or developing new technologies for space exploration that could one day enable humanity to become a multi-planetary species. Your contributions will be part of a larger effort to make the world a better place.

Choosing a career in science, especially rocket science, is not just about professional fulfillment; it's about embarking on a journey filled with lifelong learning, personal growth, global impact, effective communication, and a profound sense of purpose. By embracing the unknown and challenging established paradigms, you will join the ranks of those who have pushed the boundaries of human knowledge and capability.

Becoming a scientist, and specifically a rocket scientist, is a journey filled with excitement, challenges, and immense rewards. It requires a mindset of curiosity, a passion for discovery, and a willingness to embrace the unknown. The attractions of intellectual challenge, innovation, impact, exploration, and collaboration make this career path incredibly fulfilling.

By choosing to become a scientist, you're not just embarking on a career; you're joining a tradition of exploration and discovery that has shaped our understanding of the universe and our place in it. Your work will contribute to the advancement of knowledge, the betterment of society, and the pursuit of human excellence.

So, if you have the curiosity, the passion, and the drive, take the leap into the world of science and let your journey of discovery begin. So, are you ready to take on the challenge and become a pioneer in the fascinating world of science? The universe awaits your discoveries.

The world of science, and particularly the field of rocketry, awaits your unique skillset, your boundless curiosity, and your passion for making a difference. So, are you ready to answer the call? If the prospect of asking bold questions, pushing boundaries, and leaving your mark on the universe excites you, then don't wait, don't hold back. Grab your metaphorical lab coat. Fuel your curiosity, ignite your passion, and let it propel you towards the stars. The universe awaits, and science, especially rocket science, is your passport to explore it all. The world of science needs your unique perspective, your relentless drive, and your passion for discovery.

You are about to become a rocket scientist in training! Forget everything you think you know about limitations – we're blasting past them! Here, you'll wield a superpower: the **vision of a true rocket scientist!**

Imagine the world, not as it is, but as it could be. We don't just dream; we **dream the impossible** and then chase those dreams to the furthest reaches of the cosmos! Challenges are like puzzles waiting to be cracked, roadblocks become mere stepping stones on our launchpad to greatness. **Setbacks? Those are just fuel for innovation!**

We don't operate on blind faith – healthy skepticism is our guiding light. We're not chasing quick wins, but breakthroughs that will echo through the ages. The rules? They're just suggestions, my friend. We're here to **rewrite the rulebook, forge a new path, and leave our fiery footprints on the universe!** Are you ready to join the mission?

Forget puny firecrackers – our rocket launches are about controlled explosions, the kind of power you'd find in a small nuclear bomb (but don't worry, it's completely contained!). These are fire-breathing monsters, and launching them is a precision act. One mistake, one off calculation, and things go south in a hurry.

Calling all Space Problem-Solvers!

SpaceX propulsion pioneer Tom Mueller captures the essence: "Launching a rocket is a symphony of precision. A thousand potential missteps, one perfect outcome." At SpaceX, we push the boundaries of space exploration, literally and figuratively. We meticulously assemble intricate spacecraft, millions of parts and kilometres of wiring, all aimed at daring missions through the unforgiving vacuum. Imagine a high-tech puzzle hurtling towards the unknown at incredible speeds!

Troubleshooting at the Final Frontier

Challenges are inevitable. Unlike a car, there's no pulling over in space. When issues arise millions of miles away, your expertise shines. You'll become a data detective extraordinaire, wielding your analytical superpowers. You'll navigate a vast ocean of information, pinpointing the culprit amongst countless possibilities. Forget greasy wrenches; this is about pure, unadulterated problem-solving brilliance.

Ready to become a troubleshooting rockstar? Get ready, Future Space Architect!

The life of a scientist is a captivating blend of intellectual challenge, boundless creativity, and the potential to make a real difference. Imagine yourself as Marie Curie, meticulously sifting through data, her relentless pursuit leading to the discovery of radioactivity. Or perhaps you see yourself as Stephen Hawking, his brilliant mind defying physical limitations to unlock the secrets of black holes. These are just a few of the countless heroes who have paved the way for aspiring scientists like you.

The future is unwritten, and you, my friend, have the pen in your hand and set your sights on the stars. After all, the next giant leap for mankind might just begin with a single, inquisitive mind like yours.

The future is unwritten, and you, have the pen

Unfurled, a canvas vast and deep,
The cosmos beckons, secrets to keep.
Your brush, a dream, paints visions bold and new,
A testament to a heart that dares to pursue.

Curiosity, a lantern bright and strong,
Guides through the shadows where answers belong.
A knight on a quest, with a spirit so keen,
You'll conquer the unknown, where mysteries convene.

Unwritten futures wait for your command,
The quill in your hand, a map in the sand.
With a steady heart, fuelled by a burning desire,
You'll write the chapters, set the cosmos on fire.

Chapter 3.

Understanding the Rocket and Role of a Rocket Scientist

Rocket Science: Embarking on Celestial Journeys

Have you ever gazed into the night sky and yearned to traverse its infinite expanse? Well, that's where rocket science comes into play. It's the amazing field that turns those starry dreams into roaring reality. But before we blast off into the nitty-gritty, let's get a feel for what this whole rocket science thing is all about.

Rocket Science: An Expansive Realm of Opportunities

Picture a realm where you can conceive and construct machines that ascend beyond the stratosphere—not merely airplanes, but rockets that plunge into the cosmic abyss! That's the might of rocket science, often referred to as astronautics, or for those who cherish a good fusion, aerospace engineering. It's an exhilarating amalgamation of science and engineering that empowers us to fabricate rockets and spacecraft, the chariots that escort us on our cosmic odysseys.

Rocket science is not just about building rockets; it's a symphony of physics, chemistry, and engineering principles all working in harmony to achieve what once seemed impossible. Imagine harnessing the raw power of combustion to propel a vehicle through the void of space. It's a marvel of human ingenuity and perseverance.

The Masterminds Behind the Mission: Rocket Scientists

Think of rocket scientists, or aerospace engineers, as the modern-day wizards who unlock the secrets of space travel. They're the masterminds who use physics and math, like a secret code, to design these incredible machines. It's their knowledge of gravity, motion, and energy that allows them to craft rockets powerful enough to escape Earth's grasp and propel us towards the stars, explore space, and return safely.

The Role of Innovation

Innovation is at the heart of rocket science. Engineers and scientists are continually pushing the boundaries of what is possible, developing new technologies and techniques to make space travel more efficient and reliable. This relentless pursuit of progress is what has enabled humanity to explore the moon, send probes to distant planets, and dream of manned missions to Mars.

The Human Element

Behind all the technology and engineering, rocket science is a profoundly human endeavour. It requires the collaboration of countless individuals, each contributing their expertise and creativity to solve complex problems. It's a testament to what we can achieve when we work together towards a common goal.

In the end, rocket science opens up a universe of possibilities. It allows us to explore new worlds, seek out new life, and perhaps one day, find a new home among the stars. It's a field that embodies the spirit of adventure and the quest for knowledge that defines us as a species. So, if you've ever dreamed of reaching for the stars, rocket science might just be the path for you. It's a challenging and rewarding journey, filled with wonder and discovery. And who knows? One day, you might find yourself among the pioneers who turn those starry dreams into a dazzling reality.

A Historical Journey: From Firecrackers to Spaceships

The story of rocket science is a fascinating one, stretching back centuries! Did you know that the first rockets were actually fireworks used by the Chinese way back in the first century? Pretty cool, right? These early rockets were simple, but they laid the foundation for what was to come. Fast forward a thousand years, and we see scientists like Isaac Newton laying down the laws of motion, the very principles that would govern how rockets fly.

The 1900s: The Dawn of the Space Age

Then came the 20th century, the era that ignited the real space race! Pioneering minds like Konstantin Tsiolkovsky in Russia and Robert Goddard in the US started experimenting with liquid-fuelled rockets, engines far more powerful than gunpowder. And guess what? Their work paved the way for the historic launch of Sputnik 1, the first artificial satellite, by the Soviet Union in 1957.

This event marked the dawn of the Space Age, a time of incredible innovation and exploration.

A Multi-Disciplinary Marvel: What Makes a Rocket Tick?

But building a rocket isn't just about slapping some metal together and throwing in a big engine. It's a complex symphony of different scientific disciplines working in harmony. Here's a taste of what goes into making a rocket tick:

Basic Principles

The Spark of Genius: Newton's Third Law and Rocket Propulsion

Imagine blowing up a balloon and releasing it without tying it closed. The air whooshes out, propelling the balloon to move in the opposite direction. This is all thanks to Newton's Third Law of Motion! It basically says that forces come in pairs: one pushing one way, the other pushing back just as hard in the opposite direction. This same idea is the secret behind rockets blasting off into space! This law states that for every action, there is an equal and opposite reaction. In a rocket, the action is the forceful expulsion of mass, usually in the form of hot, high-speed exhaust gases, out of the engine nozzle. The reaction? A powerful force pushing the rocket forward in the opposite direction. It's like a cosmic tug-of-war, where the rocket and the exhaust gases pull on each other, but ultimately, the rocket wins, blasting off into space!

Propulsion: This is all about creating the thrust, the push that sends the rocket skyward. We're talking powerful engines that burn fuel and generate hot gases, which blast out the back, propelling the rocket forward according to Newton's third law of motion (every action has an equal and opposite reaction).

Fuelling the Fire: Propellants – The Rocket's Lifeblood

Imagine a car without gasoline – that's a rocket without propellant! This is the fuel that undergoes a fiery combustion reaction to generate the force, or thrust, that propels the rocket skyward. Propellants come in three main flavours:

Solid Propulsion Systems: These are like giant firework rockets, with the fuel and oxidizer (the ingredient that helps the fuel burn) pre-mixed and packed into a solid grain, making them more reliable and easier to store. They're simple, reliable, and great for a quick burst of power, often used in booster rockets during launch. Think of the Space Shuttle's iconic solid rocket boosters that ignited with a fiery roar.

Liquid Propulsion Systems: These are the powerhouses of the rocket world. They store fuel and oxidizer as separate liquids, like kerosene and liquid oxygen. Imagine a high-performance race car with fine-tuned fuel injection – that's the level of control you get with liquid propellants. They offer more control and efficiency than solid-fuelled engines, allowing for multiple engine restarts and throttling (adjusting the engine's power output). However, they are more complex and require additional plumbing and pumps to manage the propellants. Examples include the powerful engines used on the Space Shuttle and the Falcon 9 rocket. They're often used in upper stages of rockets and spacecraft engines, like the mighty engines of the Saturn V rocket that took astronauts to the Moon.

Cryogenic propellants: are fuels and oxidizers stored at extremely low temperatures to keep them in a liquid state. These propellants, such as liquid hydrogen and liquid oxygen, are highly efficient and provide a significant amount of thrust, making them ideal for rocket propulsion. Liquid hydrogen is typically stored at extremely low temperatures of around -253 degrees Celsius (-423 degrees Fahrenheit). Liquid oxygen is stored at a somewhat higher, but still very low, temperature of approximately -183 degrees Celsius (-297 degrees Fahrenheit). These cryogenic temperatures are necessary to keep the hydrogen and oxygen in their liquid states for efficient use as rocket propellants. However, handling cryogenic propellants requires special insulation and technology to maintain their low temperatures and prevent them from evaporating before use. They are a critical component in many modern rockets, enabling long-duration missions and high-performance space exploration.

Semicryogenic propellants: are a type of rocket fuel that combines cryogenic oxidizers, like liquid oxygen, with room-temperature liquid fuels, such as kerosene. This blend offers a balance between the high efficiency of cryogenic systems and the ease of handling associated with non-cryogenic fuels. Semicryogenic propellant systems are simpler and less costly to manage than fully cryogenic ones, making them a popular choice for many launch vehicles. They provide a good compromise between performance and practicality in rocket propulsion.

Hybrid Propellants: These are the innovative new kids on the block, combining elements of both solid and liquid propellants. They offer some of the simplicity of solids with the control and efficiency of liquids. Think of a hybrid car that blends gasoline power with electric efficiency – that's the potential of hybrid propellants for future rockets.

Thrust: The Power of a Rocket Punch!

Now, let's talk about thrust – the rocket's punch that sends it soaring through the sky. Remember Sir Isaac Newton's third law of motion? Every action has an equal and opposite reaction. In a rocket, the hot gases produced by burning the propellant are expelled out of the engine nozzle at high velocity. This creates a force in the opposite direction, pushing the rocket forward, just like a fire hose spraying water pushes the firefighter back. The faster and hotter the exhaust gases, the greater the thrust generated!

Staging: Teamwork Makes the Dream Work (and Gets You to Space!)

Imagine you're on a long car journey. When you run out of fuel, you can just stop at a nearby petrol pump to refuel. But with rockets, you can't do that. You have to carry all the fuel you need from the start. This makes the rocket very heavy. Staging helps solve this problem.

Think of trying to climb Mount Everest with a backpack full of supplies for the entire journey. It would be really hard, right?

Rockets use multiple stages to make the journey more efficient. The first stage is the biggest and most powerful. It provides the thrust needed to overcome Earth's gravity. Once its fuel is used up, it is jettisoned, meaning it's detached and falls away. Then, lighter upper stages take over. These stages use less fuel and achieve higher speeds more efficiently.

Think of a relay race, with each stage handing off the baton (propellant) to the next runner (stage) to reach the finish line (orbit or beyond!). This multi-stage approach allows rockets to achieve the incredible speeds needed to escape Earth's gravity and reach space. The mighty Saturn V rocket used a three-stage configuration to take astronauts to the Moon!

Orbital Mechanics: The Cosmic Choreography

Now, reaching space is one thing, but staying there is another! This is where orbital mechanics comes in. It's the study of how objects move under the influence of gravity. Imagine throwing a ball – it follows a curved path due to Earth's gravity. By understanding these gravitational forces and the laws of physics, we can calculate the exact velocity and trajectory a rocket needs to achieve a stable orbit around Earth, the Moon, or even other planets. It's like choreographing a cosmic ballet, ensuring the rocket reaches its destination and stays there without falling back to Earth or flying off into the endless abyss.

Materials Science:

We've been diving deep into the fiery world of rocket propulsion, but a rocket needs more than just a powerful engine to reach for the stars. It needs a tough outer shell, a lightweight body, and materials that can handle the crazy conditions of space travel. That's where the amazing field of materials science comes in, and guess what? You're about to become a mini-materials scientist yourself!

The Balancing Act: Strong Yet Light Weight

Imagine trying to build a spaceship out of bricks – not exactly ideal for soaring through space, right? Rockets need to be incredibly strong to withstand the immense forces of launch and the constant vibrations of flight. But they also need to be lightweight, because every extra pound of weight means less fuel you can carry and less distance you can travel. So, materials scientists face a constant challenge: creating materials that are strong enough to handle the stresses of space, yet light enough to keep the rocket nimble.

A Universe of Materials: Alloys and Composites to the Rescue!

To meet this challenge, materials scientists have developed a whole arsenal of incredible materials:

Metal & Titanium Alloys: These are blends of different metals, like the titanium alloys commonly used in rocket bodies. Titanium is incredibly strong and lightweight, making it a perfect choice for withstanding the high pressure and heat of launch. Imagine a super-strong, lightweight metal skeleton for your rocket!

Carbon Fiber Composites: These are like the superheroes of the material world. They combine carbon fibres, incredibly strong and stiff threads of carbon, with a lightweight resin that binds them together. This creates a super-strong, lightweight material that can be moulded into various shapes for different parts of the rocket. Think of a rocket body woven from super-strong, lightweight threads!

Facing the Heat: Temperature Extremes in Space

Space may seem like a vast emptiness, but it's not exactly a walk in the park for a rocket. During launch, the rocket experiences scorching temperatures due to air friction. Then, once in space, it faces the harsh reality of extreme cold. Materials scientists develop special coatings and insulation to protect the rocket from these temperature extremes.

Heat Shield: During launch, the rocket needs protection from the scorching heat generated by air friction. Structural engineers design heat shields using special materials that can absorb or deflect heat, protecting the sensitive equipment inside. Imagine the rocket wearing a fireproof jacket during launch!

Thermal Insulation: Once in space, the temperature plummets. Structural engineers use special thermal insulation materials to keep the rocket's internal temperature stable and protect sensitive equipment from freezing. Imagine the rocket wearing a cozy thermal blanket in the frigidness of space!

Shaking Things Up: Vibration and the Importance of Material Strength

A rocket launch isn't exactly a smooth ride. The powerful engines create intense vibrations that can shake the entire structure. Materials scientists carefully analyze the different types of vibrations a rocket might experience and choose materials that can withstand them without cracking or breaking. Imagine a rocket built with materials that can handle the intense shaking of a rock concert, but for a much longer duration!

The Invisible Threat: Space Radiation Resistance

Space is filled with invisible radiation, like X-rays and gamma rays, which can damage electronics and even harm astronauts on long journeys. So, materials scientists develop special shielding materials that can absorb or deflect this radiation, protecting the sensitive equipment and crew inside the spacecraft. Imagine a rocket with a special suit of armour protecting it from the harmful rays of space!

This is just a glimpse into the fascinating world of materials science in rocketry. With new innovative materials being developed all the time, we're constantly pushing the boundaries of what's possible. So, the next time you look up at a rocket blasting off, remember the incredible materials science that went into building that powerful machine, allowing us to explore the vast unknown!

Thermodynamics:

We've been exploring the fiery guts of rocket engines and the superhero materials that hold them together. But there's another crucial player in this cosmic symphony – thermodynamics! Don't worry, it won't involve memorizing complex equations (although some basic understanding is helpful). Today, we'll unravel the fascinating dance between heat and work that makes rocket engines tick!

The Magic of Heat: Transforming Energy for Propulsion

Imagine a pot of boiling water – the heat from the stove is causing the water molecules to move frantically. That's thermal energy in action. Now, in a rocket engine, the burning propellant generates a massive amount of heat energy. But what good is all that heat if it just sits there bubbling away? That's where thermodynamics comes in! It helps us understand how to convert this thermal energy into something useful – **work**, in this case, the thrust that propels the rocket forward.

Efficiency is Key: Extracting the Most Power

Think of a car engine – if it burns fuel inefficiently, you spend more money at the pump and get less mileage. Similarly, in a rocket engine, efficiency is paramount. We want to extract the most work (thrust) from the heat energy generated by burning the propellant. Thermodynamics provides the tools to analyze this process and optimize engine design. One key concept is **exhaust velocity**. The faster the hot exhaust gases are expelled from the engine nozzle, the greater the thrust generated for the same amount of propellant. Think of blowing up a balloon – a quick, sharp burst of air sends it flying further than a slow, gentle puff.

The Rocket Equation: Balancing Efficiency and Performance

Here's where things get a little more technical (but still exciting!). The "rocket equation" is a cornerstone of rocket science, derived from principles of thermodynamics. It relates a rocket's final velocity to its initial mass, propellant mass, and exhaust velocity. In simpler terms, it helps us understand the trade-off between efficiency and performance. A more efficient engine with a higher exhaust velocity can achieve greater final velocity with the same amount of propellant. Conversely, a less efficient engine might require more propellant to achieve the same velocity.

Examples in Action: Comparing Rocket Engines

Let's see thermodynamics in action by comparing two types of rocket engines:

Solid-fuelled rockets: These engines are simpler and more reliable, but they offer less control over the combustion process. This can lead to lower exhaust velocities compared to liquid-fuelled engines. Imagine a firecracker – it burns quickly but not very efficiently.

Liquid-fuelled rockets: These engines offer more control over the combustion process, allowing for higher exhaust velocities and therefore greater efficiency. Think of a high-performance car engine – it burns fuel efficiently and generates more power.

Beyond the Basics: Optimizing Efficiency for Deep Space Exploration

Thermodynamics doesn't stop at comparing engine types. It helps us push the boundaries of performance by exploring ways to optimize combustion, reduce heat losses, and develop new types of propellants that release more energy during combustion. Every improvement in efficiency translates into carrying more payload (satellites, probes, or even astronauts) further into space.

So, you see, thermodynamics is much more than just a fancy word. It's the secret sauce that helps us convert the fiery energy of rocket propellants into the powerful thrust that propels us towards the stars. As we delve deeper into this fascinating field, we'll unlock new ways to explore the cosmos, all thanks to the magic of heat and work!

Guidance, Navigation, and Control (GNC) Systems:

We're about to delve into the nerve centre of a rocket – its Guidance, Navigation, and Control (GNC) system. Imagine a high-speed spaceship hurtling through space. How does it know where to go, keep itself pointed in the right direction, and make those critical course corrections? That's all thanks to the incredible GNC system, and you're about to become a mini-GNC specialist!

GNC: The Brain Behind the Brawn

Think of a rocket as a powerful muscle car – it has the raw power (engine) to blast off, but it also needs a skilled driver (GNC) to steer it on the right path. The GNC system is the complex network that integrates three vital functions:

Guidance: This is like the rocket's roadmap. It figures out where the rocket needs to go based on pre-programmed instructions or by receiving signals from ground control. Imagine feeding the destination coordinates into a spaceship's navigation system.

Navigation: Just like a ship uses a compass, a rocket relies on a sophisticated navigation system to determine its current location and orientation in space. This information is crucial for the GNC system to make any necessary course corrections. Imagine a captain constantly checking the ship's position on a map.

Control: Once the GNC system knows where it needs to go and where it currently is, the control system takes over. It uses a combination of thrusters, fins, actuators and other mechanisms to adjust the rocket's attitude (pointing direction) and trajectory (flight path) to match the desired course. Imagine the captain turning the helm and adjusting the sails to steer the ship.

Navigating the Cosmos: A Toolbox of Techniques

Rockets have a whole toolbox of navigation tools at their disposal:

Inertial Guidance Systems (IGS): These are like internal autopilots. They use gyroscopes (spinning wheels that maintain orientation) and accelerometers (instruments that sense acceleration) to track the rocket's movement and position, even without any external reference points. Imagine a self-contained navigation system that doesn't need a signal from Earth. Today Laser based Gyroscopes, ceramic servo accelerometers, advanced sensors are used for sensing rotational velocity and linear acceleration of the vehicles.

Star Trackers: Celestial Navigators for Spacecraft

Star trackers are advanced systems used to navigate in space, much like sailors used to navigate by the stars on the open sea. These devices lock onto specific stars whose positions are precisely known. By tracking these stars, the star trackers can determine the rocket's attitude, which means its orientation or pointing direction in space.

Imagine you're a sailor navigating by constellations at night. You look up, identify familiar stars, and use their positions to figure out where you are and where you're headed. Star trackers work in a similar way. They have cameras and sensors that capture images of the star-filled sky. By comparing these images with an onboard stored catalogue of star maps, they can pinpoint the exact orientation of the spacecraft.

This information is crucial for ensuring the rocket stays on the correct path and can make precise adjustments as needed. Without star trackers, navigating the vast and dark expanse of space would be much more challenging. These celestial navigators play a vital role in the success of space missions, helping spacecraft reach their destinations accurately.

Global Navigation Satellite Systems (GNSS): While not always available in deep space, GNSS like GPS can be incredibly useful within Earth's atmosphere or near navigation satellites in orbit. They provide precise positioning data to the GNC system, ensuring the rocket stays on course during launch and early ascent phases. Imagine using a high-tech GPS system to pinpoint your location during the initial stages of the flight.

Keeping it Steady: Control Systems in Action

Once the GNC system figures out where it needs to go and where it is, it's time for the control system to take action. Here's how it works:

Thrusters: These are like tiny rocket engines that can fire in different directions. By strategically controlling the thrust from these thrusters, the GNC system can make small adjustments to the rocket's attitude and trajectory. Imagine using small manoeuvring jets to fine-tune the spaceship's course.

Fins: Some rockets, especially during atmospheric flight, use fins to control their orientation. By adjusting the angle of the fins through small movements, the GNC system can steer the rocket like a giant arrow. Imagine using rudders on a ship to adjust its direction.

The Importance of Precision: Every Millisecond Counts

In the high-stakes world of spaceflight, even tiny errors can have big consequences. The GNC system needs to be incredibly precise and reliable. Every calculation, every adjustment, has to be done with incredible accuracy to ensure the rocket reaches its destination successfully. Imagine a spaceship needing to perform a delicate maneuverer to dock with a space station – the GNC system needs to be flawless!

That's just a taste of the amazing GNC systems that guide rockets on their cosmic journeys. With constant advancements in technology, these systems are becoming ever more sophisticated, paving the way for even more daring space exploration missions. Remember, the next time you witness a rocket launch, you're not just seeing a powerful machine blast off – you're witnessing the incredible GNC system working its magic behind the scenes! We've been exploring the intricate workings of rockets – from their fiery engines to the guidance systems that steer them through the cosmos.

Next, we delve into the brain of the operation: **The Mission Computer!** This marvel of technology is responsible for the complex calculations, intricate software, and high-precision guidance that make a successful space mission possible. Here's how it all works:

The Mighty Mission Computer: Brains Behind the Brawn

Imagine a rocket as a powerful athlete – it has the strength (engine) and agility (control systems) to perform incredible feats. But just like an athlete needs a sharp mind to make strategic decisions, a rocket needs a mission computer! This powerful brain performs a multitude of tasks, all critical for a successful mission:

Crunching the Numbers: The mission computer is a math whiz, constantly performing complex calculations. It takes into account the rocket's current position, velocity, and orientation, along with the desired trajectory and mission objectives. Based on these factors, it calculates the necessary adjustments (like firing thrusters or adjusting fins) to keep the rocket on course. Think of a spaceship captain relying on a supercomputer to analyze data and make course corrections in real-time.

Software Symphony: The Guiding Force

The mission computer isn't just a calculator; it's also home to a complex suite of software. This software acts like a conductor in an orchestra, directing all the different components of the GNC system (Guidance, Navigation, and Control) to work together flawlessly. It interprets data from the navigation systems (like star trackers or GPS), sends commands to the control systems (like thrusters or fins), and constantly updates the flight path based on real-time conditions. Imagine a sophisticated program controlling every aspect of the rocket's guidance, navigation, and control with split-second precision.

Accuracy is Key: No Room for Errors

In the unforgiving environment of space, even small errors can have disastrous consequences. That's why the mission computer is programmed with incredibly high accuracy and precision. Every calculation, every software instruction, is designed to be flawless. Engineers spend countless hours testing and refining the software to ensure it performs perfectly under all conditions. Imagine a spaceship needing to perform a precise maneuverer to dock with a space station – the mission computer's calculations have to be spot on!

Beyond the Basics: Adapting to the Unexpected

While the mission computer follows a pre-programmed flight plan, it's not a rigid robot. Advanced software allows for some degree of autonomy. The computer can analyze sensor data and make minor adjustments to account for unexpected situations, like wind gusts during launch or minor course deviations. Think of a spaceship's computer being able to react to unforeseen circumstances and make small corrections on the fly.

Real-World Examples: A Glimpse into Mission Computer Action

Here are some real-world examples of how mission computers are used:

Space Shuttle Launches: The Space Shuttle had a complex mission computer that calculated the precise trajectory for launch and re-entry, ensuring a safe and smooth journey.

Mars Rovers: The rovers exploring Mars rely on mission computers to navigate the rough terrain, avoid obstacles, and perform scientific tasks autonomously.

Deep Space Probes: Probes venturing far beyond Earth's orbit depend on mission computers to execute manoeuvres, collect data, and transmit it back to Earth.

The Future of Mission Computers: Ever-Evolving Technology

The world of mission computers is constantly evolving. As we push further into space and develop more complex spacecraft, these brains will become even more powerful and sophisticated. Imagine future mission computers capable of real-time decision-making, adapting to unforeseen situations, and even learning from past experiences.

Remember, the mission computer is the unsung hero of spaceflight. This marvel of technology ensures our rockets reach their destinations, explore the unknown, and unlock the secrets of the cosmos. So, the next time you witness a spacecraft blasting off, remember the incredible mission computer quietly working its magic behind the scenes!

Control Systems: Imagine a rocket without a steering wheel! That's where control systems come in. They use sensors, computers, and tiny thrusters to keep the rocket on course and make sure it doesn't veer off into oblivion. Without a control system, a rocket would be just a giant firework soaring wildly out of control. Let us dive into the fascinating world of these systems and see how they keep our rockets pointed in the right direction, using a combination of clever engineering and cutting-edge technology!

Steering the Starship: The Importance of Control Systems

Imagine a spaceship blasting off without any way to control its direction! It wouldn't be a pretty sight (or a very successful mission). That's where control systems come in. They act like the rocket's autopilot, constantly monitoring its position and making tiny adjustments to keep it on course. Here's how they work:

Sensing the Surroundings: The control system relies on a network of sensors that act like the rocket's eyes and ears. These sensors gather data on the rocket's current orientation, velocity, and any external influences like wind or gravity. Imagine a spaceship with gyroscopes that sense its rotation, accelerometers that measure its speed, and even star trackers that lock onto specific stars to determine its position in space.

Brainpower Behind the Brawn: All the data collected by the sensors is fed into the mission computer, the rocket's brain. This computer analyses the information and compares it to the pre-programmed flight path. If there's any deviation, the computer sends out instructions to the control system.

Course Correction: Taking Action! This is where things get exciting! The control system uses various mechanisms to make adjustments and keep the rocket on course. Here's where your hydraulic and electro-mechanical actuators come into play:

Hydraulic Actuators: These are like powerful muscles that use pressurized fluid to move control surfaces like fins or rudders. Imagine a giant syringe pushing oil to adjust a massive spaceship fin. Think of them for larger, high-power adjustments during launch or atmospheric flight.

Electro-Mechanical Actuators (EMAs): These are more precise and efficient cousins of hydraulic actuators. They use electric motors to move control surfaces with great accuracy. Imagine a spaceship using high-tech electric motors for fine-tuning its attitude and manoeuvres, especially in deep space.

Working Together: A Symphony of Systems

The control system doesn't operate in isolation. It works in perfect harmony with other crucial systems:

Guidance System: This system provides the desired flight path for the rocket, like a roadmap in space. The control system uses this information to make any necessary adjustments. Imagine the guidance system being the map and the control system being the driver on a spaceship.

Navigation System: This system helps the rocket determine its current location and orientation in space. This information is crucial for the control system to understand how much and in which direction it needs to adjust. Imagine the navigation system being the GPS and the control system being the autopilot on a spaceship.

Real-World Examples: Control Systems in Action

Control systems are the silent heroes of countless space missions:

Space Shuttle Launch: During launch, the control system uses fins and rudders controlled by hydraulic actuators to steer the Space Shuttle through the thick atmosphere.

Deep Space Probes: Probes venturing far beyond Earth's atmosphere rely on EMAs for precise control during manoeuvres and scientific data collection.

The Future of Control Systems: Adapting and Advancing

Control systems are constantly evolving. As we explore further into space, these systems will need to become even more sophisticated. Imagine future control systems capable of anticipating and reacting to unexpected situations, like a spaceship automatically adjusting for a micrometeoroid impact.

So, there you have it. Control systems are the workhorses that keep our rockets flying true. With a combination of sensors, computers, and powerful actuators, these systems ensure our rockets reach their destinations and help us explore the vast unknown!

Orbital Mechanics:

Gear up for a celestial adventure, because we're diving into the fascinating world of orbital mechanics – the key to understanding how objects, like our rockets and even planets, move and dance around each other under the powerful grip of gravity! This incredible field of science is what allows us to calculate the perfect trajectories, design stable orbits, and ultimately ensure our rockets reach their cosmic destinations, be it the Moon, Mars, or even beyond!

Gravity's Symphony: The Conductor of Space Motion

Imagine throwing a ball in the air. It goes up, then falls back down, all thanks to gravity. But in space, things get a little more complex. Orbital mechanics helps us understand how gravity, acting like an invisible conductor, orchestrates the movement of celestial bodies. It's what keeps the Moon orbiting Earth, planets orbiting the Sun, and even artificial satellites zipping around our planet.

The Art of the Trajectory: Getting There is Half the Fun

Think of a rocket launch – it's not just a straight shot up! Orbital mechanics helps us calculate the perfect trajectory, like aiming a giant slingshot, to propel a rocket into the desired orbit. This involves considering factors like:

Escape Velocity: This is the minimum speed a rocket needs to overcome Earth's gravity and achieve orbit. Imagine throwing a ball hard enough so it never falls back down, but instead keeps circling the planet.

Orbital Parameters: Once in orbit, the specific path a rocket takes depends on factors like altitude, inclination (the angle of the orbit relative to the equator), and eccentricity (how circular the orbit is). Imagine the difference between a close, circular orbit around Earth and a highly elliptical path reaching far out into space.

Designing Orbits: The Celestial Highway

Orbital mechanics doesn't just help us get things into space; it also helps us design the specific orbits we want them to follow. Here are some fascinating orbital possibilities:

Geostationary Orbits: These orbits are like celestial parking spots. A satellite placed in a geostationary orbit stays fixed above a specific point on Earth's equator, making them ideal for communication satellites. Imagine a satellite hovering over a specific spot on Earth, always in view, like a cosmic guard post.

Low Earth Orbits (LEO): These orbits are closer to Earth, making them ideal for scientific research satellites and the International Space Station. Think of a satellite zipping around Earth at a relatively low altitude, collecting valuable data.

Interplanetary Transfer Orbits: These are the cosmic highways that allow spacecraft to travel between planets. Orbital mechanics helps us calculate the precise path and timing needed to send a spacecraft on a journey to Mars or beyond. Imagine a rocket following a calculated trajectory, like a celestial road map, to reach another planet.

Real-World Examples: Orbital Mechanics in Action

Orbital mechanics plays a crucial role in every space mission:

Apollo Missions: Landing humans on the Moon involved complex orbital calculations to ensure a smooth lunar rendezvous and safe return.

Space Probes: Sending probes to distant planets like Voyager 1 requires meticulously planned trajectories based on orbital mechanics principles.

International Space Station (ISS): Maintaining the ISS in its correct orbit requires constant monitoring and adjustments based on orbital mechanics calculations.

The Future of Orbital Mechanics: Pushing the Boundaries

Orbital mechanics is a constantly evolving field. As we venture further into space and explore new celestial bodies, these calculations will become even more sophisticated. Imagine using orbital mechanics to design missions to asteroids, establish lunar colonies, or even send probes to distant star systems.

So, remember, orbital mechanics is the language of the cosmos. By understanding the dance of gravity and celestial motion, we can unlock the secrets of space travel and chart a course towards a future filled with incredible cosmic adventures!

This is all about understanding how objects move under the influence of gravity. It's what allows us to calculate trajectories, design orbits, and ensure our rockets reach their destination, whether it's the Moon or Mars.

The Symphony of Systems: A Rocket's Inner Workings

A rocket may look like a sleek, powerful machine, but it's actually a complex orchestra of different systems, each playing a vital role in its successful mission. Here's a breakdown of some key players:

Structural Engineering: The forces a rocket experiences during launch and flight are incredible. Let us delve into the essential world of structural engineering – the invisible backbone that holds a rocket together. Imagine a powerful engine blasting off, but without a strong, lightweight body, it would crumble under the immense forces of space travel. That's where structural engineers come in, wielding their knowledge of materials and physics to create the ultimate spacefaring skeleton!

The G-Force Gauntlet: Facing the Forces of Flight

Ever been on a roller coaster? Now imagine that feeling amplified a thousand times over! During launch and flight, a rocket experiences incredible G-forces (the force of gravity) pushing and pulling on its body. Structural engineers have to account for all these forces:

Liftoff: As the rocket blasts off, immense thrust pushes it upwards, putting a tremendous strain on the lower portions of the vehicle. Imagine a giant hand pushing the bottom of the rocket with incredible force.

Aerodynamic Forces: Once the rocket enters the atmosphere, air resistance creates drag, trying to slow it down. This force can put stress on the entire structure, especially the nose cone and fins. Imagine the rocket pushing through thick air, like swimming through molasses.

Engine Vibrations: Powerful engines create intense vibrations that can shake the entire rocket. Structural engineers need to design the body to absorb these vibrations without cracking or breaking. Imagine a rocket engine causing the whole structure to vibrate, like a powerful speaker shaking the floor.

Standing Tall Under Pressure: Deflection and Vibration Control

A rocket needs to be rigid enough to withstand the immense forces of launch and flight, but not so rigid that it becomes brittle. Structural engineers use clever design techniques to manage deflection and vibrations:

Stress Distribution: The goal is to distribute the stress (force per unit area) evenly throughout the structure. This prevents any one part from becoming overloaded and failing. Imagine spreading the weight of a heavy object across a large surface area to avoid creating a hole.

Stiffeners and Ribs: These are like the internal reinforcements of a rocket's body. They add rigidity to specific areas that experience high stress, preventing excessive bending or twisting. Imagine adding beams and supports to a building to make it more stable.

Real-World Examples: Structural Engineering in Action

Structural engineering plays a vital role in every successful space mission:

Space Shuttle: The iconic Space Shuttle's lightweight yet strong body, made from aluminium alloys and reinforced carbon fibre composites, allowed it to withstand the intense heat and G-forces of launch and re-entry.

Falcon Heavy: This powerful rocket by SpaceX utilizes a combination of high-strength steel and advanced composite materials to handle the immense forces generated by its multiple engines.

The Future of Structural Engineering: Lighter, Stronger, Farther

The quest for lighter and stronger materials is never-ending. As we push the boundaries of space exploration, structural engineers will develop even more advanced materials and design techniques. Imagine building rockets with materials that are even stronger and lighter, allowing us to travel further and explore more of the cosmos!

So, remember, the invisible hand of structural engineering. Now, we're blasting off into the incredible world of aeronautical engineering – the science that unlocks the secrets of flight! This field is the foundation for building rockets that soar through the atmosphere and beyond. But before we launch into the cosmos, let's get familiar with some key concepts that make flight possible

– pitch, yaw, roll, lift, and drag! Buckle up, because we're about to become junior aeronautical engineers!

Aeronautical Engineering:

Understanding Thrust in Rockets

Thrust is the force that propels a rocket forward, allowing it to overcome gravity and atmospheric drag to reach space. It is generated by the expulsion of exhaust gases produced during the combustion of rocket propellants.

How Thrust is Generated

Combustion Process:

Inside the rocket engine, fuel and an oxidizer are combined and ignited in the combustion chamber. This chemical reaction produces high-pressure, high-temperature gases.

Expulsion of Exhaust Gases:

These gases are expelled at high speed through the rocket's nozzle. The nozzle is designed to accelerate the gases to extremely high velocities, converting thermal energy into kinetic energy.

Newton's Third Law of Motion:

According to Newton's Third Law, for every action, there is an equal and opposite reaction. The action of expelling gases downward results in an equal and opposite reaction that pushes the rocket upward.

Components of Thrust Generation: Combustion Chamber:

The area where fuel and oxidizer are burned, creating hot gases.

Nozzle:

A specially shaped tube through which the hot gases are expelled. The nozzle accelerates the gases to high speeds, directing them out of the rocket.

Factors Affecting Thrust

Amount of Propellant:

More propellant generally means more thrust, as there is more mass to expel at high speed.

Exhaust Velocity:

Higher exhaust velocities result in greater thrust. The design of the nozzle and the efficiency of the combustion process are critical in achieving high exhaust velocities.

Chamber Pressure:

Higher pressure in the combustion chamber increases the force with which the gases are expelled, thereby increasing thrust.

Overcoming Gravity and Drag

For a rocket to lift off:

The rocket must generate enough thrust to exceed its weight. A thrust-to-weight ratio greater than 1 is necessary for liftoff.

Minimizing Drag:

Rockets are designed to be aerodynamic to minimize air resistance. During ascent, the engines produce enough thrust to overcome this drag.

Thrust in rockets is a force generated by the expulsion of exhaust gases from the combustion of propellants. This force, explained by Newton's Third Law of Motion, propels the rocket upward. The design of the combustion chamber, nozzle, and type of propellant are critical in producing effective thrust. Thrust vector control ensures the rocket remains stable and on course during flight. By generating sufficient thrust to overcome gravity and atmospheric drag, rockets can reach space and fulfil their missions.

The Fantastic Forces in Play

Imagine a rocket on the launchpad, ready to defy gravity. To achieve flight, it needs to overcome some important forces:

Lift: This is the hero of the story, the invisible force that counteracts gravity and pushes the rocket upwards. Lift is generated by the rocket's shape of its body as it moves through the air. Think of an airplane wing slicing through the air, creating lift just like a bird's wing.

Drag: This is the villain, the force that opposes the rocket's forward motion. Air resistance creates drag, and it tries to slow the rocket down. Imagine a car driving through thick mud – that's drag in action!

Thrust: This is the rocket's muscle, the powerful force generated by its engines that propels it forward. Think of a fire hose blasting water – that's the thrust pushing the rocket in the desired direction.

Keeping it Steady: The Art of Control

Now, a rocket isn't just a giant firework soaring out of control. To navigate through the sky, it needs to control its orientation using three crucial movements:

Pitch: This is like nodding your head. By tilting its nose up or down, the rocket controls how much lift it generates and can climb or descend. Imagine a spaceship tilting its nose up to gain altitude.

Yaw: This is like turning your head from side to side. By adjusting its yaw, the rocket controls its direction left or right. Imagine a spaceship turning slightly to avoid an asteroid!

Roll: This is like rolling a barrel on the ground. By rolling on its axis, the rocket can keep its wings level for optimal lift generation. Imagine a spaceship keeping its wings perfectly horizontal for stable flight.

Real-World Examples: Putting it All Together

Let's see these concepts in action with real-world examples:

Airplane Take off: During take off, the airplane increases its angle of attack (the angle between the wing and the oncoming airflow) to generate more lift and overcome its weight. It also uses rudders and ailerons (control surfaces) to maintain pitch, yaw, and roll for a smooth ascent.

Rocket Launch: During launch, a rocket's powerful engines generate immense thrust to overcome gravity. The rocket also uses fins and thrust vectoring (directing the engine exhaust) to control its pitch, yaw, and roll for a stable climb through the atmosphere.

Aeronautical Engineering: Building on these Principles

Aeronautical engineers use their knowledge of these forces and control principles to design rockets that are aerodynamically efficient. They consider factors like:

Body Shape Design: The shape and size of the overall body, affect lift generation. Engineers design fins, body shape of the rocket, that optimize lift for different types of rockets.

Control Surfaces: These are movable parts like fins, rudders, and ailerons that allow the rocket to control its pitch, yaw, and roll. Engineers design these surfaces for precise and efficient control.

Overcoming Gravity:

A rocket must generate enough thrust to overcome Earth's gravitational pull. The thrust-to-weight ratio must be greater than 1 for the rocket to lift off.

Overcoming Atmospheric Drag:

During ascent, rockets encounter air resistance or drag. The rocket's shape (aerodynamics) and speed influence the amount of drag. Rockets are designed with streamlined shapes to minimize drag, and their engines produce sufficient thrust to overcome this force.

Centre of Gravity This is the point where the rocket's weight is evenly balanced. Aeronautical engineers ensure the centre of gravity is in the optimal position for stable flight.

The Future of Aeronautical Engineering: Pushing the Boundaries

Aeronautical engineering is constantly evolving. As we develop new propulsion systems and explore reusable rockets, engineers will need to design vehicles with even greater efficiency and manoeuvrability. Imagine future rockets that can take off and land vertically, or even rockets that can fly at hypersonic speeds! So, you've now taken your first steps into the fascinating world of aeronautical engineering! By understanding lift, drag, pitch, yaw, roll, and how engineers use these concepts, you're well on your way to becoming a master of rocket flight! Remember, these principles are the foundation for building rockets that can take us on incredible journeys across the cosmos!

Instrumentation and Measurement Systems: A rocket is like a high-performance car – it needs constant monitoring! These systems gather vital data on everything from engine performance and fuel levels to the temperature inside the spacecraft. Sensors placed throughout the rocket feed information back to the control centre, allowing engineers to ensure everything is functioning smoothly.

Communication Systems: Communication is key, especially when you're hurtling through space millions of miles away. Rockets rely on robust communication systems to transmit data and telemetry back to Earth, allowing mission control to monitor the spacecraft and send commands if needed. This often involves powerful radio antennas and sophisticated communication protocols.

Pyrotechnic Systems: A Comprehensive Guide

Embark on the fascinating world of pyrotechnic systems, an essential component in the realm of rocketry. As an aspiring rocket scientist, mastering this subject is crucial for the successful deployment and operation of rockets. With enthusiasm, I will guide you through the intricacies of pyrotechnic systems, providing detailed explanations and examples to fuel your understanding.

Introduction to Pyrotechnic Systems

Pyrotechnic systems are designed to produce controlled explosive effects for various applications in rocketry. These systems play pivotal roles in stages such as ignition, separation, and deployment. Understanding the science behind these controlled explosions will enhance your ability to design and implement effective rocket systems.

Components of Pyrotechnic Systems

Initiators (Igniters): Initiators are the starting point of any pyrotechnic event. They generate the initial spark required to ignite the pyrotechnic composition. For example, in a rocket launch, the initiator ignites the solid propellant, setting the stage for the rocket's ascent.

Pyrotechnic Compositions: These are chemical mixtures that produce heat, light, gas, and sound upon combustion. The composition is carefully formulated to ensure a controlled reaction. A common example is the use of black powder in igniters, which burns rapidly to produce the necessary thrust.

Delay Mechanisms: Delay mechanisms are used to control the timing of subsequent pyrotechnic events. For instance, a delay charge might be used in a staging rocket to ensure that the first stage has fully burned out before the second stage ignites.

Transfer Lines: These are conduits that transmit the flame or pressure from one part of the system to another. An example is the use of flexible hoses to carry the flame from the initiator to the main pyrotechnic charge.

Containment Vessels: These vessels house the pyrotechnic composition and are designed to withstand the pressure generated during combustion. They ensure that the reaction occurs in a controlled manner, directing the force where needed.

Detailed Example: Rocket Stage Separation

Let's delve into a practical example to illustrate how pyrotechnic systems work in rocket stage separation.

Initiation: Upon reaching a predetermined altitude, an electronic signal triggers the initiator. This initiator contains a small amount of pyrotechnic composition that ignites, producing a flame.

Transfer of Flame: The flame travels through transfer lines to the separation charge located between the rocket stages.

Separation Charge: The separation charge, typically composed of a fast-burning pyrotechnic composition, ignites and produces a rapid buildup of gas pressure.

Physical Separation: The generated pressure forces the stages apart. The containment vessel ensures that the pressure is directed in such a way that the stages separate cleanly without damaging the rocket.

Delay Mechanism: A delay mechanism might be employed to ensure that the second stage does not ignite immediately, allowing for a brief period of stabilization.

Safety Considerations

Safety is paramount when dealing with pyrotechnic systems. Here are some key points to consider:

Controlled Environment: Always handle pyrotechnic materials in a controlled environment to prevent accidental ignition.

Proper Storage: Store pyrotechnic materials in appropriate containers and environments to prevent degradation and accidental ignition.

Testing: Conduct thorough testing of pyrotechnic components to ensure reliability and predictability.

Safety Protocols: Follow strict safety protocols and guidelines during the handling, assembly, and deployment of pyrotechnic systems.

Mastering pyrotechnic systems is a thrilling and essential part of becoming a rocket scientist. By understanding the components and their functions, you can design and implement effective and safe pyrotechnic systems for various rocketry applications. Embrace the challenge with enthusiasm, and let your journey into the world of pyrotechnics ignite your passion for rocketry.

Beyond the Basics: A Universe of Specialization

This is just a glimpse into the fascinating world of rocket science. As you delve deeper, you'll discover even more mind-blowing concepts and technologies. Remember, the universe is waiting to be explored, and with your curiosity and the power of rocket science, you can be a part of that incredible journey!

Thermal Protection Systems: These shields protect the spacecraft from the scorching heat of atmospheric re-entry or the intense radiation of space.

Payload Integration: This involves carefully integrating the spacecraft or scientific instruments into the rocket, ensuring they are securely mounted and can withstand the launch environment.

We've just begun our rocket science adventure, and there's a whole universe of intricate systems to explore. Remember, rocket science is a constantly evolving field. New technologies and innovations are emerging all the time, pushing the boundaries of what's possible. So, if you're passionate about space exploration, there's always something new to learn and contribute to!

This is just the beginning of your rocket science odyssey. Keep exploring, keep learning, and who knows, maybe one day you'll be the one designing the next generation of spacecraft that will take us further into the cosmos! Hey there, space enthusiast! Launching a rocket isn't just about the fiery beast itself. It's a complex ballet, meticulously choreographed by a hidden orchestra – the **ground systems**. These are the unsung heroes that prepare the rocket for its journey and ensure a flawless liftoff.

Today, we'll delve into this fascinating world and see how these ground systems get your rocket ready to chase the stars!

The Launch Pad – A Stage for Rocket Dreams

Imagine a massive platform, a concrete jungle with towers and steel structures reaching towards the sky. That's the **launch pad**, the rocket's starting point. It provides a sturdy base and a safe environment for all the pre-launch activities. Here are some key players on this launch pad stage:

Mobile Launcher Platform (MLP): This massive steel structure acts as a temporary home for the rocket. It allows engineers to access the entire vehicle for checkups, fueling, and final preparations.

Umbilical Arms: These are giant, flexible tubes that connect the rocket to the launch pad. They provide essential fluids like fuel and oxidizer, as well as electrical connections for communication and data transfer. Imagine them as the rocket's umbilical cord, nourishing it before it takes flight.

Deflector: This impressive structure, often filled with water, diverts the hot exhaust plume from the rocket engine away from the launch pad, protecting it from the fiery blast. Think of it as a giant heat shield, keeping the launch pad cool.

Testing, Testing... 1, 2, 3! – Integrated Rocket Evaluation

Before launching your precious cargo into space, you need to be absolutely sure everything is working perfectly. That's where the magic integrated rocket evaluation comes in. Ground systems play a crucial role here:

Ground Checkout Equipment: This is a fancy term for a collection of specialized tools and instruments. They're used to check every single system within the rocket, from the engines and propulsion systems to the electrical and communication systems. Think of them as the rocket's personal doctor, giving it a thorough checkup before liftoff.

Launch Control Center: This is the mission control for the launch. Here, engineers and scientists monitor all the data coming from the rocket and ground systems in real-time. They can identify any potential issues and make adjustments before launch. It's the nerve center of the entire operation, where every heartbeat of the rocket is meticulously tracked.

Launch Day! The Ground Systems Take Center Stage

The big day arrives! The rocket is fueled, all systems are a go, and the countdown begins. Ground systems shine in this moment:

Fueling Systems: These complex systems meticulously pump the rocket with the precise amount of fuel and oxidizer it needs for liftoff. It's a delicate balancing act; too little fuel, and the rocket won't reach orbit. Too much, and it becomes inefficient.

Ignition Systems: When the countdown reaches zero, a spark ignites the rocket engine, unleashing a torrent of fire and fury.

Ground systems ensure a smooth and controlled ignition, sending the rocket on its journey.

Mission: Control! Keeping Your Rocket on Course with Essential Systems

Just launched your magnificent rocket, then only the real work is just beginning! To ensure a safe and successful journey, we rely on a trio of critical ground systems: **range safety, telemetry and telecommand, and radar systems**. Let's dive into how these systems work together to keep your rocket on course and bring it back home (or, well, at least not somewhere it shouldn't go!).

Range Safety – Guardians of the Skies

Imagine a group of watchful eagles, constantly scanning the heavens. That's essentially the role of **range safety**. Their top priority? **Safety, safety, safety!** Here's how they keep things in check:

Destruct System: This might sound ominous, but it's a crucial failsafe. If the rocket veers off course and poses a threat to populated areas or valuable property, the range safety team can activate the destruct system, terminating the flight in a controlled manner. Think of it as a giant emergency brake for an out-of-control rocket.

Tracking Systems: Range safety uses advanced radars and telescopes to precisely track the rocket's trajectory. If anything goes wrong, they can quickly assess the situation and determine the best course of action.

Telemetry & Telecommand – A Spacetime Conversation

Now, let's talk about communication! Just like you wouldn't send your child on a long trip without a phone, we need to stay in touch with our rocket. This is where **telemetry and telecommand** come in:

Telemetry: This system acts as the rocket's voice. Sensors onboard constantly collect data on everything from engine performance to fuel levels. This data is then transmitted back to Earth in real-time, allowing us to monitor the rocket's health and make adjustments if needed. Imagine it as a constant stream of updates from the rocket, keeping us informed.

Telecommand: Think of this as your way of talking back to the rocket. The ground control team can use telecommand to send instructions to the rocket's onboard computers. These commands can range from minor adjustments to course corrections or even activating onboard systems. It's your way of sending instructions up to the rocket, like telling it to fire its thrusters or deploy its solar panels. The commands include the commands even to destruct the vehicle in the event of a malfunction and the vehicle veers off to populated areas.

Radar Systems – All-Seeing Eyes in the Sky

Finally, we have our trusty **radar systems**. These act as the watchful eyes of the operation, constantly tracking the rocket's position and velocity:

Tracking Radars: These powerful radars use radio waves to pinpoint the rocket's location with incredible precision. They can even track the rocket's speed and direction, ensuring it stays on its intended course. Imagine them as a high-tech spotlight, keeping the rocket constantly in view.

Telemetry Radars: These specialized radars are specifically designed to receive the data stream from the rocket's telemetry system. They work in conjunction with ground stations to ensure all that crucial information is received loud and clear. Think of them as giant ears tuned to the rocket's whispers, picking up on every detail.

The Grand Symphony of Spaceflight

These three systems work together in beautiful harmony, conducting the grand symphony of spaceflight. Range safety ensures a safe journey, telemetry and telecommand keep the lines of communication open, and radar systems provide constant vigilance. With these systems working seamlessly, your rocket can soar through the cosmos with confidence, reaching new heights and achieving the seemingly impossible

Launch Monitoring Systems: As the rocket takes flight, a network of radars, cameras, and telemetry systems track its trajectory and performance. This crucial information helps ensure a safe and successful launch.

The Symphony of Success

Ground systems may not be the glamorous stars of the show, but they're the silent orchestra that makes every launch a success. They're a testament to human ingenuity, a complex web of technology that transforms dreams of space travel into reality. So, the next time you witness a rocket majestically rise into the sky, remember the unsung heroes – the ground systems – that made it all possible!

In conclusion, rocket science is an amazing mix of imagination, precision, and constant innovation. It turns dreams of space exploration into reality and shows the best of human creativity and teamwork. By learning the basics of propulsion and tackling tough engineering problems, rocket science opens up endless possibilities. We explored the complex technology and engineering needed to design and build vehicles that can travel into space. From understanding propulsion to overcoming the strong forces during launch and flight, we saw the careful craftsmanship and innovative thinking required to make rockets that can leave Earth and journey into the cosmos. For those excited about exploring space, becoming a rocket scientist offers a challenging but rewarding path filled with wonder and discovery. As we advance in this incredible field, the stars are no longer out of reach—they're our next goal in our ongoing search for knowledge and adventure.

Chapter 4

Academic Background of rocket Scientists

Science: The Foundation of Rocket Science

You, future ROCKET SCIENTIST, get ready! We've started with the basics of rockets, and now it's time to dive into the amazing SCIENCE and ENGINEERING journey that will make you a real rocket scientist! Get ready to explore new areas of knowledge, because this is your mission control to becoming a SPACE EXPLORATION SUPERHERO.

Just like a sturdy launchpad, your journey begins with a strong foundation in science. Here are the key scientific disciplines that fuel rocket science:

Physics: This is the language of the universe! Mastering physics allows you to understand the forces at play during launch, how rockets move in space (orbital mechanics), and the effects of gravity. Imagine calculating the trajectory of your rocket to Mars – that's physics in action!

Chemistry: Rockets are all about chemical reactions. Understanding the properties of propellants (rocket fuel) and how they burn efficiently is crucial. Imagine formulating a special type of fuel that allows your rocket to travel further – that's the power of chemistry!

Mathematics: This is the code that unlocks the secrets of the universe. You'll use advanced math to design and analyze rocket structures, calculate trajectories, and optimize performance. Think of solving complex equations to ensure your rocket reaches its destination perfectly – that's the beauty of math!

Engineering: Building Your Rocket Science Toolkit

Once you've got the scientific base, it's time to build your engineering toolkit. Being a rocket scientist involves a lot of engineering, but don't worry! This guide will break it down for you step-by-step. I'll explain all the important parts of engineering you'll need to know to reach for the stars!

Aerospace & Aeronautical Engineering: The Heart and Soul of Rocket Science

Aerospace and aeronautical engineering are at the very core of rocket science, embodying the essence of designing, developing, and perfecting vehicles capable of exploring the final frontier. This field covers a vast array of disciplines, from the overall design of spacecraft to the intricacies of propulsion systems and guidance control. Envision yourself crafting the next generation of spacecraft—that's aerospace engineering at its finest!

At the forefront of rocket design and development, aeronautical engineering delves into the study of aircraft and spacecraft dynamics. This involves mastering the principles of aerodynamics, propulsion systems, and structural analysis—each of which is paramount to the successful creation and operation of rockets.

Aerodynamics:

Understanding the behaviour of airflow over a rocket's surface is crucial. The aerodynamics of a rocket affects its stability and performance during ascent. Engineers must consider factors such as drag, lift, and turbulence. By optimizing the shape and surface of the rocket, they can minimize air resistance, reduce fuel consumption, and ensure a smoother ascent. Advanced computational models and wind tunnel testing are often employed to simulate and refine these aerodynamic properties.

Propulsion Systems:

Propulsion systems are the engines that drive rockets into space. Engineers in this field must understand various types of propulsion, including chemical rockets, ion thrusters, and other advanced technologies. This involves studying the combustion processes, fuel mixtures, and exhaust dynamics to achieve maximum efficiency and thrust. Innovations in propulsion technology can lead to more powerful, reliable, and cost-effective rockets. For example, liquid fuel engines, solid rocket boosters, and hybrid systems each have unique advantages and challenges that aerospace engineers must navigate.

Structural Analysis:

The structural integrity of a rocket is essential for withstanding the immense forces experienced during launch and flight. Aerospace engineers perform rigorous structural analysis to ensure that every component can endure these stresses without failure. This includes selecting appropriate materials, designing load-bearing structures, and conducting stress tests. The goal is to create a rocket that is both strong and lightweight, maximizing its payload capacity while ensuring safety and durability.

Guidance and Control Systems:

Precision in navigation and control is critical for a successful mission. Engineers design sophisticated guidance and control systems that use sensors, gyroscopes, and onboard computers to maintain the rocket's trajectory and orientation. These systems must be highly accurate, capable of making real-time adjustments to account for variables such as atmospheric conditions and gravitational forces. The interplay between these guidance systems and the rocket's propulsion and aerodynamic design ensures that the vehicle follows its intended path from launch to destination.

Crafting the Future:

Aerospace and aeronautical engineers are the visionaries behind the next generation of spacecraft. They push the boundaries of technology and innovation, transforming concepts into reality. Their work involves not only theoretical knowledge but also practical application, extensive testing, and continuous improvement.

Imagine designing a spacecraft that can travel to Mars, withstanding the harsh environment of space, landing on a distant planet, and returning safely. This is the pinnacle of aerospace engineering—a blend of creativity, precision, and relentless pursuit of excellence.

Mastering the Field:

To excel in aerospace and aeronautical engineering, one must master a wide range of subjects. This includes fluid dynamics, thermodynamics, control theory, and materials science. Advanced degrees and hands-on experience in designing and testing aerospace systems are often necessary. The field is ever-evolving, with new technologies and methodologies continually emerging, making lifelong learning and adaptation essential.

In conclusion, aerospace and aeronautical engineering are the heart and soul of rocket science. These disciplines encompass everything from designing the overall vehicle to perfecting propulsion systems and guidance control. By mastering the principles of aerodynamics, propulsion, and structural analysis, aerospace engineers create the vehicles that will carry us into the next era of space exploration. Their work not only enhances our understanding of the cosmos but also pushes the boundaries of human capability, paving the way for future generations of space explorers.

Mechanical Engineering

Mechanical Engineering is indispensable in the design, fabrication, and functionality of rockets. This field encompasses a wide range of disciplines, each crucial to overcoming the unique challenges presented by space exploration. By delving into thermodynamics, fluid mechanics, structures, machine design, and material science, engineers can develop the expertise needed to create rockets that withstand extreme conditions and perform reliably.

Thermodynamics plays a vital role in understanding and managing the heat generated during rocket propulsion and re-entry into Earth's atmosphere. The principles of thermodynamics help engineers design systems that can efficiently manage thermal energy, ensuring that components do not overheat and fail under the intense conditions of a launch or space travel.

Fluid mechanics is equally critical, particularly in the propulsion system. The behaviour of liquids and gases under various pressures and temperatures determines how fuel is delivered and combusted within the rocket engines. Engineers must optimize the flow of propellants to ensure efficient combustion, which directly influences the amount of thrust generated. This requires precise calculations and simulations to model the complex interactions within the engine's combustion chamber.

Structures and material science are foundational to the physical integrity of the rocket. Engineers must design the rocket's body to withstand immense forces during launch, including the vibrations and stresses caused by rapid acceleration.

Machine design involves creating the mechanical systems and components that make up the rocket. This includes everything from the intricate mechanisms that control engine nozzles to the deployment systems for satellite payloads. Engineers must ensure these machines operate flawlessly in the harsh environment of space, where extreme temperatures, vacuum conditions, and radiation pose significant challenges.

Consider the propulsion system as a specific example. This system relies heavily on the principles of fluid dynamics to ensure efficient fuel combustion and thrust generation. Engineers must design fuel injectors, combustion chambers, and nozzles that maximize the conversion of chemical energy into kinetic energy, propelling the rocket forward. This involves detailed analysis and testing to refine the design and achieve optimal performance.

Mechanical engineers also address the challenges of re-entry. As a rocket or spacecraft returns to Earth, it encounters tremendous aerodynamic heating. Engineers must design thermal protection systems that shield the vehicle from these intense temperatures, preventing structural damage and ensuring the safety of any onboard crew or payload.

In summary, mechanical engineering provides the tools and knowledge needed to tackle the diverse and demanding challenges of rocketry. From the fundamental principles of thermodynamics and fluid mechanics to the practical aspects of machine design and material science, mechanical engineers play a pivotal role in making space exploration possible. Their expertise ensures that rockets can withstand the rigors of launch, operate efficiently in space, and return safely, advancing our ability to explore and utilize the final frontier.

Electrical & Electronics Engineering

Rocketry demands a robust comprehension of electrical systems and circuitry, forming the backbone of a successful launch and space mission. Electrical engineering imparts essential knowledge about avionics, telemetry, telecommand, guidance, and control systems—each a critical component in the operation of a rocket.

Consider the rocket's sophisticated navigation system. It relies on a network of precise electronic controls that guide the vehicle through the vast expanse of space. Telemetry systems are another crucial aspect, responsible for transmitting data from the rocket to ground control. This data includes vital information about the rocket's status, such as fuel levels, engine performance, and environmental conditions. Tele-command systems, on the other hand, enable ground control to send commands to the rocket, instructing it to perform specific actions. Guidance and control systems work in tandem to keep the rocket on its intended path. The control system then executes these adjustments, using actuators and thrusters to steer the rocket. Additionally, pre-launch operations are critical for ensuring a successful mission. This involves a thorough checkout of the launch vehicle to verify that all systems are functioning correctly. Engineers conduct a series of tests, examining everything from the rocket's engines to its electrical systems.

In essence, a profound understanding of Electronics engineering is indispensable for anyone involved in rocketry. The intricate dance of electronic systems—from navigation to telemetry and beyond—forms the heart of space exploration, guiding our vehicles through the void and ensuring that humanity's reach continues to extend into the cosmos.

Chemical Engineering: The Cornerstone of Rocket Propellants and Fuel Technologies

Chemical engineering is integral to the development of rocket propellants and fuel technologies, serving as the cornerstone for creating the powerful energy sources that propel rockets into space. Engaging in the synthesis and formulation of high-energy compounds is crucial for achieving the performance and reliability required for successful space missions.

Synthesis of High-Energy Compounds:

Chemical engineers specialize in the synthesis of high-energy compounds that serve as rocket propellants. This involves a deep understanding of chemical reactions, thermodynamics, and material properties. Engineers must design and optimize chemical processes to produce fuels that release maximum energy while maintaining stability and safety. These high-energy compounds are the heart of rocket propulsion, providing the necessary thrust to overcome Earth's gravity.

Formulation of Rocket Propellants:

The formulation of rocket propellants is a complex process that requires precise control over the chemical composition and physical properties of the fuel. Chemical engineers work to balance various factors, such as energy density, combustion efficiency, and stability. They also need to consider the physical state of the propellant—whether it is solid, liquid, or hybrid—as each type has unique advantages and challenges. Solid propellants, for example, offer simplicity and reliability, while liquid propellants provide greater control and higher performance.

Innovations in Propellant Technologies:

Chemical engineers are at the forefront of developing new propellant technologies that enhance thrust and efficiency while minimizing environmental impact. Picture the development of a new type of propellant that not only delivers superior performance but also reduces the emission of harmful byproducts. This could involve the use of alternative fuels, such as those derived from renewable resources or engineered to produce fewer pollutants. Innovations like these are essential for sustainable space exploration and reducing the environmental footprint of rocket launches.

Environmental Considerations:

Minimizing the environmental impact of rocket propellants is a significant concern for chemical engineers. Traditional rocket fuels can produce pollutants that harm the environment, such as greenhouse gases and toxic residues. Engineers are exploring green propellant technologies that aim to reduce these negative effects. For instance, using cryogenic fuels like liquid hydrogen and liquid oxygen results in cleaner combustion, producing water vapor as the primary byproduct. Additionally, research into eco-friendly additives and alternative propellant formulations is ongoing to create more sustainable options for future missions.

Safety and Stability:

Safety is paramount in the development and handling of rocket propellants. Chemical engineers must ensure that the fuels they create are stable under various conditions, preventing accidental ignition or decomposition. This involves rigorous testing and quality control measures to ensure the propellants meet stringent safety standards. Engineers also design storage and handling systems that minimize risks during transportation and loading onto the rocket.

Interdisciplinary Collaboration:

Chemical engineering in rocketry is a highly interdisciplinary field, requiring collaboration with experts in mechanical engineering, materials science, and aerospace engineering. Together, they work to integrate the propellants into the overall rocket design, ensuring compatibility and optimal performance. This collaborative effort is essential for advancing rocket technology and achieving successful missions.

Real-World Applications:

Consider the development of the Space Shuttle's reusable solid rocket boosters, which used a composite propellant to achieve the necessary thrust while maintaining safety and reliability. Another example is the innovative use of cryogenic propellants in rockets like the Saturn V, which propelled astronauts to the moon. These advancements are a testament to the critical role of chemical engineering in space exploration.

Future Directions:

The future of chemical engineering in rocketry holds exciting possibilities. Researchers are exploring advanced propellant formulations, such as metalized fuels that offer higher energy densities and novel hybrid propellants that combine the best features of solid and liquid fuels. Additionally, the push towards sustainable space exploration is driving the development of environmentally friendly propellants that do not compromise performance.

In conclusion, chemical engineering is the cornerstone of rocket propellants and fuel technologies. By mastering the synthesis and formulation of high-energy compounds, chemical engineers create the powerful fuels that drive space exploration. Their innovations not only enhance thrust and efficiency but also address environmental and safety concerns, paving the way for the next generation of rockets and sustainable space missions.

Computer & Software Engineering: The Digital Backbone of Rocket Science

In the digital age, computer and software engineering are vital components of rocket science, underpinning everything from simulation and modelling to real-time data analysis and control systems. These fields are essential for ensuring the precision, reliability, and success of space missions. Engineers in these domains develop sophisticated algorithms, create advanced software, and process vast amounts of data to support every aspect of rocket design, testing, and operation.

Rocket Simulation and Modelling:

Computer engineering enables the creation of detailed simulation models that predict a rocket's behaviour under various conditions. These simulations are crucial for understanding how a rocket will perform during launch, flight, and landing. Engineers use complex algorithms to model physical phenomena such as aerodynamics, propulsion, structural dynamics, and thermal properties. By running these simulations, they can identify potential issues, optimize designs, and validate performance before building and launching the actual rocket.

Software Development:

Software engineers develop the applications and systems that control rockets and analyze mission data. This includes everything from the flight control software that guides the rocket's trajectory to the onboard systems that monitor and adjust engine performance in real-time. These software systems must be highly reliable and capable of operating under the harsh conditions of space. Engineers use rigorous testing and validation processes to ensure that the software performs flawlessly, as any errors could lead to mission failure.

Real-Time Data Analysis:

During a rocket launch and flight, vast amounts of data are generated by sensors and instruments on the rocket. Computer engineers develop systems to collect, process, and analyze this data in real-time. This enables mission control to monitor the rocket's status, detect any anomalies, and make quick decisions if necessary. Real-time data analysis is critical for ensuring the rocket stays on course and operates safely throughout its journey.

Algorithms and Machine Learning:

Advanced algorithms and machine learning techniques are increasingly being used in rocket science. These technologies can improve the accuracy of simulations, optimize flight trajectories, and enhance decision-making processes. For example, machine learning algorithms can analyze historical flight data to identify patterns and predict potential issues, allowing engineers to address them proactively. Additionally, optimization algorithms help design more efficient flight paths, reducing fuel consumption and increasing mission success rates.

Simulation Models:

Imagine creating a simulation model that predicts a rocket's trajectory with unparalleled accuracy. This involves not only understanding the physics of rocket flight but also developing complex mathematical models and computational algorithms. Engineers use these models to simulate every aspect of a mission, from launch to orbit insertion and beyond. By fine-tuning these simulations, they can achieve a level of precision that ensures the rocket reaches its intended destination.

Software for Mission Planning:

Mission planning software is another critical tool developed by software engineers. This software helps plan the entire mission, from pre-launch preparations to post-mission analysis. It includes modules for trajectory planning, payload integration, and risk assessment. By using mission planning software, engineers can create detailed plans that account for all possible scenarios, ensuring that the mission proceeds smoothly and efficiently.

Data Processing and Visualization:

Handling the vast amounts of data generated during a rocket mission requires robust data processing systems. Engineers develop tools to filter, organize, and analyze this data, making it accessible and useful for decision-making. Visualization tools are also essential, allowing engineers to interpret complex data through graphs, charts, and other visual representations. These tools help identify trends, detect anomalies, and communicate findings to the broader team.

Embedded Systems and Control:

Embedded systems are the specialized computers that control the various subsystems of a rocket. These include everything from engine controllers to navigation systems. Engineers design embedded systems to be highly reliable and capable of operating autonomously. They must ensure that these systems can handle the specific requirements of space travel, such as extreme temperatures, radiation, and limited power availability. Control systems, guided by sophisticated software, manage the rocket's orientation, speed, and trajectory, ensuring it follows the planned path.

Integration with Other Engineering Disciplines:

Computer and software engineering are highly interdisciplinary, requiring close collaboration with other engineering fields such as aerospace, mechanical, and electrical engineering. For example, the software controlling a rocket's propulsion system must be integrated with the physical engine components designed by mechanical engineers. This integration ensures that all systems work together seamlessly, maximizing the rocket's performance and reliability.

Cybersecurity:

In the era of digitalization, cybersecurity is a critical concern for rocket missions. Engineers must protect the software and data systems from cyber threats that could compromise the mission. This involves implementing robust security measures, including encryption, secure coding practices, and regular security audits. Ensuring the integrity and confidentiality of mission-critical data is essential for the success and safety of space missions.

Future Trends:

The future of computer and software engineering in rocketry is filled with exciting possibilities. Advances in artificial intelligence, quantum computing, and big data analytics promise to further enhance the capabilities of simulation models, real-time data analysis, and autonomous control systems. These technologies will enable even more precise and efficient missions, paving the way for new achievements in space exploration.

In conclusion, computer and software engineering are the digital backbone of rocket science. By mastering algorithms, software development, and data processing, engineers create the tools and systems that drive the success of space missions. Their work in simulation, real-time analysis, and control systems ensures that rockets perform reliably and accurately, pushing the boundaries of what is possible in space exploration.

In the digital age, computer engineering is vital for rocket simulation, modeling, and real-time data analysis. Acquaint yourself with algorithms, software development, and data processing. Imagine creating a simulation model that predicts a rocket's trajectory with unparalleled accuracy.

Materials Science: The Backbone of Rocket Construction

The selection of materials is a pivotal aspect of rocket construction, directly impacting the performance, safety, and success of space missions. Materials science explores the properties of various substances to ensure they can withstand the harsh conditions of space travel, including extreme temperatures, high pressures, and intense vibrations. Engineers meticulously choose and develop materials that meet the stringent demands of rocketry, balancing factors such as strength, weight, durability, and thermal resistance.

Understanding Material Properties

Materials science involves a deep understanding of the physical and chemical properties of different substances. This includes studying how materials respond to stress, strain, heat, and other environmental factors. Engineers must ensure that the materials used in rockets maintain their integrity under the most challenging conditions. This involves rigorous testing and analysis to verify that materials will not crack, deform, or degrade during the mission.

Advanced Composites: Lightweight and High-Strength

One of the most significant advancements in materials science for rocketry is the development and use of advanced composites. These materials combine two or more distinct substances to create a new material with superior properties. For instance, carbon fiber-reinforced polymers (CFRP) are widely used in rocket construction due to their exceptional strength-to-weight ratio. CFRPs offer the necessary strength to withstand launch forces while being much lighter than traditional materials like steel or aluminium. This reduction in weight allows rockets to carry more payload and reduces the amount of fuel needed, enhancing overall efficiency.

Thermal Protection Systems

Thermal protection is a critical concern for rockets, especially during re-entry into the Earth's atmosphere. The intense friction generated by high-speed travel through the atmosphere produces extreme heat, which can damage or destroy the rocket. Materials scientists develop specialized thermal protection systems (TPS) to shield the rocket from these temperatures. For example, the Space Shuttle used reinforced carbon-carbon (RCC) tiles on its nose and leading edges, which can withstand temperatures over 1,500 degrees Celsius. Similarly, ablative materials are designed to absorb and dissipate heat by gradually burning away, protecting the underlying structure.

High-Temperature Alloys

In addition to composites, materials scientists also develop high-temperature alloys that can endure the extreme conditions within rocket engines. These alloys, often made from nickel, titanium, and other metals, maintain their strength and stability at very high temperatures. They are used in critical engine components, such as nozzles and combustion chambers, where the materials are exposed to intense heat and pressure during fuel combustion.

Resistance to Radiation

Spacecraft are subjected to high levels of radiation from the sun and cosmic rays. Prolonged exposure to radiation can degrade materials and affect the performance of onboard systems. Materials scientists develop radiation-resistant materials and coatings to protect the rocket and its payload. These materials must shield sensitive electronics and instruments from radiation damage, ensuring they function correctly throughout the mission.

Durability and Longevity

The durability and longevity of materials are also crucial factors. Rockets often face repeated stress cycles during launch, orbit, and re-entry phases. Materials must be resilient enough to endure these cycles without fatigue or failure. Engineers conduct extensive fatigue testing to ensure that materials can withstand the demands of multiple launches and long-duration missions.

Innovation in Material Development

Materials science is an ever-evolving field, with continuous research and innovation leading to the development of new materials with enhanced properties. Nanomaterials, for example, offer the potential for even lighter and stronger composites. Researchers are also exploring smart materials that can adapt to changing conditions, such as self-healing materials that can repair minor damages autonomously.

Interdisciplinary Collaboration

Materials science is inherently interdisciplinary, requiring collaboration between chemists, physicists, engineers, and other specialists. This collaborative approach ensures that the best materials are selected and optimized for each specific application within the rocket. For example, the integration of materials science with aerospace engineering helps in designing more efficient and robust structures, while collaboration with chemical engineering aids in developing better fuel and propulsion systems.

Case Study: The Space Shuttle

A notable example of materials science in action is the Space Shuttle program. The Shuttle's structure utilized advanced materials like aluminium-lithium alloys for the primary airframe and CFRP for various components. The thermal protection system comprised thousands of silica tiles and RCC panels, showcasing the diverse application of materials science to solve complex engineering challenges.

Future Directions

The future of materials science in rocketry holds exciting possibilities. Researchers are exploring new frontiers such as metamaterials, which have unique properties not found in nature, and 3D printing technologies for rapid prototyping and manufacturing of rocket components. These advancements promise to further enhance the performance, reliability, and cost-effectiveness of future space missions.

In conclusion, materials science is the backbone of rocket construction, providing the essential knowledge and innovations needed to create rockets capable of withstanding the rigors of space travel. By selecting and developing advanced materials, engineers can build rockets that are strong, lightweight, and resilient, paving the way for continued exploration and discovery in the final frontier.

Systems Engineering: The Holistic View of Rocket Science

Systems engineering provides a holistic view of the rocket as an integrated entity, ensuring that all components and subsystems work together seamlessly. This discipline involves coordinating different engineering domains, such as propulsion, avionics, and structural components, to create a cohesive and efficient rocket. Systems engineers play a crucial role in orchestrating the seamless interaction between these diverse elements, ensuring the success of space missions.

Holistic Integration

Systems engineering looks at the rocket as a whole rather than focusing on individual parts. This comprehensive perspective ensures that every component and subsystem is designed to function together optimally. Systems engineers analyze the interactions between different elements, identifying potential conflicts and resolving them before they become critical issues. This approach minimizes the risk of failures and enhances the overall performance of the rocket.

Coordination of Engineering Domains

One of the primary responsibilities of systems engineers is to coordinate various engineering domains. For example, the propulsion system must work harmoniously with the avionics and structural components. This requires a deep understanding of each domain and how they interrelate. Systems engineers act as the bridge between different engineering teams, facilitating communication and collaboration to ensure that all systems are compatible and work together as intended.

Orchestration of Seamless Interaction

Envision a systems engineer as the conductor of an orchestra, ensuring that each instrument plays its part in harmony with the others. In rocket science, this means ensuring that the propulsion system provides the necessary thrust while the avionics system accurately guides the rocket, and the structural components withstand the stresses of launch and space travel. Systems engineers develop detailed plans and protocols to manage these interactions, ensuring that every system performs its role at the right time.

Design and Development Processes

Systems engineering involves comprehensive design and development processes. Systems engineers start with high-level requirements, breaking them down into detailed specifications for each subsystem. They use modelling and simulation tools to predict how the entire system will behave, identifying potential issues and optimizing the design. This iterative process involves constant testing and validation to ensure that the rocket meets all performance criteria.

Risk Management

Managing risk is a critical aspect of systems engineering. Systems engineers identify potential risks early in the design process and develop strategies to mitigate them. This might involve designing redundant systems to ensure reliability, conducting extensive testing to uncover vulnerabilities, and implementing safety protocols to protect both the rocket and its payload. Effective risk management ensures that the rocket can withstand unexpected challenges and complete its mission successfully.

Lifecycle Management

Systems engineering encompasses the entire lifecycle of the rocket, from initial design and development through manufacturing, testing, launch, and mission operations. Systems engineers oversee each phase, ensuring that the rocket meets all requirements and performs as expected. This lifecycle approach ensures that the rocket remains reliable and effective throughout its operational life.

Interdisciplinary Collaboration

Systems engineering is inherently interdisciplinary, requiring collaboration with experts from various fields. Systems engineers work closely with aerospace engineers, mechanical engineers, electrical engineers, computer scientists, and other specialists. This collaborative approach ensures that all aspects of the rocket are considered and optimized, leading to a more robust and efficient system.

Real-World Applications

Consider the example of the Saturn V rocket, which successfully carried astronauts to the moon during the Apollo missions. The success of the Saturn V was due in large part to effective systems engineering. Systems engineers coordinated the complex interactions between the rocket's powerful engines, precise guidance systems, and resilient structural components, ensuring that all parts worked together to achieve the mission's goals.

Future Directions

The future of systems engineering in rocketry holds exciting possibilities. Advances in artificial intelligence and machine learning are being integrated into systems engineering processes, enabling more sophisticated modelling and simulation, real-time data analysis, and autonomous decision-making. These technologies promise to further enhance the efficiency and reliability of rocket systems, paving the way for more ambitious space missions.

In conclusion, systems engineering provides a holistic view of the rocket as an integrated entity, ensuring that all components and subsystems work together seamlessly. By coordinating different engineering domains and orchestrating their interactions, systems engineers create rockets that are efficient, reliable, and capable of achieving their mission objectives. Their comprehensive approach and interdisciplinary collaboration are essential for the continued success and advancement of space exploration.

Environmental Engineering: Addressing Ecological Impacts in Rocketry

In the modern era, environmental considerations are becoming increasingly significant in rocketry. Environmental engineering plays a crucial role in addressing the ecological impacts of rocket launches and space missions. This field focuses on developing sustainable practices and technologies to minimize the environmental footprint of space exploration. From creating eco-friendly propellants to managing the environmental effects of rocket launches, environmental engineers are at the forefront of making space travel more sustainable.

Eco-Friendly Propellants

One of the primary areas of focus in environmental engineering for rocketry is the development of eco-friendly propellants. Traditional rocket fuels, such as hydrazine and kerosene, can produce harmful emissions and leave a significant carbon footprint. Environmental engineers are researching and developing alternative propellants that are less harmful to the environment. For example, green propellants like liquid methane and bio-derived fuels offer the potential to reduce emissions and decrease the overall environmental impact of rocket launches.

Reducing Carbon Footprint

Environmental engineering aims to reduce the carbon footprint of space missions. This involves not only developing cleaner fuels but also optimizing the efficiency of rocket engines to reduce fuel consumption. Engineers work on improving the combustion process and developing advanced propulsion systems that offer higher efficiency and lower emissions. By reducing the amount of fuel needed for each launch and improving the overall efficiency of rocket systems, the carbon footprint of space missions can be significantly decreased.

Minimizing Launch Site Impact

Rocket launches can have a substantial impact on the local environment, including noise pollution, chemical contamination, and habitat disruption. Environmental engineers work to mitigate these effects by designing launch pads and facilities that minimize ecological disturbance. This can include measures such as using soundproofing technologies to reduce noise pollution, implementing containment systems to prevent chemical spills, and designing launch sites to avoid sensitive habitats. Additionally, post-launch site restoration plans are developed to rehabilitate any areas affected by the launch.

Sustainable Manufacturing Practices

The manufacturing of rockets and spacecraft also has environmental implications. Environmental engineers promote sustainable manufacturing practices to reduce waste, conserve resources, and minimize pollution. This can involve using recyclable materials, reducing the use of hazardous substances, and implementing energy-efficient production processes. By adopting green manufacturing techniques, the environmental impact of rocket production can be significantly reduced.

Lifecycle Analysis

Environmental engineering encompasses a comprehensive lifecycle analysis of rockets and spacecraft. This involves evaluating the environmental impact of every stage of a rocket's life, from raw material extraction and manufacturing to launch, operation, and disposal. Engineers use this analysis to identify opportunities for reducing environmental impact at each stage. For instance, designing rockets for easier disassembly and recycling at the end of their life can help minimize waste and environmental harm.

Addressing Space Debris

Space debris, or space junk, is an increasing environmental concern. Environmental engineers work on strategies to mitigate the creation of space debris and manage existing debris in orbit. This includes developing technologies for debris removal, designing spacecraft that minimize the risk of fragmentation, and implementing policies for responsible end-of-life disposal of satellites and other space objects. Effective management of space debris is essential to protect the space environment and ensure the sustainability of space activities.

Regulatory Compliance and Policy Development

Environmental engineers also play a role in ensuring compliance with environmental regulations and contributing to the development of policies that promote sustainable space activities. This can involve working with governmental and international organizations to establish standards for environmental protection in space exploration. By advocating for policies that prioritize environmental considerations, engineers help shape a more sustainable future for space missions.

Real-World Applications

An example of environmental engineering in action is the development of the SpaceX Falcon 9 rocket, which uses liquid oxygen and RP-1 (a refined form of kerosene) as propellants. SpaceX has also focused on making its rockets reusable, significantly reducing the need for manufacturing new rockets for each launch and thereby lowering the overall environmental impact. Additionally, NASA's Green Propellant Infusion Mission (GPIM) is testing non-toxic, environmentally friendly propellants for future spacecraft.

Future Directions

The future of environmental engineering in rocketry holds promise for even more sustainable practices and technologies. Advances in green chemistry, renewable energy sources, and biodegradable materials are likely to further reduce the environmental footprint of space missions. Continued research and innovation in this field will be essential for balancing the demands of space exploration with the need to protect our planet.

In conclusion, environmental engineering is increasingly important in rocketry, addressing the ecological impacts of rocket launches and space missions. By developing eco-friendly propellants, reducing the carbon footprint, minimizing launch site impact, and promoting sustainable practices, environmental engineers are making significant strides in creating a more sustainable future for space exploration. Their efforts ensure that as we reach for the stars, we do so with a commitment to preserving the environment here on Earth.

Industrial Engineering: Optimizing Production Processes and Supply Chain Management for Rocket Manufacturing

Industrial engineering plays a crucial role in the field of rocketry by optimizing production processes and managing supply chains. Efficiency and cost-effectiveness are paramount in the manufacturing of rockets, where every component must meet stringent quality standards to ensure mission success. Industrial engineers streamline assembly lines, enhance productivity, and maintain high-quality standards, making significant contributions to the aerospace industry.

Streamlining Production Processes

Industrial engineers are tasked with optimizing the production processes involved in rocket manufacturing. This includes designing efficient assembly lines where each step is carefully planned to minimize waste and reduce production time. By implementing lean manufacturing principles, engineers eliminate unnecessary steps, reduce bottlenecks, and ensure a smooth flow of materials and components. This streamlining not only enhances productivity but also improves the overall reliability of the final product.

Supply Chain Management

Effective supply chain management is critical in the aerospace industry, where the timely delivery of high-quality materials and components is essential. Industrial engineers develop strategies to manage the complex network of suppliers, manufacturers, and logistics providers. They ensure that all parts are delivered on time and meet the required specifications. By optimizing the supply chain, engineers can reduce costs, minimize delays, and maintain the quality and integrity of the rocket components.

Quality Control and Assurance

Maintaining stringent quality standards is vital in rocket manufacturing. Industrial engineers implement robust quality control and assurance processes to ensure that every component meets the necessary specifications and tolerances. This involves rigorous testing, inspection, and validation at various stages of production. Engineers use statistical process control techniques to monitor production processes and identify any deviations from quality standards. By ensuring that only the highest quality components are used, industrial engineers contribute to the overall reliability and safety of rockets.

Enhancing Productivity

Productivity enhancement is a key focus of industrial engineering. Engineers use various techniques, such as time and motion studies, to analyze work processes and identify opportunities for improvement. By redesigning workflows, optimizing labour utilization, and implementing automation where feasible, industrial engineers can significantly boost productivity. This is particularly important in the aerospace industry, where the demand for faster production times must be balanced with the need for precision and quality.

Cost-Effectiveness

Achieving cost-effectiveness without compromising on quality is a major challenge in rocket manufacturing. Industrial engineers employ cost-benefit analysis and other financial modelling techniques to evaluate different production methods and materials. They strive to find the optimal balance between cost and performance, ensuring that rockets are produced within budget while meeting all technical requirements. By reducing waste, improving efficiency, and negotiating better terms with suppliers, industrial engineers help lower the overall cost of rocket production.

Case Study: SpaceX's Manufacturing Innovations

A prime example of industrial engineering in action is SpaceX's approach to rocket manufacturing. SpaceX has revolutionized the aerospace industry by implementing innovative production techniques and achieving remarkable cost reductions. The company's use of vertical integration, where most components are manufactured in-house, allows for greater control over quality and production schedules. Additionally, SpaceX's emphasis on reusability, with rockets like the Falcon 9 designed to be flown multiple times, showcases the successful application of industrial engineering principles to achieve cost-effectiveness and efficiency.

The Path to Becoming a Rocket Scientist

As you embark on this exhilarating journey to become a rocket scientist, immersing yourself in diverse engineering disciplines is essential. Each branch of engineering offers unique insights and skills that are integral to the successful design, development, and launch of rockets. From the precision of materials science to the holistic approach of systems engineering, and the efficiency-driven focus of industrial engineering, these fields collectively contribute to the advancement of rocketry.

Dedication and Perseverance

Achieving the zenith of scientific achievement in rocketry requires dedication and perseverance. It involves a continuous commitment to learning, adapting to new technologies, and overcoming challenges. The path may be demanding, but the rewards are immense. Contributing to space exploration and advancing human knowledge are among the most fulfilling pursuits one can undertake.

In conclusion, industrial engineering is vital for optimizing production processes and managing supply chains in rocket manufacturing. By enhancing productivity, maintaining quality standards, and achieving cost-effectiveness, industrial engineers play a crucial role in the aerospace industry. As you delve into this and other engineering disciplines, you will gain the skills and knowledge needed to excel in the exciting field of rocketry. With dedication and perseverance, you can reach the pinnacle of scientific achievement and contribute to humanity's exploration of the cosmos.

The academic qualifications of a rocket scientist are diverse and multifaceted, encompassing a wide range of disciplines that collectively contribute to the successful design, development, and deployment of rockets. From the fundamentals of physics and mathematics to specialized knowledge in aerospace engineering, materials science, and engineering disciplines like Computer Mechanical, Electronics, Chemical, Systems engineering and environmental science, each field offers unique insights and skills vital to rocketry. Pursuing advanced degrees and engaging in continuous learning are essential to stay at the forefront of technological advancements and innovation. Aspiring rocket scientists must cultivate a strong foundation in these disciplines, coupled with practical experience and a passion for exploration. With dedication, perseverance, and a commitment to excellence, you can ascend to the pinnacle of achievement in this exhilarating field, playing a pivotal role in advancing humanity's reach into the cosmos.

Chapter 5

History of Rocketry and Early Experiments:

From Fireworks to First Flights

The idea of using explosions for propulsion has a long history. As early as the 13th century, the Chinese were experimenting with gunpowder-powered rockets for military purposes. These were essentially glorified fireworks, but they laid the foundation for future advancements. Fast forward to the 17th century, and we have visionaries like Isaac Newton formulating the laws of motion that would become the cornerstone of rocket science.

The 19th and 20th Centuries: The Rise of Rocket Pioneers

The 19th and 20th centuries saw a surge in rocket development. Scientists like Konstantin Tsiolkovsky in Russia and Robert Goddard in the US laid the groundwork for modern rockets.

Konstantin Tsiolkovsky (1857-1935): Often regarded as the father of astronautics, Tsiolkovsky was a Russian scientist who developed the theoretical foundations of rocketry and space travel. Tsiolkovsky theorized the concept of the "rocket equation," a mathematical formula that relates the final velocity of a rocket to its propellant mass, exhaust velocity, and the initial mass of the rocket itself. This equation became crucial for designing efficient rockets.

Robert H. Goddard (1882-1945): An American physicist and engineer, Goddard is credited with building and launching the world's first liquid-fuelled rocket in 1926. His work laid the groundwork for modern rocketry. Goddard conducted pioneering experiments with liquid-fuelled rockets and demonstrated the feasibility of using liquid propellants for sustained flight, achieving much higher thrust than gunpowder rockets.

Hermann Oberth (1894-1989): A German scientist, Oberth's work in rocketry and space exploration influenced many of the early pioneers in the field. His book, "The Rocket into Planetary Space," published in 1923, provided a comprehensive analysis of the technical challenges and potential

A little bit History

Buckle up for a thrilling ride through history, where we'll explore the fascinating tale of rockets, from their dark origins to their bright future! Let us start with the V-2 rocket, a weapon of war, and ends with the birth of space programs in the USA and Russia, fuelled by the very same technology!

The V-2: A Rocket Ignited by War

During World War II, Nazi Germany developed the V-2 rocket, the world's first long-range ballistic missile. This wasn't a shining example of rocketry, but a brutal weapon that rained terror on Allied cities. Though horrific, the V-2 represented a significant leap in rocket technology. Imagine a powerful, 40-foot-tall metal beast capable of reaching supersonic speeds and delivering a devastating payload.

A Race to the Cosmos: Capturing the V-2 Legacy

As the war ended, both the United States and the Soviet Union scrambled to capture this revolutionary technology and the minds behind it. Top German rocket scientists, including Wernher von Braun, were recruited by both sides, sparking an incredible space race.

The USA: From Captured V-2s to the Moon

The US established Operation Paperclip, a secret mission to acquire V-2 rockets and German expertise. These captured V-2s became the foundation for America's early space program. Imagine these captured rockets being like stepping stones, leading the US on a path towards the stars.

Early Steps: The US used modified V-2s for scientific research, studying the upper atmosphere and even launching the first American satellite, Explorer 1, in 1958.

Building on the Legacy: The knowledge gained from the V-2s paved the way for the development of more powerful rockets like the Saturn V, the mighty machine that propelled astronauts to the Moon during the Apollo missions.

The Soviet Union: A Rival Rises

The Soviet Union wasn't far behind. They established their own rocket program, capturing V-2 technology and recruiting German scientists. The space race was heating up!

Sputnik's Shock: The Dawn of the Space Race

The Launch of Sputnik 1

On October 4, 1957, the Soviet Union launched Sputnik 1, the world's first artificial satellite, into orbit. This event marked the beginning of the space age and set off a series of events that would become known as the Space Race.

Sputnik 1: Design and Specifications:

Sputnik 1 was a metal sphere, about the size of a beach ball, measuring 58 centimetres (22.8 inches) in diameter. It weighed approximately 83.6 kilograms (184 pounds).

It was equipped with four external radio antennas to broadcast radio pulses.

Sputnik 1's primary mission was to demonstrate the feasibility of launching an artificial satellite and to study the Earth's upper atmosphere.

The satellite was launched atop an R-7 intercontinental ballistic missile (ICBM) from the Baikonur Cosmodrome in Kazakhstan.

Global Reactions

The launch of Sputnik 1 sent shockwaves around the world, especially in the United States. The implications of the Soviet Union's technological achievement were profound.

United States: The successful launch demonstrated that the Soviet Union had not only mastered rocket technology but also possessed the capability to launch nuclear warheads via ICBMs. Americans were startled and concerned about their own technological lag, leading to widespread public and governmental anxiety.

International Response:

The rest of the world watched in awe and apprehension as the Soviet Union celebrated its achievement. The event triggered a re-evaluation of scientific and technological capabilities globally.

The Beep Heard Around the World

One of the most memorable aspects of Sputnik 1 was its radio signal, a simple, repetitive beep. These beeps could be picked up by radio operators around the world, symbolizing the presence of the satellite in orbit.

Public Fascination: Amateur radio operators and the general public tuned in to listen to Sputnik's beeps. The beeping sound became an iconic representation of humanity's leap into space.

Scientific Data:

While the beeping served as a psychological triumph, it also had scientific purposes. The signals helped track the satellite's orbit and study the ionosphere.

The Space Race Begins

Sputnik's success ignited a fierce competition between the United States and the Soviet Union, known as the Space Race. This period saw rapid advancements in space technology and numerous attempts to outdo each other.

US Response:

The United States government responded by accelerating its own space program. The National Aeronautics and Space Administration (NASA) was established in 1958 to coordinate America's space activities.

The US also launched its own satellites, starting with Explorer 1 on January 31, 1958.

Sputnik 2 Laika, a dog.

The Soviets followed up with the launch of Sputnik 2 on November 3, 1957. This satellite carried Laika, a dog, making her the first living creature to orbit the Earth. This further intensified the competition.

Funny Moments and Anecdotes

The early days of the Space Race were not without their humorous and lighter moments, often stemming from the novelty and challenges of space exploration.

Satellite Overflight Fears:

In the United States, there were amusing yet serious debates about whether Sputnik's overflights constituted a violation of US airspace. The satellite's repeated passes overhead were a new phenomenon, leading to both paranoia and curiosity.

Media Frenzy:

The media in both the Soviet Union and the United States played up the significance of the space race. In the US, there were cartoons and jokes about Sputnik, portraying it as a metallic "moon" that had suddenly appeared in the skies.

Beep Mania:

The beeping sound from Sputnik 1 became a cultural phenomenon. It was incorporated into music, radio shows, and even used as sound effects in movies, symbolizing the technological leap and the global intrigue with space.

The launch of Sputnik 1 was a pivotal moment in human history, marking the dawn of space exploration. It ignited the Space Race between the Soviet Union and the United States, leading to rapid technological advancements and a renewed focus on science and engineering. While the event had serious geopolitical implications, it also brought about a wave of excitement, curiosity, and even humour, as humanity took its first steps into the vast unknown of space. The simple beeping of Sputnik 1's radio signal echoed not just across the airwaves but across the hopes and imaginations of people around the world, forever changing our view of what was possible.

The Space Race: Yuri Gagarin and Alan Shepard

Yuri Gagarin's Historic Journey

Background: Yuri Gagarin, a Soviet Air Force pilot, was selected from a pool of over 200 candidates to be the first human in space. His training involved rigorous physical and psychological tests to ensure he could withstand the stresses of space travel.

Vostok 1 Mission Launch Date: April 12, 1961

Spacecraft: Vostok 1; Launch **Site:** Baikonur Cosmodrome, Kazakhstan

Journey into Space: At 9:07 AM Moscow time, Vostok 1 blasted off with Gagarin aboard. The launch was smooth, and Gagarin's cheerful voice was broadcasted back to Earth, reporting that all systems were functioning normally.

Orbit: Gagarin's spacecraft reached orbit, making him the first human to journey into outer space and orbit the Earth. The spacecraft completed one full orbit in 108 minutes.

Experiences in Orbit: Gagarin experienced weightlessness for the first time, a sensation that he described as feeling "very pleasant." He also observed the Earth's curvature and the vastness of space, marking a monumental achievement in human history.

Re-entry: The re-entry process was automatic. Vostok 1 re-entered Earth's atmosphere, and Gagarin ejected from the capsule at an altitude of about 7 kilometres, parachuting safely to the ground.

Landing: Gagarin landed in a field near the Volga River, where he was greeted by local farmers.

His safe return was celebrated as a triumph for the Soviet Union and a significant milestone in the Space Race.

Alan Shepard's, USA, Planned Journey

Background: Alan Shepard, a Navy test pilot, was chosen by NASA to be the first American astronaut to travel into space. His mission, named Freedom 7, was part of Project Mercury, NASA's first human spaceflight program.

Freedom 7 Mission:

Planned Launch Date: Originally set for May 2, 1961, but delayed to May 5, 1961 due to weather and technical issues.

Spacecraft: Mercury-Redstone 3 Launch **Site:** Cape Canaveral, Florida

Pre-Launch Preparations:

Shepard underwent extensive training and simulations to prepare for the mission. On the morning of May 5, 1961, he was suited up and strapped into the Mercury capsule. As Shepard waited in the capsule for the launch, there were numerous delays. He had been in the capsule for several hours, and the countdown continued to be delayed due to technical issues.

Nature Calls: Shepard eventually felt the need to urinate, but the spacecraft's design did not include a provision for this. He asked mission control for permission to urinate in his suit, to which they reluctantly agreed, realizing there was no other option.

Urination: Shepard urinated in his suit, and the liquid was absorbed by the suit's lining. This incident highlighted the need for better waste management systems in future missions.

Launch: At 9:34 AM Eastern time, Freedom 7 was launched. The Redstone rocket performed flawlessly, propelling Shepard into space.

Suborbital Flight: Unlike Gagarin's orbital flight, Shepard's mission was a suborbital trajectory. He reached an altitude of 187.5 kilometres and experienced about five minutes of weightlessness before descending.

Splashdown: Shepard's capsule re-entered the atmosphere and splashed down in the Atlantic Ocean. He was recovered by the USS Lake Champlain, marking a successful mission.

Gagarin's Achievement: Yuri Gagarin's successful orbit of the Earth was a monumental achievement for the Soviet Union and demonstrated their advanced capabilities in space exploration. Gagarin became an international hero and a symbol of Soviet prowess.

Shepard's Flight:

Alan Shepard's successful suborbital flight demonstrated the United States' resolve and technological capabilities. Although it came after Gagarin's historic journey, it was a critical step for NASA and paved the way for future missions.

Continued Rivalry:

The Space Race continued to intensify, with both nations striving to achieve further milestones, including lunar exploration. The achievements of Gagarin and Shepard marked the beginning of human space exploration and laid the groundwork for the eventual Apollo missions and the moon landing.

Historical Events After Yuri Gagarin's Space Flight

Yuri Gagarin's Space Flight and Its Impact

Yuri Gagarin's successful orbit of Earth on April 12, 1961, was a significant milestone in the Space Race. It demonstrated the Soviet Union's advanced space capabilities and increased the pressure on the United States to catch up and surpass Soviet achievements.

Immediate Reactions:

The United States was both shocked and motivated by Gagarin's flight. The American public and government realized the urgency of accelerating their space program.

The United States' Response

Alan Shepard's Flight:

On May 5, 1961, less than a month after Gagarin's flight, Alan Shepard became the first American in space. His suborbital flight aboard Freedom 7 was a critical step in restoring American confidence and demonstrating NASA's capabilities.

John F. Kennedy's Vision:

In response to the Soviet achievements, President John F. Kennedy sought to regain American leadership in space exploration. He understood that a bold goal was necessary to galvanize public support and drive technological advancements.

Kennedy's Famous Speech: On May 25, 1961, President John F. Kennedy delivered a historic speech before a joint session of Congress. In this speech, he laid out an ambitious goal for the United States: to land a man on the Moon and return him safely to Earth before the end of the decade.

Kennedy Said: "I believe that this nation should commit itself to achieving the goal, before this decade is out, of landing a man on the Moon and returning him safely to the Earth. No single space project in this period will be more impressive to mankind, or more important for the long-range exploration of space; and none will be so difficult or expensive to accomplish."

Significance of the Speech:

Kennedy's declaration was a bold and inspiring commitment. It set a clear, ambitious target that would drive American efforts in space exploration.

The speech highlighted the competitive nature of the Space Race and the symbolic importance of space exploration in demonstrating technological and ideological superiority during the Cold War.

Advancements and Milestones Leading to the Moon Landing

NASA's Apollo Program:

Following Kennedy's speech, NASA launched the Apollo program, which was specifically designed to achieve the goal of landing a man on the Moon.

The program involved extensive research and development, including the creation of the Saturn V rocket, which would become the most powerful rocket ever built.

Key Milestones:

Apollo 1 Tragedy:

On January 27, 1967, a cabin fire during a pre-launch test of Apollo 1 killed astronauts Gus Grissom, Ed White, and Roger B. Chaffee. This tragedy highlighted the dangers of space travel and led to significant safety improvements.

Apollo 8:

On December 21, 1968, Apollo 8 became the first manned mission to orbit the Moon. Astronauts Frank Borman, James Lovell, and William Anders provided stunning images of Earthrise from lunar orbit, capturing the world's imagination.

Apollo 11:

On July 20, 1969, Apollo 11 successfully landed on the Moon. Astronauts Neil Armstrong and Edwin "Buzz" Aldrin became the first humans to walk on the lunar surface, while Michael Collins orbited above in the command module.

Armstrong's famous words, "That's one small step for man, one giant leap for mankind," echoed Kennedy's vision and marked a triumphant moment in human history.

Legacy of Kennedy's Vision

President Kennedy's declaration and the subsequent achievements of the Apollo program demonstrated the power of setting ambitious goals and the importance of national commitment to scientific and technological advancement. The Moon landing not only fulfilled Kennedy's vision but also inspired generations of scientists, engineers, and explorers, solidifying America's leadership in space exploration and showcasing the potential of human ingenuity and determination

From Weapon to Wonder: A New Era Dawns

The V-2's dark origins may be a stark reminder of the horrors of war, but its captured technology became the seed for a new era of exploration. The US and Soviet space programs, fuelled by the V-2 legacy, pushed the boundaries of human achievement.

The Future: A Legacy that Lives On

Today, the V-2's influence is still felt. The basic principles behind its design are echoed in modern launch vehicles. The space race may have ended, but international collaboration in space exploration continues.

So, space explorer, the story of rockets is a complex one, filled with both darkness and light. The V-2 may have been born from war, but its captured technology ultimately ignited a passion for exploration that continues to this day. As we venture further into the cosmos, remember the lessons learned from the past, and strive to use this incredible technology for the betterment of humanity!

The Future of Rocketry: Pushing the Boundaries

Rocket science is a constantly evolving field. Today, we're seeing advancements in reusable launch vehicles, more efficient engines, and even alternative propulsion methods like ion engines. The future of rocketry is bright, promising to unlock new frontiers in space exploration and revolutionize our understanding of the universe.

So, remember, the power of rockets is rooted in a simple yet brilliant principle – Newton's Third Law. With each fiery blast, we inch closer to the stars, fuelled by a relentless curiosity and the boundless potential of human ingenuity. Keep reaching for the stars, and who knows, maybe you'll be the one who designs the next generation of rockets that takes us even further!

Key Contributions to Modern Technology and Exploration

The development of rocketry has led to numerous technological advancements and achievements in space exploration, transforming our understanding of the universe and enabling practical applications that benefit society.

Key Contributions:

1. Satellite Technology:

The launch of the first artificial satellite, Sputnik 1, by the Soviet Union in 1957, marked the beginning of the space age. Satellites have since become indispensable for communication, weather forecasting, navigation (GPS), and Earth observation.

2. Human Spaceflight:

The pioneering efforts of NASA and other space agencies have made human space exploration possible. Milestones include Yuri Gagarin's historic orbit of Earth in 1961, the Apollo moon landings (1969-1972), and the continuous human presence on the International Space Station (ISS) since 2000.

3. Deep Space Exploration:

Robotic spacecraft and probes have explored distant planets, moons, and other celestial bodies. Notable missions include the Voyager probes, which have travelled beyond our solar system, and the Mars rovers, which continue to explore the Martian surface.

4. Technological Innovations:

Advances in materials science, electronics, and computer technology have been driven by the demands of rocketry and space exploration. These innovations have had far-reaching impacts on various industries, including aviation, telecommunications, and medical imaging.

Chapter 6.

The Story of Rockets in India

Early Beginnings

Tipu Sultan and Mysorean Rockets:

The history of rocketry in India dates back to the late 18th century during the rule of Tipu Sultan, the ruler of the Kingdom of Mysore.

The Mysorean rockets, developed under his reign, were an advanced form of military technology. These rockets were made of iron tubes that held the propellant and were capable of carrying explosive payloads.

These rockets were effectively used against the British East India Company during the Anglo-Mysore Wars, particularly in the Battle of Pollilur (1780) and the Battle of Seringapatam (1799).

The Genesis of India's Space Program:

Jawaharlal Nehru's Vision:

Fast forward a couple of centuries. The world is buzzing with the excitement of the Space Age. The Soviet Union launches Sputnik, the first artificial satellite, and then Yuri Gagarin becomes the first human in space. India, with its rich scientific heritage, couldn't stay grounded!

In 1962, the Indian National Committee for Space Research (INCOSPAR) was formed, laying the foundation for the future Indian Space Research Organisation (ISRO). The journey began with a humble step: launching **sounding rockets**. These smaller rockets didn't reach orbit, but they were crucial for studying the upper atmosphere and gaining valuable experience in rocket science.

Jawaharlal Nehru, the first Prime Minister of India, envisioned a strong scientific and technological base for India's development. He believed that advancements in science and technology were crucial for the country's progress and modernization. Nehru's establishment of the Indian National Committee for Space Research (INCOSPAR) in 1962 was a significant step towards realizing this vision.

Key Personalities

Dr. Homi J. Bhabha:

Dr. Homi J. Bhabha, known as the father of India's nuclear program, played a pivotal role in the early years of India's space endeavours. He was instrumental in advocating for the development of both nuclear energy and space technology. As the founder of the Tata Institute of Fundamental Research (TIFR) in 1945, Bhabha established a strong foundation for scientific research in India.

Dr. Vikram A. Sarabhai:

Dr. Vikram A. Sarabhai is often regarded as the architect of the Indian space program. He was a visionary scientist and an influential figure in promoting space research in India. Sarabhai's leadership and strategic vision were crucial in shaping the direction of India's space efforts. He emphasized the practical applications of space technology for the development of the country.

Establishment of INCOSPAR

Indian National Committee for Space Research (INCOSPAR):

INCOSPAR was established in 1962 under the Department of Atomic Energy (DAE). The committee was tasked with formulating and executing a space research program for India.

Dr. Vikram Sarabhai was appointed as the first Chairman of INCOSPAR. Under his guidance, the committee laid the groundwork for future space activities in India.

Thumba Equatorial Rocket Launching Station (TERLS):

One of the first significant achievements of INCOSPAR was the establishment of the Thumba Equatorial Rocket Launching Station (TERLS) in 1963. Thumba, located near Thiruvananthapuram in Kerala, was chosen for its proximity to the magnetic equator, making it ideal for studying the equatorial electrojet (a stream of charged particles in the ionosphere).

TERLS was inaugurated by Dr. Vikram Sarabhai and Dr. Homi Bhabha. The facility became the focal point for India's early rocket launches and space research activities.

Early Rocket Launches:

The first sounding rocket launch from Thumba took place on November 21, 1963. The Nike-Apache rocket, supplied by NASA, was launched to study the upper atmosphere.

These early launches marked the beginning of India's journey into space research and experimentation. The data gathered from these missions provided valuable insights into the Earth's atmosphere and ionosphere.

International Collaborations

Collaboration with NASA:

INCOSPAR established a collaborative relationship with NASA and other international space agencies. This cooperation was essential for acquiring technology, expertise, and resources during the nascent stage of India's space program.

NASA provided some technical assistance, equipment, and training to Indian scientists and engineers, facilitating the development of indigenous capabilities.

United Nations Support:

The United Nations played a supportive role in India's space endeavours. The UN provided technical expertise and facilitated international cooperation in space research.

Formation of ISRO

By the late 1960s, India's space program had made significant strides under INCOSPAR. Recognizing the need for a dedicated organization to oversee space research and development, the Indian Space Research Organisation (ISRO) was established on August 15, 1969. Dr. Vikram Sarabhai was appointed as the first Chairman of ISRO. His leadership and vision continued to drive the organization's mission to harness space technology for national development.

Dr. Vikram Sarabhai: Architect of India's Space Program

Embark on a captivating journey through the life and vision of Dr. Vikram Sarabhai, the pioneering scientist who laid the foundations of India's space program. With enthusiastic fervor, I will unravel the story of his visionary goals, his contributions, and the legacy he left behind.

Dr. Vikram Sarabhai: A Brief Biography

Dr. Vikram Sarabhai was born on August 12, 1919, in Ahmedabad, Gujarat, India, into a prominent industrialist family. His early education took place at the Gujarat College in Ahmedabad, after which he went to England to study at the University of Cambridge. There, he earned a Tripos in Natural Sciences in 1940. With the onset of World War II, Sarabhai returned to India, where he continued his research at the Indian Institute of Science under the guidance of Nobel laureate Dr. C.V. Raman. In 1947, he returned to Cambridge to complete his Ph.D. in cosmic ray physics.

Sarabhai's Vision for India's Space Program

Dr. Sarabhai's vision for India's space program was revolutionary and forward-thinking. He believed that a robust space program was essential for the nation's development and independence. Here’s a detailed look at his vision and the principles that guided him:

Space for Societal Development: Sarabhai envisioned using space technology to address the socio-economic challenges of India. He believed that satellites could be utilized for communication, weather forecasting, and resource management, thus directly benefiting the common people.

Example: The establishment of the Indian National Satellite System (INSAT) is a testament to this vision. INSAT has been instrumental in enhancing telecommunications, broadcasting, and meteorology in India.

Indigenous Capability: Sarabhai was a strong proponent of developing indigenous capabilities in space technology. He believed that India should be self-reliant and not depend on foreign technologies for its space endeavors. The establishment of the Indian Space Research Organisation (ISRO) in 1969 under his leadership aimed to achieve self-sufficiency in satellite and rocket technology.

International Collaboration: While advocating for self-reliance, Sarabhai also understood the importance of international cooperation. He sought collaborations with other space-faring nations to accelerate India's space technology development.

India's collaboration with NASA for the Satellite Instructional Television Experiment (SITE) in 1975 demonstrated Sarabhai's approach to leveraging international expertise for national benefit.

Tragic Death and Succession

Dr. Vikram Sarabhai's illustrious career was tragically cut short when he passed away unexpectedly on December 30, 1971, in Thiruvananthapuram, Kerala. His death marked a significant loss for the scientific community and the nation.

Following Sarabhai's untimely demise, Dr. Satish Dhawan succeeded him as the chairman of ISRO. Dr. Dhawan, a distinguished aerospace engineer and scientist, brought his own expertise and vision to the organization. He was instrumental in advancing Sarabhai's dreams, ensuring the continuity and growth of India's space program.

Dr. Satish Dhawan:

Dr. Satish Dhawan was born on September 25, 1920, in Srinagar, India. He obtained his Bachelor's degree in Mechanical Engineering from the University of Punjab and a Master's degree in Aerospace Engineering from the University of Minnesota. He furthered his studies with a Ph.D. in Aeronautics and Mathematics from the California Institute of Technology (Caltech).

Under Dhawan's leadership, ISRO achieved several milestones:

Satellite Launch Vehicle (SLV): Dhawan oversaw the development of India's first satellite launch vehicle, SLV-3, which successfully placed the Rohini satellite into orbit in 1980.

Operational Satellite Systems: He played a pivotal role in the establishment of operational satellite systems like INSAT and the Indian Remote Sensing (IRS) satellites, which have had far-reaching impacts on communication and resource management in India.

Institutional Development: Dhawan emphasized the importance of institutional development and capacity building, which led to the establishment of several space research centers and institutes across India.

Dr. Vikram Sarabhai's visionary leadership and pioneering efforts laid the cornerstone for India's space program. His holistic approach, combining technological self-reliance with societal development, continues to guide ISRO's endeavors. Despite his tragic and untimely death, the legacy of Sarabhai was carried forward by capable successors like Dr. Satish Dhawan, ensuring that India remains a formidable player in the global space arena. Embrace the inspiration drawn from these scientific luminaries as you chart your path in the world of rocketry and space exploration.

The period leading up to the formation of ISRO was marked by visionary leadership, strategic planning, and international collaboration. The efforts of Jawaharlal Nehru, Dr. Homi Bhabha, and Dr. Vikram Sarabhai were instrumental in laying the foundation for India's space program. The establishment of INCOSPAR, the development of TERLS, and the early rocket launches were critical milestones that paved the way for the creation of ISRO. This early groundwork enabled India to embark on a successful journey in space exploration and technology development, positioning the country as a significant player in the global space arena.

The Story of SLV-3: Triumph through Adversity.

Let me tell an interesting event from the life of Abdul Kalam, which he has narrated in his book.

The First Launch: A Moment of Anticipation and Disappointment

Imagine the scene: It was August 10, 1979, at Sriharikota, a place buzzing with anticipation and excitement. Scientists and engineers at the Indian Space Research Organisation (ISRO) were on the brink of a historic moment – the launch of India's first

Satellite Launch Vehicle (SLV-3). Leading the efforts was the renowned aerospace scientist Dr. A.P.J. Abdul Kalam, under the visionary leadership of Dr. Satish Dhawan.

As the countdown reached zero, the SLV-3 roared to life, ascending majestically into the sky. For a few brief moments, it seemed as though India's dreams of entering the space arena were within grasp. However, fate had other plans. Shortly after liftoff, the vehicle veered off course and plunged into the Bay of Bengal.

Facing the Press: Dr. Satish Dhawan's Leadership

The failure was a significant setback, and the atmosphere at ISRO was thick with disappointment. As the leader, Dr. Satish Dhawan took it upon himself to face the media. With unwavering resolve, he addressed the press, taking full responsibility for the failure. Dhawan's composed and forthright demeanor reassured the nation and the scientific community, exemplifying his philosophy: "Credit to the team, blame to the leader."

He said, "We failed, but we did gain a lot of valuable experience and insights. We will come back stronger." His words reflected his belief in the resilience and potential of his team.

The Second Launch: A Tale of Redemption

Undeterred by the setback, ISRO's team went back to the drawing board. They meticulously analyzed the failure, identifying and rectifying the technical flaws. This rigorous process of learning and improvement culminated in a second attempt on July 18, 1980.

This time, as the SLV-3 soared into the heavens, the tension was palpable. The moments seemed to stretch endlessly as the rocket climbed higher and higher. Then, the words everyone had been waiting for crackled through the communication lines: the mission was a success. The Rohini satellite was placed into orbit, marking a significant milestone for India's space program.

A Moment of Triumph: Abdul Kalam and the Press

In a remarkable display of leadership and humility, Dr. Satish Dhawan chose Dr. A.P.J. Abdul Kalam to address the press after the successful launch. Dhawan's philosophy shone through – he had taken the blame for the failure, and now he ensured that the credit for the success was given to the team, particularly to Kalam, who had played a pivotal role in the mission's success.

Dr. Kalam, with his characteristic modesty, spoke about the hard work and dedication of the entire team. He highlighted the collaborative spirit and the relentless pursuit of excellence that had driven them to overcome the earlier failure.

The saga of SLV-3 is not just a story of technological achievement but also a profound lesson in leadership and resilience. Dr. Satish Dhawan's philosophy of taking responsibility for failures while giving credit to the team for successes fostered a culture of trust and motivation within ISRO. This ethos not only paved the way for the success of the SLV-3 mission but also laid the foundation for India's future accomplishments in space exploration.

Embrace the spirit of this story as you navigate your own journey in the field of rocketry. Remember that failures are stepping stones to success, and true leadership lies in empowering and uplifting your team.

Modern Rocketry in India - Aryabhata Satellite:

Launched on April 19, 1975, Aryabhata was India's first satellite. Named after the ancient Indian mathematician and astronomer, the satellite was built by ISRO and launched by the Soviet Union.

This marked India's entry into the space age, demonstrating the country's capabilities in satellite technology.

SLV and ASLV Programs:

The Satellite Launch Vehicle (SLV) project aimed to develop an indigenous launch vehicle capable of placing small payloads into low Earth orbit.

On July 18, 1980, SLV-3 successfully launched the Rohini satellite, making India the seventh country to achieve this capability.

The Augmented Satellite Launch Vehicle (ASLV) program followed, which aimed to improve payload capacity and reliability. Despite initial failures, it laid the foundation for future successes.

The PSLV: India's Mighty Workhorse Rocket, Explained!

Greetings, space explorer! Today, we're setting our sights on the **Polar Satellite Launch Vehicle (PSLV)**, the incredible rocket that's been the backbone of India's space program. Get ready for a deep dive into its capabilities, achievements, and why it's called the "workhorse" of ISRO (Indian Space Research Organisation)!

PSLV: A Multi-talented Rocket for Diverse Missions

Imagine a single rocket that can launch different types of satellites into various orbits. That's the beauty of the PSLV! Here's what makes it special:

Four-Stage Powerhouse: The PSLV is a 44-meter-tall marvel with alternating solid and liquid fuel stages, providing the thrust needed to overcome Earth's gravity.

Capacity Chameleon: The PSLV isn't a one-size-fits-all rocket. It comes in variants like the XL version, with stronger boosters, allowing it to carry heavier payloads. Depending on the variant and mission, it can lift between 1,425 kg to 1,800 kg to various orbits. Imagine a single rocket family adapting to launch different satellites – that's the PSLV's versatility!

Orbit Options: The PSLV is a master of orbital deliveries. It can launch satellites into:

Sun-Synchronous Polar Orbits (SSPO): Ideal for Earth observation satellites, these orbits allow them to constantly revisit the same area of Earth under similar lighting conditions. Think of weather satellites keeping an eye on our planet – that's the PSLV delivering them to their SSPO perch!

Geostationary Transfer Orbits (GTO): This is where communication satellites like TV satellites love to reside. The PSLV can inject low mass satellites into this orbit, where they appear stationary over a fixed spot on Earth.

A Stellar Track Record: PSLV's Major Launches

The PSLV boasts an impressive resume of successful missions:

Chandrayaan-1 (2008): This was a historic moment! The PSLV launched India's first lunar mission, successfully placing the Chandrayaan-1 spacecraft into lunar orbit. Imagine the thrill of the PSLV igniting India's lunar journey!

Mars Orbiter Mission (Mangalyaan) (2013): Another feather in the PSLV's cap! It launched Mangalyaan, India's first mission to Mars, making India the first Asian nation and fourth space agency overall to reach the Red Planet on its maiden attempt. Imagine the PSLV propelling India into the history books of Mars exploration!

These are just a few highlights! As of today, the PSLV has completed over **58 successful launches** with only a handful of failures, demonstrating its remarkable reliability.

The "Workhorse" Earns its Name

The PSLV is aptly nicknamed the "workhorse" of ISRO for a reason. Here's why:

Cost-Effective: The PSLV is a relatively inexpensive launch vehicle compared to some international options. This makes it a budget-friendly way to launch various satellites. Imagine achieving big things in space exploration without breaking the bank – that's the PSLV's advantage!

Reliable and Versatile: With its consistent success rate and ability to handle different payloads and orbits, the PSLV is a dependable workhorse, always ready to take on new missions.

Foundation for Growth: The PSLV's success has paved the way for the development of more powerful rockets like the GSLV (Geosynchronous Satellite Launch Vehicle) family. Imagine the PSLV as the training ground for even bolder space missions!

So, the next time you hear about an Indian satellite launch, there's a good chance the mighty PSLV was the one behind it! This incredible rocket is a testament to India's engineering prowess and its unwavering pursuit of space exploration.

Greetings, young astronaut-in-training! Today, we're embarking on a thrilling mission to explore the entire fleet of ISRO's (Indian Space Research Organisation) launch vehicles. From the reliable workhorse to the ambitious next-gen giants, get ready for a launch vehicle extravaganza!

PSLV: The Indispensable Workhorse (We Already Know This One!)

We've already covered the mighty PSLV (Polar Satellite Launch Vehicle) – the reliable and versatile rocket that's been the backbone of ISRO's launches. Remember, it can carry payloads between 1,425 kg to 1,750 kg to various orbits, making it a true space jack-of-all-trades.

GSLV Mk II (Geosynchronous Satellite Launch Vehicle Mk II): Lifting the Heavier Stuff

Now, let's meet the GSLV Mk II, the big brother of the PSLV. This three-stage behemoth boasts a powerful cryogenic upper stage, allowing it to lift heavier payloads:

Capacity: Up to about 2000 Kg to GTO (Geostationary Transfer Orbit) – that's some serious muscle! Imagine a communication satellite weighing the same as a small car, launched by the GSLV Mk II!

Launches: 14 successful launches so far, proving its reliability for critical missions.

Missions: Instrumental in launching India's heavy communication satellites like INSAT-4 series.

GSLV Mk III (LVM3): Aiming for the Bigger Leagues

The GSLV Mk III, also known as LVM3 (Launch Vehicle Mark 3), is the heavyweight champion of the ISRO fleet. This next-generation launch vehicle is a true marvel:

Capacity: A whopping 4000 Kg to GTO and a staggering 10 tones to LEO (Low Earth Orbit) – that's enough muscle to launch a small interplanetary probe! Imagine the possibilities!

Launches: As of now, the LVM3 rocket, developed by the Indian Space Research Organisation (ISRO), has completed seven launches. Here is a list of these launches along with their dates and primary payloads:

1. **LVM-3/CARE Mission** - December 18, 2014: This was the first test flight, which included the Crew Module Atmospheric Re-entry Experiment (CARE).

2. **LVM3-D1/GSAT-19 Mission** - June 5, 2017: This was the first orbital flight, which successfully launched the GSAT-19 satellite.

3. **LVM3-D2/GSAT-29 Mission** - November 14, 2018: This mission launched the GSAT-29 satellite.

4. **LVM3-M1/Chandrayaan-2 Mission** - July 22, 2019: This mission was India's second lunar exploration mission.

5. **LVM3-M2/OneWeb India-1 Mission** - October 23, 2022: This was a commercial mission for OneWeb, launching 36 satellites into low Earth orbit.

6. **LVM3-M3/OneWeb India-2 Mission** - March 26, 2023: This was another commercial mission for OneWeb, launching an additional 36 satellites.

7. **LVM3-M4/Chandrayaan-3 Moon Mission** - July 14, 2023: This mission was India's third lunar exploration mission, Chandrayaan-3.

These missions highlight the versatility and capability of the LVM3 rocket in both scientific exploration and commercial satellite deployment

Future: This powerful vehicle is envisioned for future ambitious missions, including sending heavier satellites and even human spaceflight capsules into orbit

SSLV (Small Satellite Launch Vehicle): A Newcomer for the Microsat Boom

ISRO isn't just about the big guys. The SSLV (Small Satellite Launch Vehicle) is the new kid on the block, designed specifically for launching smaller satellites:

Capacity: Up to 500 kg to Low Earth Orbit – perfect for the growing market of microsatellites. Imagine a constellation of tiny Earth observation satellites launched by the SSLV, providing valuable data!

Launches: 1 successful developmental launch so far, with more planned to demonstrate its operational capability.

Future: The SSLV aims to provide a cost-effective and dedicated launch option for the burgeoning microsatellite market.

ISRO's Launch Vehicle Fleet: A Testament to Indian Ingenuity

ISRO's diverse launch vehicle fleet showcases India's remarkable advancements in rocketry. From the reliable PSLV to the powerful GSLV Mk III and the future-oriented SSLV and NGLV, ISRO has the right tool for the job, no matter the mission.

So, the next time you witness a launch from India, you'll have a deeper appreciation for the incredible launch vehicles that make it all possible! The future of Indian space exploration is soaring high, and these launch vehicles are the powerful engines propelling it forward!

Unveiling the Wonders of ISRO's Scientific Missions: Chandrayaan, Mangalyaan & Aditya!

Greetings, space enthusiast! Today, we'll embark on a wondrous journey to explore some of ISRO's (Indian Space Research Organisation) most captivating scientific missions. Buckle up as we delve into Chandrayaan 1 & 2, Mangalyaan (India's Mars Mission), and the Aditya mission to the Sun!

Chandrayaan-1 (2008): A Moonstruck Debut

India's maiden lunar mission, Chandrayaan-1, was a historic moment. Launched by the mighty PSLV, it successfully entered lunar orbit in 2008. Here's what it achieved:

Lunar Mapping: Chandrayaan-1 carried sophisticated instruments that mapped the Moon's surface in unprecedented detail. Imagine having a high-resolution map of the Moon, revealing its craters, mountains, and plains – that's what Chandrayaan-1 delivered!

Water Detection: One of the mission's most significant discoveries was the presence of water ice on the lunar surface! This finding has crucial implications for understanding lunar geology and the possibility of future lunar settlements.

A Pioneering Legacy: Chandrayaan-1 paved the way for future Indian lunar missions and established India as a major player in lunar exploration.

Chandrayaan-2 (2019): A Bold Attempt for a Soft Landing

Chandrayaan-2 was a more ambitious mission, aiming for a soft landing on the lunar surface and deploying a rover named Vikram. While the lander Vikram didn't make a soft touchdown, the mission had several successes:

Orbital Achievements: The Chandrayaan-2 orbiter successfully entered lunar orbit and continues to study the Moon with advanced instruments. Imagine a powerful satellite circling the

Moon, sending back valuable data – that's the Chandrayaan-2 orbiter in action!

Technological Advancements: The mission demonstrated India's capability to develop complex lunar landers and rovers, paving the way for future landing attempts.

Inspiring the Next Generation: Despite the lander setback, Chandrayaan-2 showcased India's unwavering commitment to lunar exploration, inspiring future generations of scientists and engineers.

Mangalyaan (Mars Orbiter Mission) (2013): Reaching for the Red Planet

Taking a giant leap beyond the Moon, Mangalyaan, also known as the Mars Orbiter Mission, was a remarkable feat for ISRO. Launched by the PSLV, it became the first successful Mars mission from Asia on its very first attempt! Here's what it achieved:

Martian Odyssey: Mangalyaan entered Martian orbit in 2014 and has been studying the Red Planet's atmosphere, surface features, and composition ever since. Imagine a satellite orbiting Mars, capturing stunning images and valuable scientific data – that's Mangalyaan on its mission!

Budget-Friendly Breakthrough: Mangalyaan was a testament to ISRO's ability to achieve complex space missions with a relatively low budget, inspiring other space agencies.

A Global Collaboration: The mission involved international collaboration, demonstrating the power of global cooperation in space exploration.

Aditya-L1 Unveiling the Sun's Secrets

The Aditya L1 mission is India's first dedicated solar mission, launched by the Indian Space Research Organisation (ISRO). The primary objective of this mission is to study the Sun, particularly its outermost layer, the corona, and its impact on the Earth's climate and space weather.

Key Points about Aditya L1:

Launch Vehicle: The mission is launched using the Polar Satellite Launch Vehicle (PSLV), a reliable launch vehicle developed by ISRO.

Orbit and Positioning:

Aditya L1 is placed in a halo orbit around the Lagrangian point 1 (L1), which is approximately 1.5 million kilometres from Earth. This point provides a continuous view of the Sun without any interruptions caused by Earth eclipses.

Payload and Instruments:

The satellite is equipped with several scientific instruments, including:

Visible Emission Line Coronagraph (VELC): To study the corona and its dynamics.

Solar Ultraviolet Imaging Telescope (SUIT): To capture images of the solar photosphere and chromosphere.

Aditya Solar wind Particle Experiment (ASPEX): To analyze the solar wind.

Plasma Analyser Package for Aditya (PAPA): To study the plasma environment.

Solar Low Energy X-ray Spectrometer (SoLEXS) and **High Energy L1 Orbiting X-ray Spectrometer (HEL1OS)**: To observe X-ray emissions from the Sun.

Magnetometer: To measure the magnetic field at the L1 point.

Scientific Objectives:

Understanding the dynamic processes of the solar corona.
Studying the origin and development of coronal mass ejections (CMEs).
Investigating the processes that lead to solar wind acceleration.
Monitoring the solar activities and their impact on space weather.

Significance:

The Aditya L1 mission is significant as it will enhance our understanding of the Sun's behaviour and its influence on the space environment. This information is crucial for space weather prediction, which can affect satellite operations, communication systems, and power grids on Earth.

International Collaboration:

While Aditya L1 is primarily an Indian mission, it collaborates with various international space agencies and scientific institutions to share data and enhance the mission's scientific output.

The Aditya L1 mission represents a significant step for India in solar research, marking its entry into a select group of nations with dedicated solar observation capabilities.

Aditya L1 was launched on September 2, 2023. This launch marked a significant milestone for the Indian Space Research Organisation (ISRO) as it embarked on its first dedicated mission to study the Sun.

Aditya L1 reached its designated halo orbit around the Lagrangian point 1 (L1) approximately four months after its launch. This timeline included various phases of the mission, such as initial orbit raising manoeuvres, cruise phase, and finally, insertion into the halo orbit around L1. The specific date it reached the orbit was January 3, 2024.

Sun-Earth L1 Point: Aditya-L1 is positioned at the first Lagrange point (L1), a point of gravitational balance between the Sun and Earth. This vantage point will allow for continuous, unobstructed observation of the Sun's corona, the outermost layer of its atmosphere

Since its insertion into the halo orbit around the Lagrangian point 1 (L1), Aditya L1 has made several significant findings regarding the Sun and its interactions with the solar system.

Understanding Solar Flares: By studying the Sun's corona, Aditya-L1 aims to improve our understanding of solar flares and coronal mass ejections, which can disrupt satellites and communication systems on Earth. Imagine a mission that can help us predict potentially damaging solar storms – that's the importance of Aditya-L1!

Space Weather Forecasting: The data collected by Aditya-L1 will be crucial for developing better space weather forecasting models, protecting our infrastructure from solar storms.

These findings from Aditya L1 contribute significantly to our understanding of solar physics, space weather forecasting, and the Sun's influence on the solar system. The mission's continuous observation capabilities have made it a vital asset in the field of heliophysics.

ISRO's Scientific Missions: Pushing the Boundaries of Space Exploration

These are just a few examples of ISRO's remarkable scientific missions. Each one has contributed significantly to our understanding of the Moon, Mars, and the Sun. These missions showcase India's commitment to peaceful space exploration and its dedication to pushing the boundaries of scientific knowledge

Looking Ahead: ISRO's Vision for the Future

ISRO doesn't rest on its laurels. They're constantly striving for more! Here's a glimpse into their future launch vehicle plans:

Next Generation Launch Vehicle (NGLV): This ambitious project aims to develop a family of rockets with even higher payload capacities, replacing the current workhorses and catering to future space exploration needs.

Reusable Launch Vehicles (RLV): ISRO is actively developing reusable launch vehicle technologies for a more sustainable and cost-effective approach to space access. Imagine launching rockets that come back for a landing, just like a plane!

Gaganyaan:

ISRO is working on the Gaganyaan mission, which aims to send Indian astronauts (Gagannauts) to space. Scheduled for the mid-2025, this mission will mark India's entry into human spaceflight.

Space Exploration and International Collaboration:

ISRO continues to work on ambitious projects, including collaboration with international space agencies and private players.

Chapter 7

Privately Owned Launch Vehicle Startups

Skyroot Aerospace

Born from ISRO Expertise: Skyroot's Stellar Origins

A Beacon for India's Private Space Skyroot Aerospace stands out as a pioneering startup in India's burgeoning private space sector. Founded by former ISRO (Indian Space Research Organisation) scientists and engineers, Skyroot harnesses a unique blend of experience and innovative spirit to make space exploration more accessible and affordable. This dynamic team is driven by a deep understanding of the complexities of space missions, paired with a youthful enthusiasm to revolutionize space access.

Rockets with a Kick: Skyroot's Workhorses

Skyroot is not just about ambitious ideas; they are actively building the rockets to turn these ideas into reality. Here's an overview of their impressive creations:

- **Vikram Series:** Named after Vikram Sarabhai, the father of the Indian space program, this family of launch vehicles is central to Skyroot's mission. Designed as small-lift launch vehicles, the Vikram rockets are perfect for deploying small satellites into orbit. This series aims to democratize space access by offering cost-effective solutions for various missions.

- **Vikram-1:** Skyroot's first operational rocket, Vikram-1, is a solid-propellant launch vehicle. Capable of carrying payloads of around 300 kg to Low Earth Orbit (LEO), Vikram-1 represents a significant step forward for Skyroot. It combines compact design with powerful thrust, ideal for launching small satellites and supporting the growth of the small satellite market.

- Future Rockets: Skyroot's ambitions extend beyond Vikram-1. They are already developing Vikram-2 and Vikram-3, which are multi-stage rockets designed to handle higher payload capacities. These rockets are set to support more complex missions, showcasing Skyroot's commitment to advancing their technology and capabilities.

Skyroot: A Beacon for India's Private Space Boom

Skyroot Aerospace is a beacon of innovation in India's private space sector. Their focus on affordability, technological advancement, and comprehensive space solutions positions them as a significant player in the industry. Skyroot's efforts are propelling India's space ambitions to new heights, demonstrating that the future of India's space exploration involves not just ISRO but also a vibrant and collaborative private space sector.

The future of India's space endeavours is bright, with companies like Skyroot paving the way for a more dynamic and collaborative space landscape. Their innovative approach and technical expertise are opening doors to exciting new possibilities, ensuring that India remains at the forefront of global space exploration.

Skyroot Aerospace: Pioneering India's Private Space Industry

Skyroot Aerospace continues to carve out a significant place for itself in India's space landscape. Their work not only complements the efforts of ISRO but also pushes the boundaries of what's possible in space exploration through innovation, cost-effective solutions, and a commitment to advancing technology.

Expanding the Vikram Series

Skyroot's Vikram series is designed with scalability and flexibility in mind, catering to a wide range of mission profiles. The development of Vikram-2 and Vikram-3 rockets represents the company's ambition to support larger payloads and more complex missions. These multi-stage rockets will feature advanced propulsion systems and improved payload capacities, making them suitable for diverse applications, including scientific research, commercial satellite deployment, and potential interplanetary missions.

Innovation through 3D Printing

One of the standout features of Skyroot's approach is their use of 3D printing technology. By manufacturing key rocket components using 3D printing, Skyroot achieves several advantages:

- Cost Reduction: Traditional manufacturing methods can be expensive and time-consuming. 3D printing reduces both cost and lead times, allowing for faster iterations and developments.

- Customization and Flexibility: 3D printing enables the creation of complex geometries that are difficult or impossible to achieve with conventional methods. This flexibility allows for more innovative designs and the ability to tailor components to specific mission requirements.

- Sustainability: Additive manufacturing generates less waste compared to traditional subtractive methods, aligning with sustainable manufacturing practices.

Developing Critical Space Electronics

Skyroot is committed to developing critical space electronics in-house, which is a strategic move to enhance reliability and reduce dependency on external suppliers. By building their own avionics and control systems, Skyroot ensures that their rockets can be tailored to specific mission needs, providing greater control over the integration and performance of their systems. This self-reliance also strengthens India's position in the global space industry, showcasing the capability to produce advanced space technologies domestically.

Promoting Private Sector Collaboration

Skyroot Aerospace advocates for a collaborative approach within India's private space sector. By fostering partnerships and encouraging cooperation among private companies, Skyroot aims to create a robust ecosystem that accelerates technological advancements and reduces costs through shared resources and expertise. This collaborative spirit is essential for driving innovation and achieving ambitious space exploration goals.

Skyroot's Vision for the Future

Skyroot Aerospace envisions a future where space access is democratized, and innovative space technologies are within reach for a wide array of stakeholders, from small startups to large governmental agencies. Their long-term goals include:

- Supporting International Collaboration: Skyroot aims to work with international partners to expand their reach and capabilities. This includes launching foreign satellites and collaborating on joint missions.

- Developing Reusable Rockets: Inspired by global trends, Skyroot is exploring the development of reusable rocket technologies. Reusability can drastically reduce the cost of access to space, making frequent and affordable launches a reality.

- Advancing Space Research and Exploration: Beyond commercial satellite launches, Skyroot is committed to contributing to scientific research and deep space exploration. This includes potential missions to the Moon, Mars, and beyond.

Skyroot Aerospace stands as a testament to the transformative power of innovation and collaboration in the private space sector. Their efforts in developing advanced rockets, pioneering 3D printing technology, and fostering a collaborative ecosystem mark them as key players in India's space journey. With their roots in ISRO and a vision for the future, Skyroot is well-positioned to lead India's private space industry into a new era of exploration and discovery. As they continue to grow and innovate, Skyroot Aerospace not only propels India's space ambitions forward but also inspires the next generation of space enthusiasts and entrepreneurs.

Skyroot Aerospace, a pioneering private space company in India, has achieved significant milestones since its inception in 2018. Here are some of their notable achievements:

1. Launch of Vikram-S: In November 2022, Skyroot made history by launching Vikram-S, India’s first privately built rocket. This suborbital rocket successfully carried three customer payloads to space, marking a significant achievement for the company and positioning it as a key

player in the global small satellite launch market (Forbes India).

https://www.forbesindia.com/article/startups/skyroot-aerospace-creating-spacefaring-history-with-vikrams/83287/1

2. Development and Testing of the Kalam-250 Engine: On March 27, 2024, Skyroot successfully test-fired the second stage engine of its Vikram-1 rocket, named Kalam-250. This engine, constructed from high-strength carbon composite materials, achieved a peak sea-level thrust of 186 kN and is expected to reach around 235 kN in space. The test represents a crucial step towards the maiden launch of Vikram-1, scheduled for later in 2024 (India Today).

   https://www.indiatoday.in/science/story/skyroot-successfully-fires-kalam-250-engine-that-will-power-vikram-i-to-space-2520273-2024-03-28

3. 3D-Printed Cryogenic Engines: Skyroot has been at the forefront of using advanced manufacturing techniques. They successfully tested Dhawan-II, a fully 3D-printed cryogenic engine, which offers enhanced payload capacity for their Vikram lineup. This engine runs on liquid natural gas (LNG) and liquid oxygen (LOX), making it more environmentally friendly compared to traditional solid fuels (mint).

https://www.livemint.com/companies/news/skyroot-aerospace-test-fires-3d-printed-cryogenic-engine-for-2024-rocket-11680620147458.html

4. Strategic Partnerships and Investments: Skyroot has attracted significant investments, raising over $68 million in funding rounds. These funds have been instrumental in scaling up operations and accelerating research and development efforts. Strategic partnerships have also bolstered their growth, enabling them to enhance their technological capabilities and market reach (Professional Times).

   https://theprofessionaltimes.com/2024/05/19/skyroot-aerospace-from-isro-roots-to-spacefaring-heights/

5. Promoting Private Space Sector Collaboration: Skyroot is a strong advocate for collaboration within India's private space sector. They aim to foster a network of private companies working together to accelerate advancements in space exploration. This collaborative approach is essential for driving innovation and achieving ambitious space exploration goals (Forbes India).

   https://www.forbesindia.com/article/startups/skyroot-aerospace-creating-spacefaring-history-with-vikrams/83287/1

Skyroot Aerospace's achievements highlight their innovative approach and commitment to making space more accessible and affordable. Their efforts are paving the way for a more dynamic and collaborative space industry in India, contributing significantly to the country's space exploration capabilities and ambitions.

The future of India's space sector is no longer just about ISRO. Companies like Skyroot are paving the way for a more dynamic and collaborative space landscape, opening doors for exciting new space possibilities!

Agnikul Cosmos

Agnikul Cosmos: Pioneering Affordable Access to Space

Origins and Mission:

Founded in 2017 by a team of passionate engineers at IIT Madras, Agnikul Cosmos has a clear mission: to democratize access to space. They believe that space exploration shouldn't be limited to big budgets and giant corporations. Their vision is to provide affordable, reliable launch solutions for small satellites, making space more accessible for universities, startups, and research institutions. Their goal is to reduce the barriers to space exploration, enabling more entities to participate in space missions and scientific research.

The Star of the Show: The Agnibaan Rocket

Agnibaan, meaning "chariot of fire" in Sanskrit, is the brainchild of Agnikul's brilliant minds. This two-stage launch vehicle is designed for versatility. Here's what makes it special:

- **Modular Design:** Agnibaan's design allows for customization by adjusting the number of engines in the first stage, enabling it to carry payloads ranging from 100 kg to 300 kg to a 700 km orbit. This modularity provides flexibility to accommodate different mission requirements and payload sizes.

- **3D-Printed Engine:** Agnibaan boasts the world's first single-piece, 3D-printed rocket engine. This innovative approach reduces weight, complexity, and manufacturing time, making the launch process more efficient. The engine's proprietary design represents a significant advancement in aerospace manufacturing technology.

- **Semi-Cryogenic Engine:** The rocket is powered by a semi-cryogenic engine that uses a combination of liquid oxygen (LOX) and kerosene, offering a good balance between performance and cost. This engine is a testament to Indian engineering prowess, providing reliable and efficient propulsion.

- **Mobile Launch System:** Agnikul envisions a mobile launch system for their Agnibaan rockets, allowing launches from various locations in India. This flexibility is crucial for meeting diverse mission requirements and navigating regulatory landscapes. It also enhances the ability to respond quickly to launch opportunities.

Milestones and Achievements:

Agnikul Cosmos has made significant strides in its journey to revolutionize space access:

- **Sub-Orbital Success:** On June 1st, 2024, Agnikul successfully conducted a sub-orbital test flight, marking a major milestone. This launch validated the Agnibaan concept and its flight control systems, demonstrating the feasibility of their design and technology.

- **Industry Recognition:** Agnikul has attracted attention and investment from prominent figures like Anand Mahindra, chairman of the Mahindra Group. This support not only validates their work but also provides the financial backing needed for future growth and development.

- **Collaboration with ISRO:** In 2021, Agnikul signed a framework agreement with the Department of Space, granting them access to ISRO's facilities and expertise. This collaboration accelerates their development process and integrates their efforts with India's established space infrastructure.

- **Financial Milestones:** Agnikul has successfully raised significant funding, which has been instrumental in advancing their projects and scaling their operations. This financial backing underscores the confidence investors have in Agnikul's vision and capabilities.

The Future is Bright:

With their innovative spirit and a team of dedicated engineers, Agnikul is on a mission to revolutionize the small satellite launch market in India and beyond. Their next big target is an orbital mission by the end of 2025. Given their track record, Agnikul is well-positioned to achieve this goal. Their progress highlights the potential for private companies to play a significant role in space exploration, contributing to advancements in technology and expanding access to space.

Agnikul Cosmos is setting the space industry on fire with their innovative Agnibaan rockets. By leveraging advanced technologies such as 3D printing and modular design, they are making space more accessible and affordable. Their milestones, including successful test flights and industry recognition, position them as a key player in the global space industry. As they continue to innovate and collaborate, Agnikul is poised to make significant contributions to space exploration and the small satellite market.

Stay tuned for more exciting developments from Agnikul Cosmos, as they continue to push the boundaries of what's possible in space exploration.

The Future of Agnikul Cosmos: Innovations and Ambitions

Agnikul Cosmos continues to build on its impressive achievements, setting its sights on even more ambitious goals and innovations. Their commitment to democratizing space access and pushing the boundaries of rocket technology positions them as a transformative force in the aerospace industry.

Upcoming Missions and Technological Advancements

Orbital Missions: Agnikul Cosmos aims to conduct its first orbital mission by the end of 2025. This ambitious goal will involve the deployment of small satellites into Low Earth Orbit (LEO), showcasing their ability to support commercial, academic, and research-based payloads. Successfully achieving this milestone will validate Agnikul's technological advancements and operational capabilities, marking a significant step forward for the company.

Further Development of Agnibaan Rockets: The ongoing development of the Agnibaan series will see enhancements in payload capacity, propulsion efficiency, and modular flexibility. The company is focused on perfecting their semi-cryogenic engine technology and expanding the customization options for different mission profiles. This development will enable Agnikul to cater to a wider range of customers and mission requirements, further solidifying their market position.

Innovation in Manufacturing: Agnikul is continuously exploring innovations in manufacturing processes. Their use of 3D printing technology for creating rocket engines not only reduces production time and costs but also allows for rapid prototyping and iterative design improvements. This approach enables Agnikul to stay ahead of the curve in a highly competitive industry, providing cutting-edge solutions to their clients.

Strategic Partnerships and Ecosystem Development

Collaborations with Global Space Agencies: In addition to their collaboration with ISRO, Agnikul is seeking partnerships with international space agencies and commercial entities. These collaborations aim to leverage global expertise and resources, enhancing their technological capabilities and expanding their market reach. Joint missions and shared technological developments will play a crucial role in Agnikul's growth strategy.

Supporting a Thriving Space Ecosystem: Agnikul Cosmos is committed to fostering a robust space ecosystem in India. By promoting education, supporting startups, and encouraging public-private partnerships, Agnikul is helping to cultivate a new generation of space innovators. Their efforts include participating in educational initiatives, offering mentorship to emerging space companies, and advocating for supportive government policies.

Environmental Sustainability

Eco-Friendly Propulsion Technologies: Recognizing the environmental impact of rocket launches, Agnikul is investing in the development of eco-friendly propulsion technologies. Their focus on semi-cryogenic engines, which use liquid oxygen and kerosene, is a step towards more sustainable space travel. Future developments may include the use of alternative, greener propellants that reduce emissions and minimize the ecological footprint of launches.

Minimizing Launch Site Impact: Agnikul's mobile launch system concept not only provides operational flexibility but also aims to reduce the environmental impact on any single launch site. By rotating launch locations and employing eco-friendly practices, Agnikul can minimize habitat disruption and promote sustainable use of launch facilities.

Vision for the Future

Expanding Beyond LEO: While the initial focus is on Low Earth Orbit, Agnikul has long-term plans to expand its capabilities to Medium Earth Orbit (MEO) and Geostationary Orbit (GEO). This expansion will enable them to support a broader range of satellite missions, including communications, Earth observation, and scientific research.

Agnikul Cosmos stands at the forefront of a new era in the Indian space industry, driven by innovation, strategic vision, and a commitment to making space accessible. Their achievements so far, including the successful sub-orbital test flight and industry recognition, are just the beginning. With continued advancements in rocket technology, strategic partnerships, and a focus on sustainability, Agnikul is poised to make significant contributions to space exploration. As they aim for an orbital mission by 2025 and beyond, Agnikul Cosmos is undoubtedly a company to watch, inspiring future generations and shaping the future of space travel.

Conclusion: The Rising Tide of India's Private Space Sector

India's private space sector is experiencing an unprecedented surge, driven by innovation, strategic vision, and a collaborative spirit. Companies like Skyroot Aerospace and Agnikul Cosmos are leading the charge, demonstrating remarkable achievements in rocket development and space technology. Their efforts to democratize space access, coupled with advancements in eco-friendly propulsion systems and 3D printing, are setting new benchmarks in the industry. Strategic partnerships with ISRO and international space agencies, along with substantial investments from notable figures and institutions, further underscore the sector's potential.

The private space industry in India is not only making space more accessible and affordable but also fostering a robust ecosystem that encourages education, innovation, and sustainable practices. As these companies continue to push the boundaries of what's possible, they are poised to play a crucial role in the global space arena. The future of India's space exploration is bright, with private sector contributions paving the way for new discoveries, economic growth, and a strengthened position in the global space community.

Chapter 8

Worldwide Rocket Launching Agencies,

Where Rocket Scientists are being made.

Let's take a whirlwind tour of some of the major launch agencies making waves in the space industry:

Government Powerhouses:

National Aeronautics and Space Administration (NASA) - USA: The granddaddy of them all, NASA is synonymous with space exploration. From the iconic moon landings to the groundbreaking missions of Curiosity on Mars and Voyager probes venturing beyond our solar system, NASA has a rich history of pushing the boundaries of human knowledge.

European Space Agency (ESA) - Europe: A collaborative effort of 22 member states, ESA is a force to be reckoned with. They're behind the mighty Ariane rocket family, a workhorse for commercial and government launches, and play a crucial role in the International Space Station program.

Japan Aerospace Exploration Agency (JAXA) - Japan: JAXA is renowned for its innovative and reliable launch vehicles like the H-IIA and H-IIB rockets. They've made significant contributions to lunar exploration with the Hayabusa missions and are a partner in the International Space Station.

China National Space Administration (CNSA) - China: CNSA has made tremendous strides in recent years. They've successfully launched their own space station, Tianhe, and their Long March rocket family is a major player in the launch market. CNSA is ambitiously pursuing lunar exploration and robotic missions to Mars.

Roscosmos State Corporation for Space Activities (Roscosmos) - Russia: Heirs to the legacy of the Soviet space program, Roscosmos boasts the venerable Soyuz rockets, a mainstay for human spaceflight to the International Space Station. They're also developing next-generation launch vehicles for future missions.

Commercial Upstarts:

SpaceX - USA: Founded by Elon Musk, SpaceX is a true game-changer. They've revolutionized spaceflight with their reusable Falcon 9 and Falcon Heavy rockets, slashing launch costs and making space more accessible. From sending astronauts to the International Space Station to launching Starlink internet satellites, SpaceX is a major player with ambitious plans for Mars colonization.

SpaceX's Falcon Fleet: SpaceX has revolutionized spaceflight with their **reusable Falcon 9** and Falcon Heavy rockets. Here's a breakdown of these impressive launch vehicles:

Falcon 9: This two-stage workhorse is the backbone of SpaceX's operations. It's partially reusable, with the first stage designed to land vertically after launch, minimizing launch costs. Falcon 9 can lift up to 23 metric tons (around 50,000 lbs.) of cargo to low-Earth orbit and has been instrumental in launching satellites, Dragon capsules carrying supplies and astronauts to the International Space Station, and even SpaceX's Starlink internet satellites.

Falcon Heavy: This behemoth is essentially three Falcon 9 first stages strapped together, making it one of the most powerful operational launch vehicles in the world. With a staggering payload capacity of over 63 metric tons (around 140,000 lbs.) to low-Earth orbit, Falcon Heavy is designed for missions requiring serious muscle, like launching deep space probes or large constellations of satellites. While the side boosters return and land, the center core currently does not due to the immense energy required for the launch.

Impact and Innovation:

The reusability of Falcon 9 and Falcon Heavy is a game-changer. By recovering and reflying the first stages, SpaceX significantly reduces launch costs, making space more accessible and paving the way for a more sustainable space industry.

The Future of Falcon:

SpaceX is constantly innovating. They're developing the Starship, a fully reusable launch vehicle and spacecraft system designed for deep space exploration, including missions to Mars. Starship promises even greater capabilities and paves the way for an exciting future in space travel.

So, there you have it! Falcon 9 and Falcon Heavy are two of the most significant rockets operating today, and SpaceX is a major force pushing the boundaries of space exploration

Blue Origin - USA: Led by Jeff Bezos, Blue Origin is another major player in the commercial space race. Their New Shepard rocket system focuses on suborbital space tourism, giving a taste of spaceflight to paying customers. They're also developing the powerful New Glenn rocket for orbital launches.

Beyond the Giants:

The space industry is no longer a sole domain of government giants. Here are a few other noteworthy launch agencies:

Rocket Lab - USA: This company focuses on launching small satellites to orbit using their Electron rocket. Their focus on rapid turnaround times and a streamlined launch process makes them attractive for small satellite companies and research institutions.

Virgin Orbit - USA: Richard Branson's Virgin Orbit takes a unique approach. They launch their Launcher One rocket from a modified Boeing 747 aircraft, offering flexibility in launch location and streamlined operations.

This is just a glimpse into the exciting world of launch agencies. As space exploration becomes more accessible, we can expect even more players to emerge, pushing the boundaries of technology and innovation

Chapter 9

How to Become a Rocket Scientist

Building a Strong Foundation

(Middle School & High School)

Dreaming of rocketing into the stars? That's an incredible goal! We just saw how many amazing technologies make up a rocket and its launch. Now, let's start on a different kind of journey – your path to becoming a rocket scientist!

While you're conquering school subjects, there are three super important ones that will be your rocket fuel: math, physics, and chemistry! Think of them as your own personal astronaut training program. The stronger you get in these subjects, the more you'll understand how rockets work and how to build them even cooler in the future!

Math: This is your rocket's control panel. You'll use math to figure out how much fuel you need, how fast your rocket will go, and even how to steer it in space! It's all about numbers, equations, and logic – kind of like cracking a secret code to make your rocket fly perfectly.

Physics: This is how your rocket works! Physics explains things like motion, gravity (that pesky force that keeps us on Earth!), and how forces push and pull on objects. You'll learn how rockets use fire (or other hot stuff!) to create thrust, which is the push that sends them blasting off!

Chemistry: This is all about the rocket's fuel! Chemistry helps you understand how different fuels work and how much energy they release. It's like figuring out the best rocket food to give your machine the most power to reach for the stars!

Here's the extra-cool part: These subjects are all connected! The math you use to calculate how fast your rocket goes depends on the physics of how the engine works, which in turn depends on the chemistry of the fuel you use. It's like a super team working together!

In school, put all your effort to be excellent in math, physics, and chemistry. If your school offers advanced classes in these subjects, jump right in! The more you learn now, the easier it will be to build amazing rockets later.

School isn't the only place to explore, though! Look for science fairs, math competitions, or even robotics clubs. These are fantastic ways to put your skills to the test, have some fun, and maybe even win a prize or two. Plus, you'll meet other students who share your passion for science and space – future rocket scientist buddies!

Remember, the journey to becoming a rocket scientist is an adventure. These classes and activities are like stepping stones that will take you closer and closer to your dream. Keep your curiosity burning bright, and who knows, maybe one day you'll be designing the rockets that take us on incredible missions to faraway planets!

Let's delve deeper into each subject and how it relates to rockets:

Math: Your Rocket's Control Panel

Mastering the language: Math is the language of rockets! You'll use algebra to figure out how much fuel you need for a specific flight. Imagine your rocket as a giant equation – the weight of the rocket, the amount of fuel, and the desired flight path all need to be factored in to reach your destination.

Geometry whiz: Geometry helps you understand the shapes and sizes of different rocket parts. The sleek, cone-shaped nose of a rocket isn't just for looks – it helps the rocket cut through the air with less resistance. Knowing how angles and shapes affect air flow is crucial for designing efficient rockets.

Trigonometry takes flight: This branch of math deals with angles and distances. It's vital for calculating the trajectory of your rocket – the path it takes as it blasts off and soars through space. Trigonometry helps you ensure your rocket reaches the right altitude and achieves the desired orbit.

Physics: Unveiling the Magic Behind the Launch

Understanding motion: Physics explains how rockets move! You'll learn about Newton's Laws of Motion, which basically states that every action has an equal and opposite reaction. This is the principle behind a rocket engine – the hot gas blasting out the back pushes the rocket forward with incredible force.

Conquering gravity: Ugh, gravity! This force wants to keep everything grounded, including rockets. But we have physics to help us overcome it! You'll learn how rockets use powerful engines to generate enough thrust (push) to break free from Earth's grip and reach space.

Aerodynamics: The art of slicing through air: Air might seem like nothing, but for a rocket, it's a big obstacle. Physics helps you understand aerodynamics, the way air flows around objects. By designing rockets with the right shape and using materials that minimize air resistance, you can make your rocket fly faster and farther.

Electricity and electronics: Making a Brain: To have precise direction, calculations and computations have to be done and the current position have to be sensed, control commands have to be executed.

Chemistry: The Rocket's Fuel Formula

Fuelling the fire: Chemistry is all about the different types of rocket fuels and how they work. You'll learn about the chemical reactions that occur inside a rocket engine, releasing enormous amounts of energy that propel the rocket forward.

Optimizing the burn: Different fuels have different properties. Some burn hotter, some are lighter, and some store more energy. A good rocket scientist knows how to choose the right fuel for the mission, balancing factors like efficiency, power, and safety.

Beyond the burn: Chemistry also helps us understand how propellants (the fuel and oxidizer used in a rocket engine) are stored safely and efficiently. You'll learn about different storage methods and how to handle these powerful chemicals responsibly.

Remember, these are just some starting points. As you progress in your studies, you'll delve deeper into these concepts and discover even more amazing things about the science and engineering behind rockets. The journey to becoming a rocket scientist is a thrilling one, filled with discovery and challenges that will keep you curious and excited!

Extracurricular activities are fantastic ways to take your love for rocket science beyond the classroom and get a head start on your dream career. Here are some cool options to explore, including some Massive Open Online Courses (MOOCs):

MOOCs: These free online courses can be a goldmine of information. Platforms like edX and Coursera offer courses in astronautics, aerospace engineering, and even rocket propulsion. The beauty of MOOCs is that you can learn from professors at top universities around the world, at your own pace. Some courses even offer certificates upon completion, which can look great on college applications.

Science Fairs & Competitions: These are a great way to showcase your scientific talents and passion for rockets. You can build your own model rocket, design a new type of engine, or conduct experiments on aerodynamics. Science fairs often have categories specifically for aerospace projects, and the competition can be fierce but rewarding. The best part is, you'll gain hands-on experience and learn from other young scientists.

Robotics Clubs: Building and programming robots is a fantastic way to develop practical engineering skills that are highly valued in rocket science. Robotics clubs provide a collaborative environment where you can learn about electronics, coding, and problem-solving – all essential skills for a future rocket scientist. Plus, building robots is just plain fun!

Astronomy Clubs: These clubs are a great way to expand your knowledge of space and develop your observational skills. You'll learn about stars, planets, galaxies, and the wonders of the universe – all of which are major destinations for rockets! Many astronomy clubs hold stargazing events where you can learn to use telescopes and explore the night sky.

Summer Programs & Camps: There are many summer programs and camps specifically focused on aerospace and rocketry. These programs offer intensive learning experiences where you can build rockets, participate in simulations, and even meet real rocket scientists. Some programs are even held at NASA facilities or aerospace companies, giving you a glimpse into the real world of rocket science.

Remember, the key is to be proactive and explore your interests. Look for online resources, clubs in your area, or even reach out to local universities or space organizations to see if they offer any outreach programs or workshops related to rocket science.

The more involved you are, the more you'll learn and the stronger your foundation will be. Who knows, maybe your project at a science fair or the robot you build in a club will spark an amazing idea that paves the way for future space exploration!

School Strategies for the Aspiring Rocket Scientist:

Here are some additional tips you can leverage within your regular school routine to propel yourself towards your rocket science goals:

Make Friends with Your Teachers: Math, Physics, and Chemistry teachers can be incredible resources. Let them know about your passion for rocket science. They might be able to suggest additional learning materials, recommend challenging projects, or even connect you with guest speakers in the aerospace field.

Ace Those Textbooks, But Look Beyond: Textbooks are a great foundation, but don't stop there. Look for online resources, science magazines, or even popular science books about rockets and space exploration. The more you read, the more you'll broaden your knowledge and discover exciting new areas of interest within rocket science.

Turn Class Projects into Rocket Science Experiments: Whenever possible, try to find ways to connect your school projects to your passion for rockets. For example, if you have a science fair project on motion, you could design and test different fin shapes for a model rocket to see how they affect stability.

Start a Rocketry Club (if one doesn't exist): If your school doesn't have a rocketry club, consider starting one! This is a fantastic way to get other students interested in space exploration and work on projects together. You can even reach out to local aerospace companies or universities for guidance and support.

Don't Be Afraid to Ask Questions: There's no such thing as a silly question in science! If something about rockets or space confuses you, don't hesitate to ask your teachers, librarians, or even search online forums for answers. The more curious you are, the deeper your understanding will become.

Document Your Journey: Keep a notebook or a digital journal where you record your learning experiences, project ideas, and even write down your future goals as a rocket scientist. Looking back on your progress can be incredibly motivating and help you stay focused on your dreams.

Remember, becoming a rocket scientist is a marathon, not a sprint. Enjoy the learning process, embrace the challenges, and never stop being curious about the wonders of space exploration.

With hard work, dedication, and a love for science, you can definitely achieve your dream of working on these incredible machines that take us beyond our world!

Here are some more specific tips and suggestions to fuel your rocket science aspirations within your school routine:

Sharpening Your Skills:

Math Olympiads & Competitions: Participating in math competitions like Math Olympiads not only tests your mathematical prowess but also looks impressive on college applications. The problem-solving skills honed through these competitions are invaluable for a future rocket scientist.

Coding Classes: While not directly related to rocket science, learning to code can give you a significant edge. Many aspects of modern rocketry involve computer programming for simulations, control systems, and data analysis. Even basic coding skills can be a valuable asset.

Physics Labs: Go Beyond the Textbook: Don't be passive in physics labs! Actively participate in experiments, ask questions about the principles being demonstrated, and try to relate them to rocket science. For example, when studying projectile motion, visualize it as a simplified model of a rocket launch.

Project Ideas & Inspiration:

3D Printing & Design: Many schools have access to 3D printers. Learn how to utilize 3D design software and print model rocket parts or experiment with different designs to optimize aerodynamics. This combines technology, design thinking, and practical application.

Weather Balloon Experiments: Weather balloons are a relatively inexpensive way to conduct high-altitude experiments. You could launch a small camera payload to capture footage from the edge of space or test sensor performance under different atmospheric conditions.

Research Papers & Presentations: Choose a specific topic within rocket science that interests you – like a particular type of engine or a historical rocket program. Research the topic thoroughly, write a paper summarizing your findings, and present it to your class. This hones your research and communication skills.

Community & Collaboration:

Guest Speakers: Reach out to your science teachers or school administration to see if they can invite guest speakers from local aerospace companies or universities. Hearing from professionals about their work and career paths can be incredibly inspiring.

Mentorship Programs: Look for mentorship programs offered by universities or space organizations. Being mentored by a real rocket scientist can provide invaluable guidance and help you bridge the gap between theory and real-world application.

Online Forums & Communities: Engage with online forums and communities dedicated to rocket science and space exploration.

Interact with other aspiring rocket scientists, share ideas, and learn from their experiences. Remember, collaboration is key in this field.

Remember, these are just a few suggestions to get you started. The key is to be proactive, creative, and leverage the resources available to you at school. Most importantly, have fun along the way! The journey to becoming a rocket scientist should be an exciting adventure filled with discovery and a sense of wonder.

Under Graduate Level Academics

Alright, congratulations on graduating high school! Now you're on to the exciting world of college, and with your sights set on becoming a rocket scientist, Aerospace Engineering is one of the best paths for you. This program will be your launchpad (pun intended!) to a fulfilling career designing and building the incredible machines that take us to explore the universe.

Here's a deeper dive into what you can expect in a Bachelor's degree in Aerospace Engineering:

Core Courses: The Building Blocks of Rocket Science:

Fluid Mechanics: Imagine air and gasses as super-fast moving liquids. This course will teach you how these fluids behave around objects like rockets. Understanding how air flows over a rocket's wings and body is crucial for designing efficient and stable vehicles.

Thermodynamics: This might sound fancy, but it's basically the science of heat and energy transfer. In rockets, this translates to understanding how engines convert fuel into thrust (the powerful push that propels the rocket forward). You'll learn about different types of engines, how they work, and how to optimize their performance.

Rocket Propulsion Systems: This is where things get really cool! You'll delve into the specifics of different rocket engine designs – chemical rockets, electric rockets, even future concepts like nuclear thermal rockets. This course will equip you with the knowledge to analyze different engine types and choose the best one for a specific mission.

Beyond the Basics: Specialized Courses for Future Rocket Scientists

Structural Analysis: Rockets need to be incredibly strong yet lightweight to reach space. This course teaches you how to design and analyze the structures of rockets, ensuring they can withstand the immense forces of launch and spaceflight without adding unnecessary weight.

Flight Dynamics and Control Systems: How do you steer a giant metal tube through the vast emptiness of space? This course covers the principles of flight dynamics – how rockets move, change course, and maintain their desired trajectory. You'll also learn about control systems that use sensors, computers, and actuators to keep the rocket on the right path.

Beyond the Classroom: Practical Experience is Key

While textbooks are essential, a good Aerospace Engineering program will offer plenty of opportunities to apply your knowledge in real-world settings. Look for programs with:

Labs: Get your hands dirty by building and testing your own model rockets or working on simulations of complex aerospace systems. These hands-on experiences are invaluable for developing practical skills.

Design Projects: Team up with classmates to design a specific type of rocket or spacecraft for a simulated mission. These projects allow you to apply your theoretical knowledge to solve real engineering problems and develop teamwork skills.

Internships: Consider seeking internships at aerospace companies, government agencies like NASA, or research institutions during your summer breaks. Internships provide invaluable experience working on real rocket science projects and give you a glimpse into the professional world.

Remember, a Bachelor's degree is just the first step. To become a top-notch rocket scientist, consider pursuing a Master's degree in a specialized field like Astronautics or Aerospace Propulsion. This will give you a deeper understanding and make you a more competitive job candidate in the exciting world of rocket science!

While Aerospace Engineering is the core foundation, becoming a well-rounded rocket scientist requires knowledge from various engineering and science disciplines. Here's a breakdown of some key areas that will complement your studies:

Electronics and Electrical Engineering: The Nerve System of Rockets

Rockets are marvels of electrical complexity, with intricate systems that require precision and reliability. Electrical and electronics engineers are the masterminds behind these systems, designing and building the wiring, control panels, and communication equipment that keep everything functioning smoothly. Here's a more detailed look at the key areas of study and how they contribute to rocket science:

Courses in Circuits and Electronics

Circuits and Electronics:

- **Overview:** This foundational course covers the basic principles of electrical circuits, including the function and interaction of components like resistors, capacitors, and transistors.

- **Application in Rockets:** Understanding these components is crucial for developing systems that control power distribution, propulsion systems, and other critical functions in a rocket. For example, circuits are used in the power management systems that ensure consistent and reliable power delivery to all parts of the rocket.

Electromagnetism:

- **Overview:** This course dives into the principles of electromagnetism, including electric fields, magnetic fields, and how they interact.

- **Application in Rockets:** Electromagnetism is essential for designing rocket guidance systems and communication equipment. It helps engineers create systems that can reliably navigate and communicate over vast distances in space. For instance, understanding electromagnetic waves is crucial for designing antennas and other communication devices.

Courses in Electronics Engineering

Digital Electronics:

- **Overview:** This course focuses on digital circuits and microcontrollers, which are the tiny computers that manage various functions within a rocket.

- **Application in Rockets:** Digital electronics are used to control everything from engine ignition sequences to navigation and telemetry systems. Engineers learn how to design and program these systems to ensure they operate correctly under the harsh conditions of spaceflight. Microcontrollers, for example, can be used to process sensor data and make real-time adjustments to the rocket's flight path.

Analog Electronics:

- **Overview:** This course deals with the design and analysis of analog circuits, which are used for signal processing and sensor data acquisition.
- **Application in Rockets:** Analog electronics play a vital role in handling the continuous signals from various sensors throughout the rocket. These sensors monitor temperature, pressure, and other critical parameters, feeding data to the control systems. Engineers must understand how to design circuits that can accurately capture and process this data.

Further Specializations and Their Importance

Control Systems Engineering:

- **Overview:** Focuses on the design and implementation of control systems that manage the dynamic behaviour of rockets.
- **Application in Rockets:** Control systems are essential for stabilizing the rocket during launch, ascent, and descent. Engineers learn how to create feedback loops and algorithms that adjust the rocket's orientation and trajectory in real-time.

Communication Systems Engineering:

- **Overview:** Covers the principles and technologies behind wireless communication systems.
- **Application in Rockets:** Communication systems ensure that data from the rocket reaches mission control and that commands from the ground are received by the rocket. This includes telemetry, tracking, and command systems that are vital for mission success.

Power Electronics:

- **Overview:** Deals with the conversion and control of electric power using electronic devices.
- **Application in Rockets:** Power electronics are used to manage the power distribution within the rocket, ensuring that all systems receive the appropriate voltage and current. This includes managing the power from solar panels or batteries in spacecraft.

Practical Applications

Electrical and electronics engineers work on both the hardware and software aspects of these systems. They use their knowledge to create robust, efficient, and reliable systems that can withstand the extreme conditions of space. For example:

- **Designing robust circuit boards** that can operate in high radiation environments.

- **Developing algorithms** for real-time data processing and control.
- **Ensuring redundancy** in critical systems to prevent failures during missions.

By mastering these areas, engineers contribute to the creation of rockets that are not only capable of reaching space but also performing complex tasks once they get there. This interdisciplinary approach ensures that every aspect of the rocket, from launch to landing, is meticulously controlled and monitored, paving the way for successful missions.

With a strong educational foundation in these subjects, aspiring rocket scientists can develop the skills needed to design and build the sophisticated electrical systems that are the backbone of modern rocketry.

Mechanical Engineering: The Heart of Rocket Propulsion

The mechanical heart of a rocket lies in its engine and propulsion systems. Mechanical engineers are responsible for designing and building these complex machines, ensuring they function reliably under extreme conditions. Their work is crucial for the successful launch and operation of rockets. Here's an in-depth look at the essential courses and areas of study within mechanical engineering that contribute to rocket science:

Key Courses and Their Applications

Mechanics of Materials:

- **Overview:** This course focuses on understanding the properties of various materials used in rocket construction and how these materials handle stress, strain, and temperature extremes.
- **Application in Rockets:** Engineers learn to select and design materials that can withstand the intense forces and environmental conditions experienced during launch and flight. For instance, materials must endure the vibrations during liftoff and the thermal stresses of re-entry without failing.

Thermodynamics & Heat Transfer:

- **Overview:** This course builds upon core mechanical engineering principles, focusing on the generation, transfer, and management of heat within a rocket engine.
- **Application in Rockets:** Understanding thermodynamics is crucial for optimizing engine performance and efficiency. Engineers design cooling systems and manage heat dissipation to prevent engine components from overheating. For example, regenerative cooling is often used in rocket engines to keep them from reaching destructive temperatures.

Structural Engineering:

- **Overview:** Structural engineering involves designing the framework of the rocket, ensuring it is both strong and lightweight.
- **Application in Rockets:** Engineers must design structures that can withstand the immense forces of launch, such as thrust and aerodynamic pressure, while minimizing weight to maximize payload capacity. This involves using advanced materials and innovative design techniques to achieve the necessary strength without adding excessive mass.

Finite Element Analysis (FEA):

- **Overview:** This course teaches the use of computer-aided design (CAD) software and FEA tools to analyze and optimize the structural integrity of rocket components.
- **Application in Rockets:** FEA allows engineers to simulate and test how different parts of the rocket will respond to various stresses and forces. This helps in identifying potential weak points and optimizing the design to ensure reliability. For instance, FEA can predict how a rocket's body will deform under the pressure of high-speed flight.

Composite Materials:

- **Overview:** This course focuses on advanced composite materials that offer exceptional strength-to-weight ratios, making them ideal for modern rocket construction.
- **Application in Rockets:** Composites such as carbon fiber-reinforced polymers are used extensively in rocket structures because they provide high strength while being significantly lighter than traditional materials like steel or aluminium. Engineers learn how to work with these materials to create strong, lightweight components that enhance the rocket's overall performance.

Practical Applications

Engine Design: Mechanical engineers design rocket engines, ensuring they can produce the necessary thrust while operating safely under extreme temperatures and pressures. This includes everything from the combustion chamber to the nozzle design, which must be optimized for maximum efficiency and performance.

Propulsion Systems: The propulsion system of a rocket, including its fuel and oxidizer tanks, pumps, and injectors, is a critical area of focus. Mechanical engineers design these systems to ensure reliable fuel delivery and efficient combustion, which are essential for achieving the desired thrust and trajectory.

Structural Integrity: Ensuring the rocket's structural integrity involves designing components that can endure the rigors of space travel. This includes the rocket's body, fins, and any other structural elements that must withstand the forces of launch and re-entry.

Heat Management: Managing heat within the rocket is vital to prevent component failure. Engineers design cooling systems, such as heat exchangers and radiators, to dissipate heat generated by the engine and other systems.

Advanced Studies and Specializations

Mechanical engineers may also specialize in areas such as fluid dynamics, vibration analysis, and aerospace propulsion systems to further enhance their expertise in rocket science. Advanced studies and research in these areas contribute to developing more efficient and reliable rockets, pushing the boundaries of space exploration.

In summary, mechanical engineering is the backbone of rocket design and propulsion. By mastering courses in mechanics of materials, thermodynamics, structural engineering, FEA, and composite materials, aspiring rocket scientists can develop the skills necessary to create robust, high-performance rockets capable of exploring the far reaches of space.

Additional Science & Engineering Topics for Aspiring Rocket Scientists

To design and build rockets that can endure the harsh conditions of space, a strong foundation in various science and engineering disciplines is essential. Here are two additional fields of study that are crucial for aspiring rocket scientists:

Materials Science:

Understanding Material Properties: Materials science delves into the properties of different materials at a microscopic level. This field is vital for developing materials that can withstand the extreme pressures, temperatures, and radiation encountered in space.

- **Properties of Materials:** This includes studying how materials respond to stress, strain, and thermal changes. Materials scientists investigate the strength, ductility, toughness, and fatigue resistance of different substances.

- **Microscopic Analysis:** Using techniques such as electron microscopy and spectroscopy, materials scientists can understand the atomic and molecular structure of materials, which helps in predicting their behaviour under different conditions.

Applications in Rocketry:

- **High-Temperature Materials:** Rockets experience extreme temperatures, especially during launch and re-entry. Materials that can withstand high temperatures without degrading are crucial. For example, carbon-carbon composites are used in thermal protection systems for their ability to endure intense heat.

- **Radiation-Resistant Materials:** Spacecraft are exposed to high levels of cosmic radiation. Materials that can resist radiation without becoming brittle or losing their mechanical properties are essential for long-duration missions.

- **Lightweight Composites:** To maximize payload capacity, rockets need to be as light as possible without compromising strength. Advanced composites like carbon fiber-reinforced polymers offer high strength-to-weight ratios, making them ideal for rocket construction.

Computer Science:

Role in Rocketry: Modern rockets rely heavily on software for control systems, data analysis, and simulations. Understanding computer science fundamentals is crucial for developing and maintaining these systems.

- **Control Systems:** Software is used to manage the rocket's flight control, navigation, and stability. Algorithms process data from sensors and make real-time adjustments to keep the rocket on its intended trajectory.

- **Data Analysis:** During and after a mission, vast amounts of data are collected. Computer scientists develop software to analyze this data, providing insights into the rocket's performance and identifying any issues.

- **Simulations:** Before a rocket is launched, extensive simulations are run to predict how it will behave under various conditions. These simulations help engineers optimize the design and identify potential problems.

Basic Coding Skills:

- **Programming Languages:** Learning programming languages such as Python, C++, and MATLAB can be valuable. These languages are commonly used in aerospace applications for developing control systems, running simulations, and analyzing data.

- **Software Tools:** Familiarity with software tools like Simulink (for modelling and simulation) and LabVIEW (for data acquisition and instrument control) can be beneficial.

- **Algorithm Development:** Understanding how to develop and implement algorithms for control systems, navigation, and data analysis is crucial. This includes knowledge of feedback control, signal processing, and machine learning techniques.

Integrating Knowledge:

By integrating knowledge from materials science and computer science with other engineering disciplines such as mechanical and electrical engineering, you can develop a comprehensive understanding of rocket design and operation. This interdisciplinary approach is essential for addressing the complex challenges of space exploration and contributing to advancements in the field.

To become a successful rocket scientist, it's important to build a strong foundation in various scientific and engineering disciplines. Materials science helps you understand how different materials behave under extreme conditions, while computer science equips you with the skills to develop and maintain the sophisticated software systems that modern rockets rely on. By mastering these fields, you will be well-prepared to tackle the challenges of designing and building reliable rockets for space exploration.

Remember, the specific courses you take will depend on your chosen university and its program structure. However, having a basic understanding of these subjects will make you a more versatile and valuable rocket scientist in the future.

The key is to be curious and explore! Take elective courses in areas that interest you, participate in research projects that combine different disciplines, and don't be afraid to ask questions. The more knowledge you have, the better equipped you'll be to tackle the exciting challenges of rocket science! In addition to the core curriculum and coursework, there are several exciting activities you can pursue to enhance your journey towards becoming a rocket scientist:

Hands-on Learning:

Rocketry Clubs & Competitions: Look for student-run rocketry clubs at your university or consider starting one if it doesn't exist. These clubs often participate in national competitions like the Intercollegiate Rocket Engineering Competition (IREC), where you can design, build, and launch your own model rockets. This is a fantastic way to gain practical experience in all stages of rocket development, from design to launch.

High-Powered Rocketry (HPR): If you're looking for a bigger challenge, consider getting involved in High-Powered Rocketry (HPR) after obtaining the necessary safety certifications. This allows you to build and launch rockets reaching much higher altitudes, experiencing the thrill of real rocket propulsion.

3D Printing & Design Challenges: 3D printing technology is revolutionizing rocketry. Learn 3D design software and participate in design challenges focused on creating innovative rocket components or lightweight structures for space exploration.

Research & Development:

Undergraduate Research Opportunities: Many universities offer research opportunities for undergraduate students. Seek out professors working on projects related to aerospace engineering, rocket propulsion, or space exploration. Participating in research allows you to contribute to real scientific advancements, gain valuable mentorship, and potentially co-author research papers for publication.

NASA Internships & Programs: The National Aeronautics and Space Administration (NASA) offers various internship and fellowship programs for undergraduate students. These programs provide the opportunity to work alongside leading aerospace professionals on cutting-edge projects, gaining invaluable experience in the real world of rocket science.

Industry Internships: Don't limit yourself to government agencies! Major aerospace companies also offer internship programs for students. This gives you a chance to learn about the industry's current projects, work on real-world engineering challenges, and potentially land a full-time job after graduation.

Networking & Professional Development:

Professional Societies: To aid in becoming a rocket engineer, several well-known professional bodies offer student memberships. These organizations provide valuable resources, networking opportunities, and educational support that are crucial for aspiring rocket engineers. Here are some of the most prominent professional bodies with student memberships:

1. American Institute of Aeronautics and Astronautics (AIAA)

- **Description:** AIAA is one of the world's largest technical societies dedicated to aerospace engineering. It offers a range of benefits for student members, including access to technical papers, scholarships, competitions, and networking events.

- **Website:** AIAA
- https://www.aiaa.org/

2. Institute of Electrical and Electronics Engineers (IEEE)

- **Description:** IEEE is a leading professional association for electronic engineering and electrical engineering. It supports students with educational resources, technical communities, and professional development opportunities.
- **Website:** IEEE
- https://www.ieee.org/

3. American Society of Mechanical Engineers (ASME)

- **Description:** ASME promotes the art, science, and practice of multidisciplinary engineering. For students, ASME offers scholarships, design competitions, mentoring programs, and access to technical resources.
- **Website:** ASME
- https://www.asme.org/

4. Society of Automotive Engineers (SAE) International

- **Description:** SAE International focuses on advancing mobility engineering. It provides student members with access to technical papers, networking events, and career development tools.
- **Website:** SAE International

5. Royal Aeronautical Society (RAeS)

- **Description:** Based in the UK, RAeS is dedicated to the global aerospace community. Student members benefit from access to industry journals, conferences, and educational workshops.
- **Website:** RAeS
- https://www.sae.org/

6. The Planetary Society

- **Description:** The Planetary Society is a non-profit organization that promotes the exploration of space. It offers student memberships with benefits like access to educational materials, participation in space advocacy, and networking with professionals in the field.
- **Website:** The Planetary Society
- https://www.planetary.org/

7. International Astronautical Federation (IAF)

- **Description:** IAF is an international organization that brings together scientists, engineers, and professionals in the space sector. It offers student memberships with access to global conferences, technical committees, and educational resources.
- **Website:** IAF
- https://www.iafastro.org/

Joining these professional bodies as a student member can provide aspiring rocket engineers with a wealth of knowledge, networking opportunities, and career support essential for their professional development in the aerospace industry.

Mentorship Programs: Seek out mentorship from professors, researchers, or even working professionals in the aerospace industry. A good mentor can provide valuable guidance, career advice, and help you navigate the path towards becoming a successful rocket scientist.

Attend Lectures & Talks: Many universities and aerospace organizations host lectures and talks by leading figures in the rocket science and space exploration fields. Attending these events allows you to learn from the best, get inspired by their work, and potentially make valuable connections.

Remember, a well-rounded education goes beyond textbooks and exams. These activities will help you develop practical skills, gain valuable experience, and build your network within the exciting world of rocket science. So, roll up your sleeves, embrace the challenges, and get ready to launch your career towards the stars!

Here are some additional activities you can pursue to supercharge your path to becoming a rocket scientist:

Deep Dives Through Research:

Independent Research Projects: Don't wait for professors to assign research. Identify a specific area within rocket science that fascinates you – perhaps a novel rocket propulsion concept or a material optimization challenge for future space vehicles. Dedicate time to independent research, reading scientific papers, and potentially conducting simulations or basic experiments to explore your chosen topic. Independent research shows initiative and a genuine passion for the field.

Literature Reviews & Paper Presentations: Stay up-to-date on the latest advancements in rocket science. Conduct literature reviews, summarizing and analyzing recent research papers published in top aerospace journals. Consider presenting your findings at student research conferences or even submitting them for publication in academic journals. This demonstrates your research skills and ability to communicate complex scientific concepts.

Sharpening Your Skills Through Workshops:

Specialized Workshops: Look for workshops offered by universities, research institutions, or even private companies focusing on specific areas of rocket science like rocket propulsion systems, control systems, or advanced materials for spacecraft. These workshops provide intensive learning opportunities from industry experts and allow you to gain hands-on experience with cutting-edge technologies.

Software Training & Simulations: Modern rocket science relies heavily on specialized software for design, simulation, and analysis. Seek out workshops or online tutorials to learn industry-standard software programs used for rocket design, control systems simulation, or computational fluid dynamics (CFD) for analyzing airflow around rockets. Mastering these tools will make you a more valuable asset in the workforce.

Volunteer at Conferences & Events: Attending conferences is a great way to learn and network. However, consider volunteering at these events as well. This allows you to interact with leading professionals, gain valuable organizational experience, and potentially receive free or discounted conference registration.

Remember, becoming a rocket scientist is not just about grades and textbooks. It's about demonstrating your passion, initiative, and well-rounded skillset. By actively engaging in these additional activities, you'll set yourself apart from the crowd and showcase your commitment to achieving your dream of working on these incredible machines that propel us towards the unknown.

Here are some additional details to fuel your rocket science aspirations:

Building a Stellar Online Presence:

Professional Networking Sites: Consider creating profiles on professional networking sites like LinkedIn. Craft a compelling profile highlighting your educational background, relevant skills, and research interests. Connect with professors, industry professionals, and other aspiring rocket scientists. These platforms can be valuable tools for staying updated on job openings, networking opportunities, and industry trends.

Personal Website or Blog: If you're passionate about sharing your knowledge and experiences, consider creating a personal website or blog dedicated to rocket science. Write articles about topics that interest you, analyze recent advancements in the field, or even showcase your research projects. This demonstrates your communication skills and can attract the attention of potential employers or collaborators.

Communication & Teamwork:

Technical Writing & Presentations: As a rocket scientist, you'll need to effectively communicate complex technical concepts to colleagues, managers, and even the public. Seek opportunities to hone your technical writing skills by participating in research paper writing competitions or contributing to your university's aerospace engineering journal. Practice giving clear and concise presentations about your research findings at conferences or workshops.

Teamwork & Collaboration: Rocket science is rarely a one-person show. Successful missions rely on the collaboration of diverse teams with expertise in different areas. Develop your teamwork skills by actively participating in group projects, joining student design teams, or volunteering for projects that require collaboration with individuals from different engineering disciplines.

Staying Inspired & Engaged:

Space Exploration News & Podcasts: Immerse yourself in the world of space exploration. Subscribe to reputable news sources and podcasts dedicated to space exploration. Stay updated on current events, new discoveries, and upcoming missions. This constant engagement will fuel your passion and keep you motivated on your journey.

Attend Space Camps & Citizen Science Programs: Consider attending space camps or citizen science programs offered by organizations like NASA or private companies. These programs offer unique opportunities to learn from astronauts and scientists, participate in simulations, and even contribute to real scientific research projects.

Remember, the journey to becoming a rocket scientist is a marathon, not a sprint. Embrace the challenges, celebrate the milestones, and never stop learning and exploring the wonders of space exploration. With dedication, perseverance, and a thirst for knowledge, you can definitely achieve your dream of working on the incredible machines that take us beyond our world!

Seeking mentorship is a fantastic way to accelerate your journey towards becoming a rocket scientist. Here are some specific strategies to find the perfect mentor:

Identifying Potential Mentors:

University Professors: Your professors, especially those specializing in aerospace engineering, rocket propulsion, or related fields, are excellent starting points. Look for professors actively engaged in research or with industry connections. They can provide invaluable guidance based on their experience and expertise.

Industry Professionals: Reach out to professionals working at aerospace companies, government agencies like NASA, or research institutions. You can find contact information through company websites or professional networking platforms like LinkedIn. Look for individuals with expertise in areas that align with your interests, such as specific rocket propulsion systems or spacecraft design.

Alumni Networks: Many universities have active alumni networks in the aerospace industry. Connecting with successful alumni can provide valuable insights into career paths, potential challenges, and the skills needed to excel in the field. Alumni might even be willing to become mentors themselves.

Approaching a Potential Mentor:

Do Your Research: Before reaching out, research your potential mentor's work and expertise. Tailor your introductory email or message, briefly explaining your academic background and research interests.

Express Your Enthusiasm & Goals: Be clear about your passion for rocket science and your aspirations for the future. Explain why you believe their mentorship would be beneficial and what you hope to learn from them.

Be Respectful of Time: Mentors are busy professionals. Offer to meet during their office hours or suggest a convenient online platform for communication. Keep your initial contact message concise and professional.

Building a Successful Mentoring Relationship:

Set Clear Expectations: Once a mentor-mentee relationship is established, have an initial conversation setting clear expectations. Discuss how often you'll communicate, what types of guidance you seek, and how you'll manage your time together.

Be Proactive & Engaged: Don't be passive! Come prepared with questions, actively participate in discussions, and show initiative. Mentorship is a two-way street, and your enthusiasm will inspire your mentor to invest time and effort in your development.

Show Appreciation & Maintain Contact: Express your gratitude for your mentor's time and guidance. Keep them updated on your progress, achievements, and any new challenges you encounter. Maintaining a long-term relationship can benefit you throughout your career.

Additional Resources:

University Mentoring Programs: Many universities have formal mentorship programs specifically designed to connect students with professionals in their field of study. Explore your university's career centre or relevant engineering department for such programs.

Professional Societies: Organizations like AIAA or ASME often have mentorship programs connecting aspiring engineers with experienced professionals. These programs can be a great way to find a mentor who shares your specific interests within the vast field of rocket science.

Remember, finding the right mentor can be life-changing. Be persistent, professional, and show your genuine passion for rocket science. There are incredible minds out there waiting to guide and support you on your exciting journey to the stars!

Here are some more points to consider when seeking mentorship and exploring additional avenues to fuel your rocket science aspirations:

Mentorship Beyond Traditional Boundaries:

Online Mentorship Platforms: Several online platforms connect aspiring professionals with mentors in various fields, including aerospace engineering. These platforms offer a convenient way to find mentors who might not be geographically close but share your specific interests within rocket science.

Reverse Mentorship: While seeking guidance from experienced professionals is valuable, consider "reverse mentorship" as well. Offer to mentor younger students interested in rocket science. Sharing your knowledge and experiences can solidify your understanding and potentially lead to new collaborations or research ideas.

Beyond Mentorship: Building Your Support Network:

Student Design Teams: Join student design teams at your university that participate in national or international competitions like the Rocket Engineering Competition (REC) or the Design, Build, Fly (DBF) Challenge. These teams provide invaluable hands-on experience in all aspects of rocket design, construction, and launch. You'll collaborate with fellow students from diverse engineering backgrounds, fostering teamwork and communication skills.

Hackathons & Innovation Challenges: Participate in hackathons or innovation challenges focused on aerospace engineering or space exploration. These events provide an intense and collaborative environment where you can develop innovative solutions to real-world problems alongside other passionate students and industry professionals.

Open-Source Rocketry Projects: The open-source movement is alive and well in rocketry! Consider contributing to open-source projects developing software for rocket simulations, design tools, or even hardware components. This allows you to gain practical experience, collaborate with a global community, and potentially make a significant contribution to the advancement of rocket science.

Remember: Don't be afraid to step outside the box and explore unconventional avenues to learn and grow. The key is to be proactive, network with like-minded individuals, and continuously seek opportunities to expand your knowledge and skillset in the fascinating world of rocket science!

Higher Education (College & Beyond)

Bachelor's Degree: Your primary focus should be a Bachelor's degree in Aerospace Engineering or in any branch of engineering we discussed so far. This program will equip you with the technical knowledge required for rocket science.

Master's Degree (Optional, but highly recommended): A Master's degree in a specialized field like Astronautical Engineering or Aerospace Propulsion will give you a deeper understanding and make you a more competitive job candidate. It can also open doors to research opportunities.

Absolutely! Here's a detailed breakdown on continuing education after your Bachelor's degree to become a top-notch rocket scientist.

Master's Degree: Deepen Your Expertise

While a Bachelor's degree provides a solid foundation, a Master's degree in a specialized field especially employed in rockets is highly recommended. Think of it as a focused deep dive into a specific area of rocket science, making you a much more competitive candidate in the job market.

Benefits of a Master's Degree:

Advanced Knowledge: Master's programs delve deeper into complex topics like rocket propulsion systems, spacecraft design, orbital mechanics, and advanced control systems. This in-depth knowledge positions you as an expert in your chosen field.

Research Opportunities: Master's programs often culminate in a thesis project, offering valuable research experience. You'll work under the guidance of professors on cutting-edge research, potentially leading to publications in academic journals and presentations at conferences.

Career Specialization: Master's programs offer various specializations like Astronautics (focusing on spacecraft design and operation), Aerospace Propulsion (deep dive into different engine types and technologies), or Control Systems (expertise in guidance and navigation). This specialization makes you a perfect fit for specific job roles within the aerospace industry.

Choosing the Right Master's Program:

Consider Your Interests: Identify your area of passion within rocket science. Are you fascinated by spacecraft design or the intricacies of rocket propulsion systems? Choose a program that aligns with your specific interests and career goals.

Research the Program: Look for universities with reputable aerospace engineering programs and strong faculty expertise in your chosen specialization. Consider factors like program curriculum, research opportunities, faculty mentorship, and career placement services offered by the university.

Funding Options: Master's degrees can be expensive. Explore scholarship opportunities offered by universities, research grants, or financial aid options. Consider contacting professors directly to inquire about potential research assistantships that can help offset program costs.

Alternative Paths: Expanding Your Skillset

While a Master's degree is a traditional path, other options can equip you with valuable skills and knowledge:

Professional Certifications: Certain professional certifications may be beneficial depending on your career goals. Explore certifications offered by organizations like the American Institute of Aeronautics and Astronautics (AIAA) or the National Society of Professional Engineers (NSPE) in specific areas like spacecraft structures or propulsion systems.

Online Courses & Specialization Programs: The online learning landscape offers a wealth of resources. Consider enrolling in online courses or specialization programs from reputable universities or platforms like Coursera or edX. These programs can provide focused learning in specific areas of rocket science and can be completed at your own pace.

Remember, the choice between a Master's degree and alternative options depends on your individual goals, learning style, and financial situation. Regardless of the path you choose, the key is to continuously enhance your knowledge and skillset to become a well-rounded rocket scientist.

Post-Graduate Specialization in Rocket Science: Engineering & Science Courses

As you embark on your Master's degree journey towards becoming a rocket scientist, here are some specific engineering and science courses, categorized by potential areas of specialization:

1. Astronautical Engineering:

Spacecraft Design & Analysis: This course delves into the principles of spacecraft design, covering topics like structural analysis, thermal control systems, orbital mechanics, and mission planning. You'll learn how to design and analyze spacecraft for various missions, ensuring they can withstand the harsh environment of space.

Spacecraft Guidance, Navigation & Control (GNC): Master the complexities of spacecraft navigation and control. This course covers topics like attitude determination, orbital mechanics, control system design, and sensor systems. You'll learn how to ensure a spacecraft maintains its desired orientation and trajectory throughout its mission.

Astrodynamics: This advanced course focuses on the motion of celestial objects and spacecraft in space. You'll learn about orbital mechanics, spacecraft trajectory optimization, and interplanetary mission planning. This knowledge is crucial for designing efficient and successful space missions.

2. Aerospace Propulsion:

Advanced Propulsion Systems: Dive deeper into the world of rocket engines! This course explores advanced propulsion concepts like nuclear thermal rockets, electric propulsion systems, and hypersonic air-breathing engines. You'll gain a comprehensive understanding of the physics and engineering principles behind these cutting-edge technologies.

Combustion Processes & Propulsion: This course delves into the fundamentals of combustion, a critical aspect of traditional chemical rocket engines. You'll study topics like propellant chemistry, combustion theory, and engine performance optimization. This knowledge is essential for designing efficient and reliable chemical rockets.

Computational Fluid Dynamics (CFD) for Propulsion: Master the use of advanced computational tools for analyzing and optimizing rocket engine performance. This course teaches you how to utilize CFD software to simulate complex fluid flow within combustion chambers and engine nozzles.

Other Specialized Areas:

Spacecraft Structures & Materials: This course focuses on the design and analysis of spacecraft structures, considering factors like strength, weight, and resistance to the harsh space environment. You'll learn about advanced materials like composites and their applications in spacecraft construction.

Space Mission Design & Systems Engineering: This course equips you with the skills to plan and design complete space missions. You'll learn about system engineering principles, mission planning tools, and how to integrate various subsystems into a cohesive spacecraft design.

Remote Sensing & Space Instrumentation: Gain expertise in acquiring data from space. This course covers principles of remote sensing, spacecraft instrumentation, and data analysis techniques. This knowledge is valuable for designing spacecraft carrying scientific instruments for space exploration.

Remember: This is not an exhaustive list, and specific course offerings may vary depending on your chosen university program. However, it provides a solid foundation for understanding the exciting specialization options available at the postgraduate level in your journey towards becoming a rocket scientist!

Here are some additional specialized engineering and science courses you might encounter in your postgraduate studies as a future rocket scientist:

Advanced Control Systems: This course goes beyond the basics of spacecraft guidance and control, delving into advanced control theory, robust control design techniques, and nonlinear control systems. This equips you to handle complex spacecraft dynamics and ensure precise manoeuvring in challenging space environments.

Spacecraft Communication Systems: Master the art of communicating with spacecraft across vast distances. This course covers topics like radio wave propagation in space, satellite communication systems, error correction techniques, and spacecraft telemetry. This knowledge is crucial for maintaining communication with spacecraft throughout their missions.

Spacecraft Power Systems: Learn how to design and analyze spacecraft power systems. This course explores topics like solar cell arrays, battery technology, power management systems, and nuclear power sources for spacecraft. Understanding these systems ensures reliable power generation for all onboard operations during a space mission.

Spacecraft Thermal Control: Space is a harsh environment with extreme temperature variations. This course teaches you how to design and analyze thermal control systems for spacecraft. You'll learn about insulation techniques, radiators, and active thermal control systems, ensuring optimal temperature conditions for sensitive spacecraft components.

Computational Mechanics for Aerospace Applications: This course delves into advanced computational tools used in aerospace engineering. You'll learn how to utilize finite element analysis (FEA) software for complex structural analysis of spacecraft components, as well as computational methods for simulating fluid flow and heat transfer within rocket engines.

Spacecraft Reliability & Risk Management: Space exploration is inherently risky. This course equips you with the knowledge to design reliable spacecraft and manage risks associated with space missions. You'll learn about fault tolerance techniques, redundancy design principles, and probabilistic risk assessment methods.

Planetary Atmospheres & Entry Systems: Planning missions to other planets requires understanding their atmospheres. This course explores the composition and dynamics of planetary atmospheres, along with spacecraft re-entry physics and thermal protection systems. This knowledge is crucial for designing spacecraft capable of safely entering and operating within planetary atmospheres.

Astrobiology: This interdisciplinary field explores the possibility of life beyond Earth. You'll learn about the search for habitable exoplanets, potential biosignatures for life detection, and the challenges of planetary protection to avoid contaminating celestial bodies with Earthly organisms. While not directly related to spacecraft design, a basic understanding of astrobiology can be valuable for future space exploration missions.

Space Policy & Law: As space exploration expands, understanding the legal and regulatory frameworks becomes increasingly important. This course explores international space law, treaties governing space activities, and ethical considerations related to space exploration. This knowledge can be valuable for professionals working in the space industry.

Here's a breakdown on research and preparation for doctoral programs to propel you towards the pinnacle of rocket science:

Research: Fuelling Your Doctoral Journey

Earning a doctoral degree positions you as a leading expert in your chosen field within rocket science. However, excelling in a Ph.D. program requires a strong foundation and a well-defined research focus. Here's how to strategically leverage research:

Identify Your Research Niche: During your Master's studies, delve into research projects that resonate with you. Discuss potential research topics with professors, explore current advancements in the field, and identify a specific area where you can contribute meaningful research.

Connect with Potential Ph.D. Advisors: Research faculty profiles at universities renowned for their aerospace engineering programs. Identify professors whose research aligns with your interests. Reach out to them via email, expressing your interest in their work and exploring potential Ph.D. opportunities in their research group.

Start Building Your Research Profile: Don't wait for a Ph.D. program to begin contributing to research. Collaborate with professors on ongoing research projects during your Master's. Present your research findings at conferences or co-author research papers for publication in academic journals. Building a strong research profile showcases your passion, expertise, and potential for doctoral-level research.

Preparation: Sharpening Your Skills for Ph.D. Success

Master the Fundamentals: Ensure you have a solid grasp of core aerospace engineering principles, advanced mathematics, and physics. Strong foundational knowledge equips you to tackle complex research problems in your chosen doctoral specialization.

Develop Strong Research Skills: Beyond theoretical knowledge, refine your research skills. Learn advanced research methodologies, data analysis techniques, and scientific writing. Mastering these skills will ensure you can effectively conduct your Ph.D. research and communicate your findings to the scientific community.

Strengthen Your Communication Skills: A successful doctoral candidate excels in both written and oral communication. Sharpen your technical writing skills to produce research papers and grant proposals. Practice presenting your research findings clearly and concisely at conferences and seminars. Effective communication will be crucial for securing funding, collaborating with colleagues, and disseminating your research.

Develop Teaching Experience: Consider gaining some teaching experience, even if it's assisting with undergraduate courses. This not only enhances your understanding of core concepts but also hones your communication and presentation skills, valuable assets when defending your dissertation.

Additional Tips:

Standardized Tests: Some Ph.D. programs require standardized tests like the GRE (Graduate Record Examinations). Research the specific requirements of your chosen programs and prepare accordingly.

Financial Aid & Scholarships: Doctoral programs can be expensive. Explore funding opportunities like research assistantships, teaching assistantships, and scholarships offered by universities, research institutions, and aerospace companies.

Remember: Earning a Ph.D. in rocket science is a marathon, not a sprint. Embrace the challenges, actively build your research profile, and demonstrate your dedication to pushing the boundaries of knowledge. With perseverance and a passion for exploring the unknown, you'll be well on your way to becoming a leading expert in the fascinating world of rocket science!

Developing the Right Skills

Technical Skills: You'll need strong analytical and problem-solving abilities. Proficiency in computer-aided design (CAD) software and data analysis tools is a plus.

Soft Skills: Excellent communication, teamwork, and critical thinking skills are essential. The ability to translate complex scientific concepts into clear and concise language is important.

Gaining Experience

Internships: Seek internship opportunities at aerospace companies, government agencies like NASA, or research institutions. This will provide valuable hands-on experience and help you build your network.

Personal Projects: Take the initiative and work on personal projects related to rocket science. This demonstrates your passion and allows you to develop your skills. Consider building and launching model rockets or participating in rocketry competitions.

Finding a Job

Research Job Openings: Government agencies, aerospace companies, and private space exploration firms all employ rocket scientists. Look for openings that match your skills and interests.

Utilize online job boards and career fairs focused on the aerospace industry.

Networking: Connect with professionals in the field. Attend industry events, conferences, and online forums. Build relationships and let people know about your goals and aspirations.

The above are only a small area where acquiring knowledge and skill will really help you in advancing your career as a rocket Scientist. Remember, the specific courses you take will depend on your chosen specialization and university program. However, these subjects showcase the diverse and fascinating areas of study you can explore in your postgraduate journey to becoming a well-rounded rocket scientist! The journey to becoming a rocket scientist requires dedication, hard work, and a love and passion for science and space. But with the right guidance and a strong foundation, you can achieve your dream of working on these incredible machines that propel us towards the stars!

Chapter 10

What Makes a Rocket Scientist

The Necessity of Academic Excellence in Becoming a Rocket Scientist

1. Foundation of Knowledge: Academic excellence provides a strong foundation in the essential subjects of mathematics, physics, chemistry, and engineering principles. These subjects are crucial for understanding the complex theories and principles that underpin rocket science. For instance, mastering calculus and differential equations is necessary for modelling the trajectories of rockets and understanding orbital mechanics.

2. Advanced Technical Skills: Excelling academically allows students to develop advanced technical skills. Courses in thermodynamics, fluid mechanics, and materials science provide the theoretical background and practical knowledge needed to design, analyze, and test rocket components. For example, understanding the principles of fluid dynamics is essential for optimizing the efficiency of rocket engines.

3. Research and Innovation: Academic excellence fosters a research-oriented mindset, enabling aspiring rocket scientists to contribute to innovations in the field. Universities and research institutions often provide opportunities to participate in cutting-edge research projects, which can lead to new technologies and methodologies in rocket science. Engaging in research also helps students develop problem-solving skills and the ability to think critically.

4. Access to Resources: Top academic performance often grants access to better educational resources, including scholarships, advanced laboratories, and mentorship from leading experts in the field. These resources are invaluable for gaining hands-on experience and deepening one's understanding of complex topics. Access to state-of-the-art laboratories allows students to experiment with real-world applications of their theoretical knowledge.

In addition to academic excellence, becoming a successful rocket scientist requires a combination of personal traits and professional skills. Here are a few key traits that make an effective rocket scientist:

1. **The Fire of Desire**

There is a famous story of a boy who visited a monk in search of wise advice.

Praful Sastri and the Monk

Once upon a time, in a charming village cradled at the foot of a majestic mountain, lived a boy named Praful Sastri. His heart brimmed with dreams, and his mind buzzed with ambition. Praful yearned for a life of wealth and success, far beyond the modest means of his upbringing.

Rumours swirled through the village of a wise monk who resided atop the mountain, a sage whose wisdom could unlock the secrets of the universe. Determined and eager, Praful set out at dawn, his heart pounding with anticipation. The climb was steep and arduous, but his resolve was unshakable, his spirit aflame with hope.

As the sun reached its zenith, Praful arrived at the tranquil monastery, his breath taken away by the serenity that enveloped the place. The monk, an ancient figure with eyes that sparkled like stars, greeted him with a warm smile.

"Welcome, young traveller," the monk said, his voice a soothing melody. "What brings you to my peaceful abode?"

Praful, barely able to contain his excitement, replied, "Wise monk, I seek the secret to making money. Please, show me the way!"

The monk's eyes twinkled with a mysterious understanding. He led Praful to a crystal-clear stream, its waters shimmering like liquid silver in the sunlight. The monk knelt by the stream and gestured for Praful to do the same. Without warning, the monk seized Praful's head and plunged it into the water.

Praful's world exploded into chaos. Panic surged through him as his lungs burned for air. His heart raced, and desperation clawed at his chest. Just when he thought he couldn't endure another second, the monk released him. Praful surfaced, gasping, each breath a precious gift.

The monk's voice, calm and profound, broke through Praful's frantic thoughts. "Tell me, young one, what did you desire most when you were underwater?"

"Air," Praful choked out, his voice raw with emotion. "I needed to breathe. I felt like I was going to die without it."

The monk nodded, his gaze piercing and wise. "That, Praful, is the key to achieving your dreams. To find wealth, you must desire it with the same intensity as you desired air. Your longing must be as fierce, as vital, as the very breath you take."

Tears filled Praful's eyes as the monk's words sank into his soul. He understood that his journey to success was not merely a quest for riches, but a passionate pursuit driven by an unquenchable fire within.

With a heart overflowing with gratitude and determination, Praful descended the mountain. Each step felt lighter, each breath more purposeful. He vowed to chase his dreams with the same fervour he had felt beneath the water. And in time, through relentless dedication and a burning desire, Praful Sastri transformed his dreams into a dazzling reality, his life a testament to the power of unwavering passion and relentless pursuit.

The Essence of Desire:

When Praful asks the monk for the secret to making money, the monk's unconventional response—holding Praful's head underwater—serves as a powerful metaphor. Let's dive into the essence of desire, shall we? Buckle up, because this is going to be an incredible ride!

Imagine yourself standing before a wise old monk, Praful, yearning to unlock the secrets of immense wealth. You crave the freedom, the power, the feeling of accomplishment that comes with financial success. But the monk, instead of handing you a dusty old business manual, does something completely unexpected. He dunks your head right into the cool, refreshing water!

Now, hold on a second! This isn't some kind of crazy hazing ritual. This, my friend, is a potent metaphor, a life lesson disguised as a little splash in the pond. Because in that very moment, when your head goes under, everything fades away. All those daydreams about great food, fancy cars and luxurious vacations? Gone. The anxieties about exams and deadlines? Poof! All you can think about, all you can crave with every fiber of your being, is that sweet, life-giving air.

This, Praful, is the essence of desire we're after! This raw, primal focus, where everything else melts away and only one thing matters. It's the desperation that kicks in when you're gasping for breath, the all-consuming need that fuels the greatest achievements.

Think about it! When you truly, madly, deeply desire to become a scientist, it becomes your north star. It guides your every move, pushes you past your perceived limits, and ignites a fire within you that won't be quenched. Just like the desperate need for air, this unwavering focus is the key that unlocks the door to achieving your goal.

Let that **burning desire to be a scientist**, be your oxygen, your reason to push forward, to break barriers, and to rise above the ordinary. Because when you have that kind of focus, my friend, there's nothing you can't achieve! Remember, the power to create the outcome you want, to reach unimaginable heights, lies dormant within you. It just needs that spark, that desperate, air-like **desire**, to ignite the flame of unstoppable ambition! Now, go forth and conquer your goals with the fierce focus of someone who's just had their head dunked! The story of Praful Sastri and the wise monk beautifully illustrates the profound necessity of strong desire in achieving one's goals. At its core, the tale conveys a timeless truth: genuine success is fuelled by an intense, almost primal desire that drives an individual to push beyond their limits.

2. Unyielding Focus:

Once upon a time, in a small village nestled between rolling hills, there lived a young boy named Arjun. Arjun was fascinated by the stars. Every night, he would lie on his back and gaze at the sky, dreaming of traveling to distant planets and exploring the vast universe. His passion for the stars was unmatched, but in his village, the idea of becoming an astronomer was considered far-fetched and unrealistic.

One day, an elderly wise man visited the village. He had traveled the world and had a wealth of knowledge about many subjects, including the stars. Arjun eagerly sought him out and poured out his heart, sharing his dream of exploring the cosmos. The wise man listened intently and then said, "Arjun, to achieve your dream, you must have unwavering focus. Like the archer who aims at the bullseye, your mind must be set on your goal without distraction."

Arjun was puzzled. "But how can I achieve such focus when there are so many distractions around me?" he asked.

The wise man smiled and decided to teach Arjun a lesson. He took Arjun to a nearby forest and handed him a small bowl filled to the brim with water. "Walk through the forest and return to me without spilling a drop," he instructed.

Arjun carefully started his journey, eyes fixed on the bowl. As he navigated the forest path, he encountered chirping birds, rustling leaves, and even a deer crossing his path. But he did not let his attention waver. He kept his focus on the bowl of water, ensuring it remained steady and full.

When he finally returned to the wise man, not a single drop had spilled. The wise man looked at him with approval. "Tell me, Arjun, what did you see in the forest?" he asked.

Arjun thought for a moment and then replied, "I saw nothing but the bowl of water. I was so focused on my task that I didn't notice anything else."

The wise man nodded. "That, my boy, is the power of focus. When your mind is set on your goal, distractions lose their power over you. Your journey to the stars will be filled with challenges and diversions, but if you keep your focus as you did with the bowl of water, you will achieve your dreams."

Inspired by the wise man's lesson, Arjun dedicated himself to his studies with renewed determination. He focused on learning everything he could about astronomy, often staying up late into the night to read and observe the stars. His unwavering focus paid off, and years later, he became a renowned astronomer, making significant contributions to the understanding of the cosmos. Arjun's story spread far and wide, inspiring many others to pursue their dreams with the same level of dedication and focus. And as he continued to explore the universe, he never forgot the wise man's lesson—that with focus, even the most distant stars can be reached.

Strong desire channels our energy and attention towards our goals, much like Praful's intense need for air. Combined with the intense focus of Arjun keep the distractions away and aligns our actions with our ambitions. This kind of desire and focus is critical because the path to achieving significant goals is often fraught with obstacles and setbacks. Without a deep-seated desire and focus on our objectives, it's easy to become discouraged and give up when faced with challenges.

3. Resilience

The Story of Maya Reaching for the Stars

In a bustling city, amidst towering buildings, there lived a young girl named Maya, a young girl with eyes that sparkled with curiosity. Unlike other children who dreamt of grand houses or fancy clothes, Maya dreamt of laboratories filled with bubbling concoctions and microscopes that unveiled hidden worlds. She craved to be a scientist, to unlock the mysteries of the universe.

However, her path wasn't paved with gleaming beakers. Maya's family struggled financially, and science seemed like a distant luxury. Textbooks were a dream, replaced by borrowed library copies, and experiments were conducted with scavenged materials – baking soda volcanoes erupting in chipped mugs.

One day, at a school science fair, Maya presented her "rainbow in a jar" experiment – a mesmerizing display of oil and water, cleverly manipulated to form a colorful spectrum. Despite the ingenuity, the judges awarded the top prize to a project with expensive equipment. Dejected, Maya slunk away, tears stinging her eyes.

An old scientist, with kind eyes and a shock of white hair, noticed her. He gently knelt beside her; his voice warm like sunshine. "Disappointed, are we?" he asked. Maya sniffled, nodding. The scientist smiled. "Science," he said, "is not about fancy tools. It's about a curious mind and a spirit that never gives up. Every failed experiment teaches you something. It's a stepping stone, not a roadblock."

His words struck a chord in Maya. She realized that the scientist was right. The challenges were there to be overcome, not surrendered to. She would have to work harder, be more resourceful, but her dream wouldn't be deterred. Fuelled by this newfound resilience, Maya devoured every scrap of scientific knowledge she could find. She volunteered at a local science lab, assisting with tasks and soaking up every concept like a sponge. With the support of the old scientist, she built her own makeshift equipment, her ingenuity blossoming under the harsh light of limitations.

As she further studied Maya was fascinated by the stars. Every night, she would sit by her window, gazing at the twinkling lights in the sky, dreaming of exploring the universe. Her family finances were not good and opportunities were limited, but Maya was determined to reach for the stars. As she grew older, Maya's passion for astronomy only intensified. She read every book she could find about space, planets, and stars. She learned about famous astronomers and scientists who had dedicated their lives to uncovering the mysteries of the cosmos. Despite her enthusiasm, there were many obstacles in her path.

Years passed, and Maya's knowledge grew. She excelled in mathematics and physics, subjects essential for understanding the universe. However, the road was not easy. Many villagers doubted her dreams. They told her that a girl from a small village could never become a scientist, let alone an astronomer. But Maya's determination was unwavering. After high school, Maya attended a prestigious university where she majored in aerospace engineering. Her coursework included rigorous studies in physics, mechanics, and materials science. She also took up courses in electrical engineering and computer science, understanding the importance of these fields in the realm of space exploration.

Professional Development

Upon graduating, Maya secured an internship at a leading aerospace company. Here, she worked on various projects, including the design and testing of rocket propulsion systems. Her dedication and innovative approach quickly caught the attention of her mentors. Maya's hands-on experience with cutting-edge technology and her ability to solve complex problems set her apart from her peers.

Determined to achieve her childhood dream, Maya pursued a master's degree in astronautics. During her postgraduate studies, she focused on advanced topics such as orbital mechanics, spacecraft design, and human spaceflight. Upon completion of her Master's degree, she secured a scholarship in a US University and finally she joined NASA. Her achievements were recognized and she received numerous accolades for her contributions to space exploration. She was particularly proud of her heritage and often spoke about the importance of diversity and representation in STEM (Science, Technology, Engineering, and Mathematics.) fields.

Maya Patel's journey from a starry-eyed child to a renowned astronaut is a testament to the power of dreams, hard work, and resilience. Maya's story became a beacon of hope and inspiration. It taught the villagers the power of resilience and determination. Her journey showed that no matter where you start, with unwavering commitment and hard work, you can reach the stars. She continues to inspire the next generation of scientists and explorers, proving that with determination and passion, the sky is not the limit but just the beginning.

4. The Relentless Pursuit

The Story of Albert Einstein's Resilience

In the late 19th century, in the town of Ulm, Germany, a boy named Albert Einstein was born. From a young age, Albert exhibited an insatiable curiosity about the world around him. His parents noticed his fascination with mechanical objects, and they nurtured his interest by providing him with a compass and building blocks.

Despite his early enthusiasm for learning, Albert struggled in school. He found the rigid and rote style of teaching uninspiring and often clashed with his teachers. His mind constantly wandered to the mysteries of the universe, but his poor performance in school led some to believe he would never amount to much.

Undeterred, Albert continued to explore his interests outside the classroom. He taught himself advanced mathematics and read extensively about physics. After finishing school, he faced numerous setbacks. He applied to several universities but failed the entrance exams. Instead of giving up, he enrolled in a less prestigious technical school in Aarau, Switzerland, where he thrived in a more flexible academic environment.

Albert eventually entered the Swiss Federal Polytechnic in Zurich. However, after graduating, he struggled to find a teaching position. He took a job at the Swiss Patent Office, where he worked as a clerk. This mundane job allowed him the freedom to think and develop his theories. During his time at the patent office, Albert published several groundbreaking papers in physics.

In 1905, often referred to as his "Annus Mirabilis" or "Miracle Year," Einstein published four papers that would forever change the field of physics. These papers included his theory of special relativity and the famous equation $E=mc^2$. Despite their revolutionary nature, his work initially received little attention from the scientific community.

Albert continued to persevere, and his persistence began to pay off. His theories gradually gained recognition, leading to teaching positions and collaborations with other prominent scientists. In 1915, he presented his general theory of relativity, which provided a new understanding of gravity. This theory was confirmed during a solar eclipse in 1919, catapulting Einstein to international fame.

Throughout his life, Einstein faced numerous challenges, both personal and professional. He fled Nazi Germany due to his Jewish heritage and settled in the United States, where he continued his work at the Institute for Advanced Study in Princeton. Despite the adversities, Einstein remained committed to his scientific pursuits and used his fame to advocate for peace and human rights.

Einstein's story is one of relentless resilience. His ability to overcome academic struggles, professional setbacks, and personal hardships demonstrates the power of determination and persistence. His unwavering dedication to his work not only led to groundbreaking discoveries but also inspired generations of scientists to dream big and push the boundaries of human knowledge.

Through his life, Einstein taught us that resilience is not just about enduring difficulties but using them as stepping stones to achieve our desires. His journey from a struggling student to one of the greatest scientists of all time is a testament to the extraordinary potential within each of us to overcome obstacles and make lasting contributions to the world.

5. Passion

A Tale of Passion and Dedication: The Inspiring Story of Ekalavya

In the vast ocean of Hindu mythology, the story of Ekalavya from the Mahabharata stands out as a poignant tale of passion, dedication, and the relentless pursuit of excellence. Ekalavya's story is a testament to how true dedication and a passionate heart can lead to mastery, even in the face of adversity.

Ekalavya's Desire to Learn Archery

Ekalavya was the son of a tribal chief in the forests of the Nishada kingdom. From a young age, he was deeply passionate about learning archery and becoming the greatest archer in the world. His idol and inspiration were the legendary teacher Dronacharya, who taught the royal princes of Hastinapura.

Seeking Dronacharya's Guidance:

Ekalavya approached Dronacharya and expressed his desire to become his student. However, Dronacharya, bound by his duty to the royal family, declined to teach Ekalavya, citing his commitment to the Kuru princes, particularly Arjuna.

Self-Determination and Innovative Learning

Undeterred by Dronacharya's refusal, Ekalavya decided to pursue his passion independently. His determination and resourcefulness set the stage for his remarkable journey.

Creating a teacher: Ekalavya crafted a clay statue of Dronacharya and considered it his guru. With unwavering devotion, he practiced archery in front of the statue, treating it as his living teacher.

He spent countless hours perfecting his skills, drawing inspiration and guidance from the statue. His dedication and self-discipline were unparalleled.

Mastery Through Passion

Ekalavya's relentless practice and passion for archery paid off. He became an exceptionally skilled archer, surpassing many of the trained warriors of his time.

Demonstration of Skill: One day, while practicing in the forest, Ekalavya demonstrated his incredible archery skills by silencing a barking dog without harming it. His precision and control astonished everyone who witnessed the feat. The Kuru princes, including Arjuna, saw Ekalavya's extraordinary talent and were amazed by his prowess.

The Test of Loyalty

When Dronacharya learned about Ekalavya's exceptional skills, he was both impressed and concerned. Ekalavya's abilities posed a potential challenge to his promise that Arjuna would be the greatest archer.

Guru Dakshina (Teacher's Fee): Dronacharya approached Ekalavya and acknowledged his incredible dedication and skill. He then asked for a guru dakshina, a traditional fee or offering to the teacher.

To ensure Arjuna's position as the greatest archer, Dronacharya requested Ekalavya's right thumb, knowing it would significantly affect his archery skills.

Sacrifice and Loyalty: Without hesitation and out of deep respect for his guru, Ekalavya cut off his right thumb and offered it to Dronacharya. This act of sacrifice was a testament to his unwavering loyalty and dedication to his teacher.

Legacy of Ekalavya

Despite losing his thumb, Ekalavya's passion and dedication to archery never waned. He continued to practice and adapt, becoming a symbol of perseverance and unwavering determination.

Inspiration and Influence: Ekalavya's story continues to inspire generations with its powerful message of dedication, innovation, and respect for teachers. His ability to rise above obstacles and his loyalty to his guru have made him a revered figure in Hindu mythology.

Ekalavya's story is a profound example of how passion and dedication can lead to mastery, even when faced with significant challenges. His journey from a determined student to a master archer, and his ultimate sacrifice, highlight the values of perseverance, respect, and unwavering commitment to one's goals. Let Ekalavya's story inspire you to pursue your passions with relentless dedication, find innovative ways to overcome obstacles, and remain true to your values and mentors. Just like Ekalavya, your passion and commitment can help you achieve greatness, regardless of the challenges you may face.

6. Curiosity

The Inspiring Story of Thomas Edison:

Thomas Alva Edison, one of the greatest inventors and scientists in history, is a shining example of how passion, perseverance, and relentless curiosity can lead to extraordinary success. His journey from a curious young boy to a prolific inventor is filled with lessons on dedication and the power of a passionate heart.

Early Life and Passion for Learning

Thomas Edison was born on February 11, 1847, in Milan, Ohio. From a young age, he displayed an insatiable curiosity and a passion for learning. Unlike many children, Edison was not interested in conventional schooling. His mother, recognizing his unique abilities, decided to homeschool him.

Home Schooling:

Edison's mother, Nancy, provided him with a rich learning environment. She encouraged him to read extensively and explore subjects that interested him.

By the age of 12, Edison had set up a small laboratory in his home, where he conducted numerous experiments. His passion for understanding how things worked drove him to explore and experiment constantly.

The Power of Perseverance: Edison faced numerous challenges and failures throughout his career, but his unwavering determination and passion for innovation kept him moving forward.

Early Ventures and Setbacks: Edison started his career as a telegraph operator, a job that allowed him to continue experimenting with electrical devices. He faced many failures, but each setback only fueled his determination to succeed.

One of his early inventions, an automatic vote recorder, failed to attract interest from politicians. Instead of being discouraged, Edison learned from the experience and focused on creating inventions that had practical applications and market demand.

The Light Bulb Invention

Edison's most famous invention, the incandescent light bulb, is a testament to his passion and perseverance. The journey to invent the light bulb was filled with challenges and countless experiments.

Journey to Success:

Edison and his team conducted thousands of experiments to find the right materials for the filament and the perfect design for the light bulb. It is said that they tested over 6,000 different materials before finding the right one.

After extensive trial and error, Edison finally succeeded in creating a practical and long-lasting light bulb in 1879. This invention revolutionized the world, bringing electric light to homes and businesses.

When asked about his many failures, Edison famously said, "I have not failed. I've just found 10,000 ways that won't work." This quote encapsulates his relentless pursuit of success and his positive attitude towards failure.

Innovation Beyond the Light Bulb

Edison's passion for invention did not stop with the light bulb. Throughout his life, he was awarded over 1,000 patents, contributing significantly to various fields including telecommunications, sound recording, and motion pictures.

Phonograph:

In 1877, Edison invented the phonograph, the first device capable of recording and reproducing sound. This invention amazed the world and laid the foundation for the modern music industry.

Motion Pictures:

Edison also played a crucial role in the development of motion picture technology. His inventions and improvements in cameras and projectors helped establish the film industry.

Legacy of Passion and Innovation

Thomas Edison's legacy is a testament to the power of passion, perseverance, and continuous learning. His inventions have had a profound impact on modern society, improving the quality of life and paving the way for future technological advancements.

Inspiring Generations:

Edison's story continues to inspire countless individuals to pursue their passions and never give up, no matter how many obstacles they encounter.

His life demonstrates that success is not just about having great ideas but also about having the determination to bring those ideas to life through hard work and persistence.

Thomas Edison's life is a powerful reminder of what can be achieved through passion, dedication, and an unwavering commitment to one's goals. His journey from a curious young boy to one of the greatest inventors of all time highlights the importance of perseverance in the face of failure and the relentless pursuit of knowledge and innovation. Let Edison's story inspire you to follow your passions, embrace challenges, and keep pushing forward, no matter how many times you encounter setbacks. With determination and a passionate heart, you too can achieve extraordinary success and make a lasting impact on the world.

7. An Analytical Mind at Work

The Inspiring Story of Lord Krishna and the Syamantaka Jewel

In the vast and rich tapestry of Hindu mythology, the story of Lord Krishna and the Syamantaka jewel stands out as a brilliant example of using a strong analytical mind to solve complex problems. This tale showcases how a meticulous nature and a keen eye for detail are crucial for ensuring success in major tasks.

The Legend of the Syamantaka Jewel

The Syamantaka jewel was a magnificent gem that belonged to Satrajit, a nobleman of the Yadava clan. This jewel was known for its extraordinary properties; it could produce eight measures of gold daily and was believed to bring prosperity and good fortune to its possessor. However, the jewel also carried a curse: if the possessor was unworthy or engaged in deceit, it would bring misfortune and disaster.

Satrajit and Prasena: Satrajit, unwilling to part with the jewel, kept it for himself despite Lord Krishna's suggestion that it be given to King Ugrasena for the benefit of all. One day, Satrajit's brother Prasena took the jewel and went hunting. He was attacked and killed by a lion, which then carried off the jewel. Later, Jambavan, the king of bears and a devotee of Lord Rama, defeated the lion and took the jewel to his cave.

Accusations and Investigation: When Prasena did not return, Satrajit accused Krishna of having orchestrated Prasena's death to obtain the jewel. Determined to clear his name and solve the mystery, Krishna set out to investigate.

Krishna's Analytical Approach:

Gathering Evidence: Krishna meticulously retraced Prasena's steps, starting from the last known location where he had gone hunting. He observed the tracks and clues left behind, which led him to the scene of Prasena's death. Here, he found evidence of a lion attack. **Following the Trail,** Krishna followed the lion's tracks, which led him to the cave of Jambavan. Inside the cave, he discovered the Syamantaka jewel in Jambavan's possession.

Understanding the Context: Before jumping to conclusions, Krishna engaged Jambavan in dialogue, understanding the context of how the jewel came into his possession.

Resolution and Restoration

Krishna's analytical mind and keen eye for detail enabled him to piece together the sequence of events that had led to the disappearance of the jewel. Rather than using force, he approached the situation diplomatically.

Confronting Jambavan: Krishna explained the situation to Jambavan and the misunderstanding that had arisen due to the missing jewel. Recognizing Krishna's wisdom and divinity, Jambavan not only returned the jewel but also offered his daughter Jambavati's hand in marriage to Krishna as a gesture of respect and honor.

Clearing His Name:

With the jewel in hand, Krishna returned to Dwaraka and presented it to Satrajit, thereby clearing his name of all accusations. Krishna's meticulous nature and analytical approach not only solved the mystery but also restored harmony and trust within the community.

Lessons from the Story

Analytical Mind: Krishna's ability to break down the problem, gather evidence, and follow logical steps to reach a solution demonstrates the power of an analytical mind in solving complex problems.

Attention to Detail: His meticulous nature in observing details, from the tracks of Prasena and the lion to understanding Jambavan's perspective, was crucial in resolving the issue without conflict.

Critical Thinking and Diplomacy: Krishna's approach highlights the importance of critical thinking and diplomacy. Rather than rushing to conclusions or using force, he sought to understand the entire situation, leading to a peaceful and just resolution.

Innovative Solutions:

By engaging in dialogue and reasoning, Krishna found an innovative solution that not only solved the problem but also built alliances and strengthened relationships.

The story of Lord Krishna and the Syamantaka jewel is a powerful reminder of the importance of an analytical mind, meticulous nature, and keen attention to detail. These qualities enable one to break down complex challenges, think critically, and find innovative solutions. Krishna's approach to solving the mystery of the missing jewel showcases how patience, wisdom, and a methodical approach can lead to success in major tasks. Let this story inspire you to cultivate these qualities in your own life, helping you to navigate challenges and achieve your goals with clarity and precision.

Analytical Mind in Solving Complex Problems

The Inspiring Story of Marie Curie:

Marie Curie, a pioneer in the field of radioactivity and the first woman to win a Nobel Prize, exemplifies how a strong analytical mind can solve complex problems and lead to groundbreaking discoveries. Her meticulous nature and keen eye for detail were crucial in her success.

Early Life and Education

Marie Curie, born Maria Sklodowska on November 7, 1867, in Warsaw, Poland, showed an early aptitude for mathematics and physics. Despite facing significant obstacles as a woman in a male-dominated field, her passion for science drove her to pursue higher education in Paris.

Academic Pursuits:

Curie moved to Paris to study at the Sorbonne, where she earned degrees in physics and mathematics. Her analytical mind allowed her to excel in her studies and conduct research that would change the world.

The Discovery of Radioactivity

Marie Curie's most significant contributions came from her research on radioactivity. Her analytical skills and attention to detail played a crucial role in these discoveries.

Analytical Breakthrough:

While researching the properties of uranium, Curie observed that the air around uranium compounds was electrically conductive. She hypothesized that this phenomenon was due to the emission of rays from the uranium atoms.

To investigate further, Curie meticulously measured the conductivity of various uranium compounds. Her analytical mind helped her notice that the intensity of the emitted rays depended solely on the amount of uranium present, suggesting the rays were a property of the uranium atoms themselves.

The Discovery of Polonium and Radium

Curie's analytical approach led her to explore other substances that might exhibit similar properties. Along with her husband, Pierre Curie, she focused on the mineral pitchblende, which was known to be more radioactive than pure uranium.

Meticulous Research:

Curie's keen eye for detail and meticulous nature were evident as she carefully isolated and measured the radioactivity of various components of pitchblende. This extensive and laborious process involved processing tons of pitchblende to extract minute amounts of radioactive elements.

In 1898, the Curies announced the discovery of a new element, polonium, named after Marie's homeland of Poland. Later that year, they discovered another element, radium, which was even more radioactive than polonium.

Innovative Solutions:

Marie Curie developed innovative methods to isolate these elements, overcoming significant challenges. Her analytical mind enabled her to devise techniques for purifying radium and polonium, despite their tiny concentrations in pitchblende.

Her work on radioactivity required not only critical thinking and detailed analysis but also physical endurance and relentless perseverance.

Legacy and Impact

Marie Curie's discoveries had a profound impact on science and medicine. Her pioneering work laid the foundation for the field of atomic physics and revolutionized medical treatments, particularly in cancer therapy.

Nobel Prizes:

In 1903, Marie Curie, along with Pierre Curie and Henri Becquerel, was awarded the Nobel Prize in Physics for their work on radioactivity. She became the first woman to receive a Nobel Prize.

In 1911, Curie received her second Nobel Prize, this time in Chemistry, for her discovery of radium and polonium and her investigation of their properties.

Marie Curie's story is a powerful example of how an analytical mind, combined with a meticulous nature and a keen eye for detail, can solve complex problems and lead to groundbreaking discoveries. Her dedication to science, despite significant challenges, demonstrates the importance of perseverance, critical thinking, and innovative problem-solving. Curie's legacy continues to inspire scientists and researchers worldwide, proving that with determination and analytical prowess, one can achieve extraordinary success and make a lasting impact on the world.

8. Problem-Solving Skills

The Story of Alexander the Great and the Gordian Knot

The story of Alexander the Great and the Gordian Knot is a legendary tale that exemplifies problem-solving skills, creativity, and decisive action. This ancient myth underscores how innovative thinking can overcome even the most intricate challenges.

The Legend of the Gordian Knot

Background:

The Gordian Knot was tied by Gordias, the king of Phrygia, in the town of Gordium. According to the legend, Gordias was a humble peasant who became king through divine Favor.

The knot was intricately tied to the yoke of an ancient wagon, and it was said to be impossible to untie.

Prophecy: An oracle had prophesied that the person who could untie the Gordian Knot would become the ruler of all Asia. This prophecy made the knot a symbol of ultimate power and destiny.

Alexander the Great's Quest

Alexander's Ambition: Alexander the Great, the young king of Macedon, was on a mission to conquer the known world. When he arrived in Gordium in 333 BCE, he encountered the famous knot and the associated prophecy.

Determined to prove himself and fulfil the prophecy, Alexander decided to take on the challenge of untying the Gordian Knot.

Approach and Analysis:

Alexander approached the knot and examined it closely. He understood that the complexity of the knot made it practically impossible to untie in the conventional manner. As a brilliant military strategist and an innovative thinker, Alexander sought a solution that would break through the apparent impasse.

The Bold Solution

Lateral Thinking: Instead of attempting to untie the knot in the traditional way, Alexander thought outside the box. He realized that the prophecy did not specify how the knot had to be undone, only that it must be untied. Drawing his sword, Alexander made a swift and decisive cut through the knot, effectively "untying" it by slicing it apart.

Fulfilment of the Prophecy: By cutting the knot, Alexander demonstrated his ability to think creatively and take bold action. This decisive move was seen as a fulfilment of the prophecy, signifying that he was destined to conquer Asia. The act of cutting the Gordian Knot became a metaphor for solving complex problems through innovative and unconventional means.

Impact and Legacy

Symbol of Leadership: Alexander's solution to the Gordian Knot showcased his leadership qualities, particularly his ability to confront challenges with ingenuity and decisiveness. This story has endured through the ages as a powerful symbol of problem-solving and strategic thinking.

Conquering Asia: True to the prophecy, Alexander went on to achieve unprecedented military successes, creating one of the largest empires in history. His campaigns extended from Greece through Asia Minor, Egypt, Persia, and into India.

The phrase "cutting the Gordian Knot" has become synonymous with solving a complex problem through bold and unconventional actions. It serves as an inspiration for those facing seemingly insurmountable challenges.

The story of Alexander the Great and the Gordian Knot is a timeless tale of creativity, critical thinking, and decisive action. Alexander's ability to analyze the situation, think innovatively, and take bold steps to achieve his goal exemplifies the qualities of a great leader. This legend continues to inspire us to approach challenges with a fresh perspective, finding solutions that may lie beyond conventional thinking. Just as Alexander did, we too can conquer the complexities we face by cutting through our own "Gordian Knots" with ingenuity and courage

9. The Importance of Goal Setting

Setting goals is a fundamental step towards achieving success in any endeavour. However, simply having goals is not enough. To truly maximize the likelihood of success, it is essential to set SMART goals—Specific, Measurable, Achievable, Relevant, and Time-bound. This method provides a clear and structured framework for setting and achieving goals, making them more attainable and less overwhelming. As Tony Robbins, a renowned motivational speaker, once said, "Setting goals is the first step in turning the invisible into the visible." Ever dreamed of designing rockets that soar into the cosmos? Becoming a rocket scientist takes focus and planning, just like a successful space launch. Here's where SMART goals come in – your secret weapon for achieving liftoff in your academic journey!

SMART goals are like perfectly-fuelled rockets: specific, clear, and with a defined trajectory. They take your dream of becoming a rocket scientist and break it down into actionable steps, making it feel less overwhelming and more like a thrilling mission.

Think of it this way: instead of a vague wish of "being involved in rockets," a SMART goal could be: "Ace my upcoming Physics exam to qualify for the Advanced Space Exploration program next semester." This goal is **Specific**, **Measurable** (by the exam grade), **Achievable** (considering your study habits), **Relevant** to your ultimate dream, and **Time-bound** (tied to the upcoming semester).

So, channel your inner rocket scientist and craft SMART goals to fuel your academic journey. Remember, as Neil Armstrong famously said, "That's one small step for man, one giant leap for mankind." Your SMART goals will be your small steps, leading to one giant

The Tale of Arjuna: Harnessing Fortune through Clear Goals and Determination

In the sacred land of Bharat, where the rivers Ganga and Yamuna flow and the Himalayas touch the sky, there existed a time of great heroes and divine intervention. This was the era of the Mahabharata, an epic that weaves tales of valour, wisdom, and destiny. Among its many heroes, Arjuna, the third Pandava, stood out as a beacon of unparalleled archery skill and unwavering focus.

The Divine Sage's Vision

One tranquil evening, the revered sage Vyasa, the composer of the Mahabharata, sat by the serene banks of the Ganga. His mind wandered through the threads of fate, seeking the path to ensure the Pandavas' victory in the inevitable battle of Kurukshetra. Vyasa's thoughts rested upon Arjuna; a warrior destined for greatness. He knew that for Arjuna to fulfil his destiny, he needed to harness fortune through clear, unwavering goals.

The Goal Set by Dronacharya

Years earlier, in the kingdom of Hastinapura, the young princes of the Kuru dynasty gathered in the grand gurukul of their teacher, Dronacharya. It was here that Drona, the master of martial arts, decided to test his students. Placing a wooden bird high upon a tree, he summoned the princes one by one.

"Look at the bird," Drona commanded, his voice as calm as the morning breeze. "Ready your bow and describe what you see."

The eldest, Yudhishthira, stepped forward. "I see the bird, the tree, and the sky," he replied. One by one, the princes described various aspects of the scene—the leaves, the branches, the bird, and the horizon.

When it was Arjuna's turn, he stepped forward with the elegance of a lion on the prowl. His eyes locked onto the wooden bird, and his fingers danced over his bowstring with the precision of a musician. "What do you see, Arjuna?" Drona asked.

"I see only the bird's eye," Arjuna replied, his voice steady and unwavering.

Drona smiled, recognizing the clarity and focus in Arjuna. "Release your arrow," he commanded. The arrow flew like a divine decree, striking the bird's eye with impeccable accuracy. It was then that Arjuna's goal became clear—to become the greatest archer the world had ever seen.

The Struggle for Mastery

Arjuna's journey was far from easy. He spent countless hours practicing, often through the night by the light of flickering oil lamps. His dedication was unwavering, and his mind was always on his goal. He sought the guidance of sages and deities, each teaching him new skills and imparting wisdom.

Arjuna's resolve led him to the Himalayas, where he performed severe penance to please Lord Shiva. For days he stood unmoved, his body covered in snow, his mind unwavering. Finally, Shiva appeared before him, disguised as a hunter. A fierce battle ensued, and impressed by Arjuna's prowess and determination, Shiva revealed his true form and blessed him with the divine weapon, the Pashupatastra.

The Cosmic Dance with Krishna

The pinnacle of Arjuna's journey came on the battlefield of Kurukshetra. Faced with the moral dilemma of fighting against his own kin, Arjuna's spirit wavered. It was then that Lord Krishna, his charioteer, friend, and guide, revealed the Bhagavad Gita. In this divine discourse, Krishna illuminated the path of righteousness, duty, and the importance of unwavering focus on one's goals.

Krishna's words were like the dawn breaking over the darkened sky of Arjuna's mind. "Set your heart upon your work but never its reward. Perform your duty with steadfastness and without attachment, Arjuna."

With Krishna's wisdom, Arjuna's focus sharpened. His goals were clear—to restore dharma and to achieve victory for the Pandavas. Armed with divine weapons and fortified by Krishna's guidance, Arjuna stood like an unshakable mountain amidst the chaos of war.

The Triumph of Focused Determination

The war of Kurukshetra was fierce, with the earth trembling under the clash of weapons and the cries of warriors. Arjuna, with his clear goals and relentless determination, fought valiantly. His arrows, like lightning bolts, found their mark time and again, striking fear into the hearts of his enemies. His resolve never wavered, even in the face of the greatest adversaries, including the mighty Karna and the invincible Bhishma.

When the dust of battle finally settled, it was Arjuna's unwavering focus and clarity of purpose that had paved the way for the Pandavas' victory. He had harnessed fortune through clear goals, dedication, and the wisdom imparted by Krishna.

The Legacy of Arjuna

Arjuna's tale is not merely one of epic battles and divine interventions; it is a testament to the power of setting clear goals and striving relentlessly to achieve them. His journey from a focused student under Dronacharya to the hero of Kurukshetra is a beacon for all who seek to harness their fortune.

In the land where the Ganga flows and the Himalayas stand tall, Arjuna's story continues to inspire generations. It teaches that with clarity of purpose, unwavering focus, and relentless effort, one can achieve greatness and carve their destiny. For those who dare to dream and strive with all their might, fortune indeed favours the brave.

Understanding SMART Goals

Specific: Clarity and Precision

A goal should be clear and specific, leaving no room for ambiguity. A goal as fuzzy as a pre-dawn nebula won't get you to Mars. To become a rocket scientist, you need laser focus and a roadmap as clear as a starry night. That's where specific goals come in – your launchpad to propel you towards achieving your ambitions.

Here's the key: Ditch the vague "I want to be involved in rockets" and craft a goal with the precision of a guidance system. Ask yourself the 5 Ws:

Who: Is it you, or are you collaborating with a team on a specific project?

What: Do you want to design rocket engines, master orbital mechanics, or specialize in spacecraft?

Where: Is there a specific university or research program you're aiming for?

When: Set deadlines! "Ace the AP Physics exam this year" or "Participate in a summer internship at a space agency by next June."

Why: Remind yourself why you're reaching for the stars. Is it a fascination with space travel, a desire to push technological boundaries, or a dream of colonizing Mars?

For example, instead of "I want to learn more about rockets," a specific goal could be: "Master the principles of rocket propulsion by the end of the year by taking online courses and attending the local astronomy club's lectures on rocket science." Remember, a specific goal is a focused mission, not a wandering spaceship. So, channel your inner rocket scientist, craft those detailed goals, and get ready for liftoff on your academic journey towards the stars!

Measurable: Tracking Progress

Track Your Rocket Science Journey with Measurable Milestones!

Every aspiring rocket scientist needs a mission control centre – a system to track progress and celebrate victories. That's where measurable goals come in – your dashboard to monitor your ascent towards the stars.

Forget vague notions of "learning more." Craft goals with the precision of a flight computer. Here's the trick: Use numbers to measure your progress! Instead of "get better at math," aim for "Improve my math SAT score by 100 points within the next year."

This allows you to see exactly how much closer you are to your target. Think "How many?" or "How much?" For instance, a measurable goal could be: "Successfully complete three online modules on orbital mechanics by the end of summer break."

Remember, Peter Drucker, the famed management guru, once said, "What gets measured gets managed." So, translate your rocket science dreams into measurable milestones. Track your progress, celebrate your wins, and stay motivated on your stellar journey!

Achievable: Realistic and Attainable

Goals should be realistic and attainable. While it's important to set challenging goals, they should still be possible to achieve with effort and commitment. An achievable goal is one that you have the skills, resources, and time to accomplish Achievable Ascendancy: Reaching for the Stars Within Reach!

Every aspiring rocket scientist needs a launch plan that's ambitious yet achievable. Shooting for the moon is great, but you need a spacecraft that can actually get you there! That's where achievable goals come in – your flight path that takes you steadily towards your cosmic dreams.

Don't get lost in the vastness of space with overly ambitious goals. While a challenge is good, ensure your goals are within reach with hard work and dedication. Focus on what you can achieve with your current skills and resources. For example, instead of aiming to design a new space engine right away, a more achievable goal could be: "Master the fundamentals of thermodynamics by the end of the semester, preparing me for advanced propulsion courses next year."

This step-by-step approach, as Nelson Mandela wisely said, makes the "impossible" seem possible. Break down your goals into achievable milestones, building confidence and momentum as you progress. Remember, even the most powerful rockets need a well-defined trajectory! So, craft **achievable goals, and watch your rocket science dreams take flight!**

Relevant: Aligning with Your Values

Each goal should matter to you and align with other relevant goals. They should be worthwhile and applicable to your current context and direction. A relevant goal is one that resonates with your values and long-term objectives. Fuel Your Passion: Goals Aligned with Your Stellar Ambitions!

Every aspiring rocket scientist needs a compass – a guiding force that ensures their efforts propel them towards the right celestial body. That's where relevant goals come in – your celestial map that aligns perfectly with your cosmic aspirations.

Don't waste fuel on irrelevant pursuits. Your goals should be like perfectly-calibrated rocket engines, driving you towards your ultimate dream. Make sure they resonate with your core values and long-term vision.

For example, instead of just aiming for good grades, a relevant goal could be: "Excel in physics and calculus classes this year, building a strong foundation for future studies in aerospace engineering."

This ensures your efforts contribute directly to your ultimate desire to become a rocket scientist. As Stephen Covey, the renowned author, advised, "Schedule your priorities, don't prioritize your schedule." So, choose relevant goals that fuel your passion and propel you on the most efficient course towards achieving your starry ambitions!

Time-bound: Creating a Sense of Urgency

“A goal is a dream with a deadline.” -Napoleon Hill

Every goal needs a target date, so you have a deadline to focus on and something to work toward. This part of the SMART goal criteria helps prevent everyday tasks from taking priority over your longer-term goals. A time-bound goal answers the question of “When every aspiring rocket scientist needs a countdown clock – a clear timeline for achieving their cosmic goals. As Napoleon Hill famously said, "A goal is a dream with a deadline." That's where time-bound goals come in – your mission clock that ensures a successful launch towards your stellar ambitions.

Don't let your dreams languish in the vast expanse of "someday." Give your goals a specific timeframe for blast-off! This creates a sense of urgency and keeps you focused on the prize. Instead of a vague "get better at science," aim for something more precise: "Improve my science GPA to 99.8% by the end of the school year through attending extra help sessions and participating in science fairs."

Setting deadlines lights a fire under you, just like the ignition sequence on a rocket. Remember, Benjamin Franklin's wise words still hold true: "You may delay, but time won't." So, craft time-bound goals, buckle up, and get ready to launch your rocket science journey into high gear!

APJ Abdul Kalam's Definition of a Dream

APJ Abdul Kalam, the former President of India and a renowned scientist, had a profound and inspiring view of dreams. He famously said, "Dream is not that which you see while sleeping; it is something that does not let you sleep." This definition emphasizes that true dreams are not mere fantasies that occur during sleep but are deeply ingrained aspirations that drive a person towards achieving their goals.

Dreams as Catalysts for Action

For Kalam, dreams were the first step towards achievement. They act as a catalyst that motivates individuals to work tirelessly towards their goals. He believed that dreams should be so compelling and powerful that they ignite a passion within a person, pushing them to overcome obstacles and challenges in their path.

The Role of Vision in Dreams

Kalam often spoke about the importance of having a vision. He believed that having a clear and well-defined vision was crucial for transforming dreams into reality. A vision provides direction and purpose, helping individuals to stay focused and committed. According to him, a dream becomes a reality when it is supported by a vision, detailed planning, and relentless effort.

The Journey from Dreams to Reality

Kalam's own life is a testament to his beliefs about dreams. Born into a humble background in Rameswaram, Tamil Nadu, he dreamed of flying and becoming a pilot. Though he did not become a pilot, his passion for aeronautics led him to become a leading scientist in India’s space and missile programs. His work on the SLV-III project, which successfully deployed the Rohini satellite in near-earth orbit in 1980, was a significant milestone in India’s space journey.

Kalam's journey was not without its challenges. He faced numerous setbacks and failures but his unwavering commitment to his dreams kept him going. His ability to learn from failures and persist with determination highlights the importance of resilience in achieving one’s dreams.

Inspiring Others to Dream

Throughout his life, Kalam inspired millions to dream big. He often spoke to students and young people, urging them to dream and work hard to achieve those dreams. He believed that the youth had the power to transform the nation and the world if they pursued their dreams with dedication and passion.

In his book "Wings of Fire," Kalam shares his experiences and the lessons he learned, encouraging readers to have faith in their dreams and work relentlessly towards them. He emphasizes that dreams should not just remain in the realm of imagination but should be translated into tangible actions and achievements.

The Significance of Hard Work and Perseverance

Kalam's definition of a dream underscores the importance of hard work and perseverance. He believed that dreams are realized not by wishful thinking but by sustained effort and perseverance. His message was clear: to achieve great things, one must be willing to put in the hard work, face failures, and keep moving forward with determination.

APJ Abdul Kalam's perspective on dreams serves as a powerful reminder that true dreams are those that drive us to action. They are the visions that keep us awake at night, urging us to strive for excellence and overcome challenges. His life and achievements are a testament to the power of dreams, vision, and relentless effort. By following his teachings, we can aspire to transform our dreams into reality and achieve greatness in our endeavours.

Craft Your Rocket Science Trajectory: Blast Off with SMART Goals!

Forget fuzzy dreams of "being involved in rockets." To become a rocket scientist, you need a mission control centre, a launchpad, and a flight plan as precise as a guidance system. That's where SMART goals come in – your secret weapon for rocketing towards achieving your ambitions!

SMART goals transform vague aspirations into actionable plans, just like an engineer meticulously blueprints a spacecraft. Here's the key:

Specific: Instead of "learn more about rockets," aim for "Master the principles of orbital mechanics by the end of the year."

Measurable: Track your progress! Aim for "Improve my math SAT score by 100 points within the next year."

Achievable: Be ambitious, but realistic. A goal like "Successfully complete three online modules on orbital mechanics by the end of summer break" sets you up for success.

Relevant: Ensure your goals align with your ultimate dream. Aim for "Excel in physics and calculus classes this year, building a strong foundation for future studies in aerospace engineering."

Time-bound: Light the launch sequence! Set a clear deadline like "Improve my science GPA to 99.8% by the end of the school year."

By ensuring your goals are SMART, you create a detailed roadmap for reaching your cosmic destination. These well-defined goals act as your compass, guiding your efforts and keeping you on track throughout your incredible journey to becoming a rocket scientist!

The Pygmalion Effect: Harnessing the Power of Positive Expectations in Goal Setting

In the mists of ancient Greece, where the whispers of gods mingled with the mortal realm, there lived a master sculptor named Pygmalion. Upon the sun-drenched island of Cyprus, his hands wrought wonders from stone, capturing beauty with every chisel and caress. Renowned far and wide for his unparalleled artistry, Pygmalion possessed a gift that seemed touched by the divine.

Yet, despite his extraordinary talent, Pygmalion harboured a deep disillusionment. He saw the flaws and frailties of human nature and, disheartened by the imperfections, vowed never to bind himself in marriage. Instead, he turned inward, channelling his passions into his craft. From the cool marble, he envisioned a woman of such grace and perfection that no mortal could compare.

Day turned to night, and night into day, as Pygmalion worked tirelessly in his studio. Each strike of his chisel was a declaration of his yearning, each sweep of his hand a testament to his unwavering dedication. His heart and soul poured into the creation, the statue began to take form, its beauty surpassing the wildest dreams of any who beheld it.

As the figure neared completion, it seemed almost to breathe with life. Her features were so exquisite, her form so divine, that Pygmalion named her Galatea. His heart, once hardened by disillusionment, softened and overflowed with love for his creation. He spent hours gazing upon her, wishing with all his might that she could step down from her pedestal and join him in the realm of the living.

Moved by the intensity of his devotion, Aphrodite, the goddess of love, descended from Olympus to bestow her grace upon him. Seeing the purity of Pygmalion's love and the depth of his desire, she smiled upon his earnest heart. In a moment that transcended the bounds of reality, she breathed life into the cold marble, and Galatea's eyes fluttered open.

In that instant, the impossible became possible. Pygmalion's dream was no longer confined to the realms of fantasy. Galatea stepped forth, a living testament to the power of unwavering belief and unrelenting dedication. His creation, born from stone and brought to life by love, stood before him as the perfect partner he had always envisioned.

Through sheer will, passion, and the magic of his expectations, Pygmalion transformed his dreams into reality. The tale of Pygmalion and Galatea endures as a timeless reminder that within the heart of every artist, every dreamer, lies the power to shape their own destiny and bring to life the visions they hold dear.

The Pygmalion Effect in Goal Setting

The story of Pygmalion is more than just a myth; it illustrates a powerful psychological phenomenon known as the Pygmalion Effect, or the Rosenthal Effect. This effect suggests that the expectations we hold, whether for ourselves or others, can significantly influence outcomes. In goal setting, the Pygmalion Effect demonstrates how positive expectations can lead to remarkable achievements.

Harnessing Positive Expectations

"Whether you think you can, or you think you can't—you're right," said Henry Ford, emphasizing the profound impact of our beliefs on our abilities. When setting goals, having high expectations can create a self-fulfilling prophecy where your belief in your success propels you toward achieving it.

The Garden of Goals: Cultivating Success

Imagine your goals as seeds planted in a garden. The soil represents your mindset, and the water and sunlight symbolize your expectations and efforts. When you nurture your goals with positive expectations and persistent effort, they are more likely to grow and flourish.

The Lighthouse: Guiding Your Journey

Consider the Pygmalion Effect as a lighthouse guiding your journey through the stormy seas of goal setting. The light from the lighthouse represents your high expectations, illuminating the path to your destination. Even when faced with challenges and obstacles, this guiding light keeps you focused and motivated, helping you navigate toward success.

Practical Applications: Setting Goals

Set Clear and Ambitious Goals: Define your goals with clarity and ambition. Believe in your ability to achieve them. This belief will serve as the foundation for your success.

Write Down Your Goals: Documenting goals makes them real and tangible. Keep them visible to remind yourself daily.

Visualize Success: Regularly visualize yourself achieving your goals. This mental imagery reinforces your positive expectations and keeps you motivated.

Surround Yourself with Positivity: Engage with people who believe in you and your goals. Their support and positive expectations can amplify your own.

Break Down Goals: Divide your goals into smaller, manageable tasks. Celebrate each small victory, reinforcing your belief in your ultimate success. Instead of saying, “I want to write a book,” start with "I will write 500 words a day." Each small victory leads to the completion of the larger goal.

Celebrate Milestones: Recognize and celebrate each small achievement along the way. This reinforces the belief that progress is possible through effort.

Review and Adjust: Regularly check your progress and be flexible enough to adjust your goals as needed. Circumstances can change, and your goals should adapt accordingly.

Embrace the Power of the Pygmalion Effect

The Pygmalion Effect teaches us that our beliefs and expectations can shape our reality. By setting high expectations for yourself and nurturing them with unwavering belief and effort, you can turn your goals into achievements. Just as Pygmalion brought Galatea to life through his dedication and belief, you too can bring your dreams to life. Embrace the power of positive expectations, and let them guide you on your journey to success. As you harness the Pygmalion Effect in your goal setting, you'll discover that the only limits are those you place on yourself. Believe in your potential, set ambitious goals, and watch as you achieve greatness.

Setting SMART goals is a powerful strategy for achieving success and creating your own good luck. By making your goals Specific, Measurable, Achievable, Relevant, and Time-bound, you set yourself up for success and increase the likelihood of reaching your objectives. Remember, as Henry David Thoreau once said, “What you get by achieving your goals is not as important as what you become by achieving your goals.” Embrace the SMART method, and watch as your aspirations turn into achievements, and your dreams into reality.

10. Embracing Risk: The Path to Becoming a Rocket Scientist

“To live a creative life, we must lose our fear of being wrong.” – Joseph Chilton Pearce

You ever feel that delicious shiver of excitement when you're about to try something totally new? That's the magic of risk calling your name, beckoning you to dance with the unknown! Risk isn't some monster lurking in the shadows, waiting to trip you up. It's the key that unlocks a treasure trove of possibilities, a thrilling invitation to step outside your comfort zone and explore uncharted territory.

Think about it: some of the most incredible moments in life happen when we embrace the unexpected. Maybe it's finally signing up for that salsa class you've been eyeing, the one that makes your heart thump happy little rhythms. Or perhaps it's quitting your unfulfilling job and taking a chance on a wild business idea – the one that keeps you up at night, buzzing with excitement. Sure, things might not always go exactly according to plan. But here's the secret sauce: risk isn't just about avoiding pitfalls; it's about opening doors to opportunities you might never have even dreamed of!

Imagine this: success is hiding on the other side of a shimmering curtain, just waiting for a brave soul like you to take the leap. It could be a dream job you never dared to apply for, a travel adventure that pushes your boundaries, or a creative project that sets your soul on fire. Risk is the bridge that gets you there, the courageous leap that transforms your life in ways you can't even begin to imagine.

Of course, it's not all sunshine and rainbows. Taking risks can sometimes lead to setbacks, even failures. But here's the thing: those bumps in the road are valuable lessons in disguise. They teach you resilience, build your confidence, and equip you with the wisdom to make even better decisions next time. Remember, the most successful people in the world aren't the ones who never stumbled; they're the ones who dared to dream big, took calculated risks, learned from their mistakes, and kept on climbing!

So, are you ready to embrace the thrill of the unknown? Remember, "Fortune favors the brave!" Don't let fear hold you back from experiencing the life-changing power of risk. Take a deep breath, tap into your inner courage, and get ready to unlock a world of amazing possibilities! The adventure awaits, and it's calling your name!

The Story of Apollo 11: The Importance of Taking Risks in Space Exploration

The story of Apollo 11, the mission that first landed humans on the Moon, is a powerful example of the importance of taking risks in the field of rocket science and space exploration. This mission not only marked a monumental achievement in human history but also demonstrated the necessity and value of embracing risk to achieve groundbreaking success.

Background: The Space Race

In the 1960s, the United States and the Soviet Union were locked in the Space Race, a period of intense competition to achieve significant milestones in space exploration. The launch of the Soviet satellite Sputnik in 1957 and the subsequent successful human spaceflight by Yuri Gagarin in 1961 spurred the United States to accelerate its space program.

President John F. Kennedy set a bold and ambitious goal for NASA: to land a man on the Moon and return him safely to Earth before the end of the decade. This declaration, made in 1961, put enormous pressure on NASA and its engineers to achieve what seemed almost impossible at the time.

Taking Risks: The Apollo Program

The Apollo program was fraught with risks, challenges, and uncertainties. The development of the Saturn V rocket, the spacecraft, and all the associated technologies required innovative engineering solutions and involved significant dangers.

1. **Technological Risks:**

- Saturn V Rocket: The Saturn V was the most powerful rocket ever built, standing at 363 feet tall and capable of generating 7.6 million pounds of thrust. The development and testing of such a massive and complex rocket involved numerous technical challenges and potential hazards.
- Lunar Module: The Lunar Module (LM), designed to land on the Moon and return to the Command Module in lunar orbit, was a completely new type of spacecraft. Engineers had to create a vehicle that could operate in the vacuum of space, land on an alien surface, and then lift off again.

2. Mission Risks:

- Launch and Flight: Each launch carried the risk of catastrophic failure. The Apollo 11 mission, in particular, had to navigate through multiple stages of flight, including the critical trans-lunar injection burn that set the spacecraft on its course to the Moon.
- Lunar Landing: The landing itself was an enormous risk. Neil Armstrong and Buzz Aldrin faced unknown surface conditions and had to manually navigate the Lunar Module to avoid boulders and craters, ultimately landing with only seconds of fuel remaining.

The Success of Apollo 11

On July 20, 1969, Neil Armstrong and Buzz Aldrin successfully landed the Lunar Module, Eagle, on the Moon's surface. Armstrong's famous words, "That's one small step for [a] man, one giant leap for mankind," marked a historic moment achieved through calculated risk-taking and innovative problem-solving.

The success of Apollo 11 was not just a triumph of engineering and science; it was a testament to the courage and willingness of NASA and its astronauts to face and manage significant risks. The mission required the coordination of thousands of engineers, scientists, and technicians, all working under the pressure of an ambitious and politically charged deadline.

Legacy and Lessons

The Apollo 11 mission demonstrated that taking risks is an inherent part of making significant advancements in space exploration. It highlighted the importance of rigorous planning, extensive testing, and the ability to adapt to unforeseen challenges. The success of Apollo 11 paved the way for future missions and set a precedent for pushing the boundaries of human achievement.

The story of Apollo 11 remains an inspiration, showing that with vision, dedication, and a willingness to embrace and manage risks, humanity can achieve the extraordinary.

References

- "Apollo 11 Mission Overview." NASA. Link
- https://www.nasa.gov/history/apollo-11-mission-overview/
- "Apollo 11: The Moon Landing, 1969." History.
- Chaikin, Andrew. "A Man on the Moon: The Voyages of the Apollo Astronauts." Viking, 1994.

Practical Life Examples of Taking Risks

"Success is not final; failure is not fatal: It is the courage to continue that counts." – Winston Churchill

Career Change

Many people take the risk of changing careers, leaving behind stability to pursue their passions. For instance, someone might leave a well-paying corporate job to start a small business in a different field. This decision involves significant risk but can lead to tremendous personal and professional growth.

Investing in Education

Pursuing higher education or professional certifications is another example of a calculated risk. The investment of time and money can open up new career opportunities and lead to long-term success.

Overcoming Personal Loss

Facing personal loss, such as the death of a loved one, is one of life's greatest challenges. By confronting this pain and finding ways to cope, individuals build emotional resilience that helps them navigate future hardships with greater strength.

Dealing with Professional Setbacks

Experiencing professional setbacks, such as being laid off or facing a business failure, can be devastating. However, those who use these setbacks as learning experiences often come out stronger and more resilient, ready to tackle new challenges.,

"You miss 100% of the shots you don't take."

According to Wayne Gretzky, often hailed as one of the greatest hockey players of all time, encapsulated a profound truth about success and risk in his famous quote, "You miss 100% of the shots you don't take." This simple yet powerful statement transcends the realm of sports, offering a universal lesson on the importance of seizing opportunities, embracing risk, and overcoming the fear of failure.

At its core, Gretzky's quote speaks to the inevitability of failure when one refrains from taking action. In hockey, as in life, the act of taking a shot is inherently tied to the possibility of scoring. However, without the attempt, success becomes impossible. This concept highlights a fundamental principle: inaction guarantees missed opportunities, whereas taking a chance, despite the risk of failure, opens the door to potential success.

Risk is an inherent part of any endeavor. Whether in sports, business, or personal pursuits, the willingness to take risks is crucial for growth and achievement. Gretzky's quote encourages individuals to embrace the uncertainty that comes with risk. By stepping out of one's comfort zone and taking action, even in the face of potential failure, one can discover new opportunities and achieve goals that seemed out of reach.

Overcoming the Fear of Failure

Fear of failure is a powerful deterrent that often prevents people from taking the necessary steps toward their goals. This fear can stem from a variety of sources, including self-doubt, societal expectations, and past experiences. Gretzky's wisdom challenges this fear by emphasizing the certainty of missed opportunities when one fails to act. By shifting the focus from the potential for failure to the necessity of action, individuals can overcome their fears and take the first step toward success.

The Importance of Persistence

Gretzky's quote also underscores the importance of persistence. Taking a shot and missing is a natural part of any journey. However, the act of continuously taking shots, learning from each attempt, and refining one's approach is what ultimately leads to success. Persistence is about maintaining the resolve to keep trying, even when faced with setbacks. It is through this relentless pursuit that individuals can turn potential failures into stepping stones for success.

The Broader Impact

Gretzky's quote has a broader societal impact as well. It encourages a culture of innovation and creativity. When individuals and organizations adopt a mindset that values action over inaction, it fosters an environment where new ideas can flourish, and progress can be made. This cultural shift can lead to advancements in technology, improvements in social systems, and the overall betterment of society.

"You miss 100% of the shots you don't take" is more than just a motivational quote; it is a guiding principle for success. Wayne Gretzky's words remind us that the fear of failure should never paralyze us into inaction. Instead, we should embrace risk, overcome our fears, and persistently take shots at our goals. By doing so, we open ourselves to the possibility of success and ensure that we do not miss out on the opportunities that life presents. In the end, it is the shots we take that define our journey and shape our destiny. Some of the greatest achievements in history have come from taking significant risks

11. Resilience in the Face of Challenges: The Catalyst for Success

Facing challenges and overcoming them builds resilience, making you better equipped to handle future obstacles.

Fuelling Your Journey to Become a Rocket Scientist

Every aspiring rocket scientist knows liftoff isn't always guaranteed. The path to space is paved with challenges – failed experiments, complex technical hurdles, and even the occasional launchpad mishap. These setbacks can be discouraging, but it's how you respond that truly defines your success.

This is where resilience comes in – your superpower for bouncing back from setbacks and blasting forward with even more determination. It's about embracing challenges, not as roadblocks, but as launchpads for growth. Here's why resilience is key:

It's Not About Getting Knocked Down, It's About Getting Back Up: Just like a rocket needs multiple attempts to reach orbit, you'll face setbacks in your journey. Resilience ensures you learn from failures, dust yourself off, and keep aiming for the stars.

Challenges Breed Innovation: Some of the greatest advancements in rocket science came from overcoming seemingly insurmountable problems. Think of the innovative solutions born from a failed engine test or an unexpected orbital anomaly. Resilience allows you to see challenges as opportunities to push boundaries and develop groundbreaking solutions.

Building a Growth Mindset: Resilient rocket scientists view challenges as stepping stones, not dead ends. They focus on learning from mistakes and constantly improving their skills.

Remember, the most successful rocket scientists aren't those who never face challenges, but those who overcome them with unwavering resilience. So, embrace the setbacks, learn, grow, and keep your sights set on the stars!

The Power of Resilience

Resilience is the cornerstone of a growth mindset. It is the inner strength that enables us to recover from difficulties and keep striving towards our goals. Just as a tree bends in the wind but does not break, resilient individuals adapt to challenges without losing their determination. Resilience is not about avoiding challenges but facing them head-on with courage and tenacity.

Imagine the mythical phoenix, a majestic bird that, upon reaching the end of its life, is consumed by flames only to rise anew from its ashes. This powerful metaphor illustrates resilience perfectly. The phoenix's ability to regenerate symbolizes the capacity to overcome adversity and emerge stronger.

Resilience is the booster rocket that propels aspiring rocket scientists towards the stars. It's the inner fortitude that allows you to weather the inevitable storms – failed experiments, mind-bending equations, and even the launch failures. Just like a spacecraft needs to withstand immense pressure to achieve escape velocity, resilience equips you to handle the challenges that come with pushing the boundaries of space exploration.

Here's why resilience is essential for reaching your rocket science dreams:

It's Not About a Flawless Trajectory: The path to becoming a rocket scientist isn't a smooth ride. There will be setbacks, technical glitches, and moments when your calculations defy logic. Resilience ensures you don't get thrown off course by these hurdles. It allows you to learn, adapt, and keep aiming for the cosmos.

Innovation Takes Guts and Grit: History is filled with groundbreaking advancements in rocket science that stemmed from overcoming seemingly insurmountable problems. Think of the countless engineers who toiled tirelessly to solve the issue of engine instability, ultimately paving the way for successful missions. Resilience allows you to embrace challenges as opportunities to innovate and push the boundaries of the possible.

Building a Growth Mindset for Stellar Achievements: Resilient rocket scientists don't see roadblocks; they see stepping stones. They learn from every failed experiment, every unexpected anomaly. They possess a growth mindset, constantly seeking knowledge and improvement.

The Tale of Scheherazade: Resilience in the Face of Challenges

In the heart of the ancient city of Baghdad, where minarets kissed the sky and the fragrance of spices wafted through bustling bazaars, there lived a sultan named Shahryar. His palace, adorned with the finest silks and glittering jewels, concealed a heart darkened by betrayal. Once a loving ruler, Shahryar had turned into a vengeful tyrant after discovering his queen's infidelity. In his wrath, he vowed to wed a new bride each night and have her executed by dawn.

The Whisper of Despair and the Birth of Hope

The city was shrouded in sorrow as the sultan's decree turned into a cycle of despair. Mothers wept, and fathers trembled, fearing for their daughters. Amidst this gloom, a beacon of hope emerged in the form of Scheherazade, the vizier's eldest daughter. Known for her wisdom and grace, Scheherazade was determined to end the bloodshed.

One moonlit night, she approached her father with resolve etched on her face. "Father, I shall marry the sultan and put an end to this nightmare," she declared. Her father, stricken with fear, tried to dissuade her, but Scheherazade's resilience was unwavering. She had a plan that demanded not just courage but also wit and tenacity.

The First Night: A Tapestry of Tales Begins

As the golden sun dipped below the horizon, Scheherazade entered the sultan's opulent chambers. Draped in robes of azure and gold, she appeared like a celestial vision. Shahryar, his heart hardened by betrayal, watched her with indifferent eyes. That night, Scheherazade began to weave a tale so enchanting that the very stars seemed to pause in their celestial dance to listen.

She spun the story of Ali Baba and the Forty Thieves, her voice a melodic river flowing through the sultan's stony silence. Just as dawn approached, she left the tale unfinished, her voice trailing off like the last notes of a lute. Captivated by the story and curious about its conclusion, Shahryar spared her life for another night.

The Dance of Resilience: Night After Night

Night after night, Scheherazade continued her delicate dance with destiny. She narrated tales of adventure, love, and magic—each more captivating than the last. The story of Sinbad the Sailor and his perilous voyages across uncharted seas held Shahryar spellbound, while the poignant tale of Aladdin and his magical lamp filled his heart with wonder.

With each tale, Scheherazade not only postponed her fate but also subtly wove lessons of wisdom, justice, and compassion into the fabric of her stories. Her resilience became a symphony of words, a testament to the power of hope and determination in the face of insurmountable odds.

The Turning Tide: A Heart Transformed

As the nights turned into weeks and the weeks into months, a transformation began to unfold within the sultan. The cold fortress of his heart, once impenetrable, started to thaw. Scheherazade's tales, laced with resilience and courage, touched the deepest recesses of his soul. He began to see not just the stories but also the storyteller—a woman of unparalleled strength and wisdom. The city, too, sensed the change. The air grew lighter, and the oppressive shadow that had loomed over Baghdad started to lift. Scheherazade's resilience had sparked a quiet revolution, turning despair into hope.

The Final Dawn: Triumph of Resilience

On the thousand and first night, as the first light of dawn kissed the minarets, Scheherazade concluded her final tale. The sultan, now a changed man, looked at her with eyes softened by love and gratitude. "Scheherazade," he spoke, his voice breaking the silence, "you have healed my heart and opened my eyes. No longer will I be the tyrant who brings death at dawn. You are my queen, and together we shall rule with wisdom and compassion."

The Legacy of Scheherazade

The tale of Scheherazade is not merely a story of survival; it is a powerful narrative of resilience in the face of relentless challenges. Her courage and ingenuity not only saved her life but also transformed a kingdom. Her story, passed down through generations, continues to inspire with its message: that resilience, coupled with wisdom and hope, can turn the tide of fate.

In the land where the desert sands whisper ancient secrets and the night sky is a tapestry of stars, Scheherazade's legacy endures. It reminds us that even in the darkest moments, resilience can light the path to success and change the course of destiny.

Historical Examples of Resilience

History is replete with examples of individuals who exemplified resilience in the face of daunting challenges:

The Story of Wernher von Braun: The Importance of Resilience in Rocket Science

Early Life and Ambition

Wernher von Braun was born in 1912 in Wirsitz, Germany (now Wyrzysk, Poland). From a young age, von Braun was fascinated by space and rocketry. His passion was ignited when he received a telescope as a gift from his mother, which he used to study the stars. This early fascination with space would shape his entire career and lead to significant advancements in rocketry and space exploration.

Initial Challenges and Setbacks

Von Braun faced numerous challenges throughout his career. His early experiments with rocketry were met with skepticism and technical difficulties. In the late 1920s and early 1930s, while studying mechanical engineering at the Technical University of Berlin, he joined the German Society for Space Travel (VfR). Here, he conducted rocket propulsion experiments that often resulted in failures and explosions.

Despite these setbacks, von Braun remained determined. His persistence paid off when he successfully launched small rockets using liquid fuel, an important breakthrough in rocketry. However, the political climate in Germany during the 1930s presented new challenges. Von Braun's work became entangled with the military ambitions of the Nazi regime.

World War II and the V-2 Rocket

During World War II, von Braun's expertise in rocketry was harnessed by the German military. He led the development of the V-2 rocket, the world's first long-range guided ballistic missile. The V-2 represented a significant technological achievement, but it was also a weapon of war, used to target Allied cities.

Von Braun's work on the V-2 was conducted under difficult and often morally compromising circumstances. He and his team faced immense pressure to deliver results, working under the constant threat of Nazi scrutiny. Moreover, the use of forced labour in the V-2 production and the rocket's destructive purpose left a controversial legacy.

Post-War Period and Resilience

After the war, von Braun and many of his colleagues surrendered to American forces. He was brought to the United States under Operation Paperclip, a secret program to recruit German scientists. In America, von Braun faced the challenge of rebuilding his career amidst suspicion and ethical scrutiny over his wartime activities.

Von Braun's resilience and unwavering dedication to rocketry allowed him to overcome these obstacles. He began working for the U.S. Army, where he developed the Redstone rocket, which later became the foundation for launching America's first satellite, Explorer 1, in 1958.

NASA and the Apollo Program

Von Braun's most significant contribution came when he joined NASA, where he led the development of the Saturn V rocket. This rocket was crucial for the Apollo missions, which aimed to land humans on the Moon. Despite numerous technical challenges and setbacks, von Braun's leadership and expertise were instrumental in the success of the Apollo program.

The Saturn V rocket, standing at 363 feet tall, remains one of the most powerful rockets ever built. On July 20, 1969, the Saturn V successfully launched Apollo 11, enabling Neil Armstrong and Buzz Aldrin to become the first humans to set foot on the Moon. This historic achievement was a testament to von Braun's resilience and his ability to lead and innovate under pressure.

Legacy and Impact

Wernher von Braun's journey from a young dreamer fascinated by space to a leading figure in space exploration underscores the importance of resilience. Despite facing numerous technical, ethical, and personal challenges, von Braun's dedication to his vision of space travel never wavered. His work laid the foundation for modern rocketry and space exploration, significantly advancing our understanding of space and our ability to explore it.

Von Braun's legacy is complex, marked by both extraordinary scientific achievement and controversial wartime activities. However, his story undeniably illustrates how resilience and a relentless pursuit of one's goals can lead to groundbreaking advancements. His contributions continue to inspire new generations of engineers and scientists dedicated to exploring the final frontier.

Sources

- "Wernher von Braun: A Biography" by Erik Bergaust
- "Rocket Man: Robert H. Goddard and the Birth of the Space Age" by David Clary
- NASA's biography on Wernher von Braun

Building Resilience: Practical Steps

Resilience can be cultivated through intentional practices and attitudes. Here are some strategies to build resilience and adopt a growth mindset:

Embrace Challenges: View challenges as opportunities to learn and grow. Instead of avoiding difficult tasks, confront them with determination. Each challenge you overcome strengthens your resilience.

Learn from Failure: Accept that failure is a part of the journey to success. Analyze your setbacks, extract valuable lessons, and apply them to future endeavours. Remember, every failure brings you one step closer to your goal.

Maintain a Positive Attitude: A positive outlook can significantly impact your resilience. Focus on your strengths and achievements, and remind yourself of past successes. Optimism fuels perseverance.

Seek Support: Surround yourself with supportive people who encourage and uplift you. Share your challenges with trusted friends or mentors, and seek their advice and encouragement. A strong support network can provide the resilience needed to navigate tough times.

Practice Self-Care: Physical and mental well-being are crucial for resilience. Ensure you get enough rest, exercise regularly, and engage in activities that rejuvenate your spirit. Taking care of yourself equips you to handle challenges more effectively.

The Path to Resilient Success

Resilience is not just about enduring hardships; it is about thriving despite them. By cultivating a growth mindset and embracing resilience, we can transform challenges into opportunities for growth and success. Remember the words of Winston Churchill, "Success is not final, failure is not fatal: It is the courage to continue that counts." Let resilience be the catalyst that propels you toward your goals, no matter how daunting the obstacles may seem. Embrace each challenge with the confidence that you have the strength to rise, like the phoenix, from the ashes of adversity.

Shift Your Perspective: Instead of seeing difficulties as threats, see them as chances to learn and grow.

Develop Grit: Angela Duckworth, in her book "Grit: The Power of Passion and Perseverance," emphasizes that talent alone doesn't lead to success. Grit—passion, resilience, and sustained persistence—is crucial. She states, "Enthusiasm is common. Endurance is rare." This idea challenges traditional notions that emphasize innate ability over hard work and dedication.

Michael Jordan, often regarded as the greatest basketball player of all time, was cut from his high school basketball team. Instead of giving up, he used this setback as motivation to work harder, famously saying, "I've failed over and over and over again in my life, and that is why I succeed."

Embrace these principles, and let resilience guide you to extraordinary achievements. By developing a resilient mindset, you can turn any challenge into an opportunity for growth and success.

Rising Strong: The Phoenix of Success"

I've stumbled through the twilight of my days,
Each fall a stone that marked my winding way,
Like rivers carved by countless rainy sprays,
Through trials, I've been shaped from life's rough clay.

Success, a phoenix rising from the ash,
Is born from flames of countless, searing tries,
In failure's wake, where shattered hopes may crash,
I found the wings to soar through endless skies.

In gardens where the thorns of trials grow,
Bloom roses of resilience, pure and grand,
For only through the rain can flowers show,
The vibrant hues that grace the fertile land.

Failures are but the anvils of our fate,
Where dreams are hammered into solid gold,
Through fire and time, we learn to navigate,
And craft a life that's wondrous to behold.

Chapter 11

Plan Of Action to become a Rocket Scientist

Becoming a Rocket Scientist: Your Step-by-Step Guide to Achieving Your Dream

Becoming a rocket scientist is an exciting and rewarding goal. Here's how you can turn this dream into a compelling and achievable goal, breaking it down into manageable steps:

Setting Your Goal and Planning

1. Define Your Goal Clearly

- **Specific:** Aim to become a rocket scientist specializing in a particular area, such as propulsion systems, satellite technology, or spacecraft design. Identifying your specific interest early will help you tailor your studies and extracurricular activities accordingly.
- **Measurable:** Set milestones you want to achieve along the way, such as completing certain courses, obtaining degrees, or gaining specific skills. For example, aim to excel in advanced placement courses in high school, secure internships during college, or publish research papers during your graduate studies.

- **Achievable:** Make sure your goals are realistic given your current situation and resources. Assess your strengths and areas for improvement, and plan accordingly.
- **Relevant:** Ensure that each step you take is relevant to your ultimate goal of becoming a rocket scientist. Every course you take, every project you work on, and every internship you complete should contribute to your expertise in rocketry.
- **Time-bound:** Set a timeline for your goals, such as graduating high school, getting into a good university, completing your degree, and gaining experience. Create a roadmap with specific deadlines for each milestone.

2. Break Down Your Goal into Manageable Steps

Step 1: Focus on Your Studies Now

- **Subjects:** Concentrate on excelling in mathematics, physics, and chemistry, as these are foundational for rocket science. Strong performance in these subjects will prepare you for the rigorous coursework in college.
- **Projects:** Participate in science fairs, join clubs (like a robotics or astronomy club), and work on small projects related to rocketry or space. These activities will give you practical experience and enhance your college applications.

Step 2: High School Preparation

- **Advanced Courses:** Take advanced placement (AP) or honours courses in math and science if available. These courses will challenge you academically and prepare you for college-level work.

- **Extracurriculars:** Join or form a science club, participate in STEM competitions, and engage in any available rocketry or aerospace programs. Building rockets, designing experiments, and participating in competitions will develop your technical skills and teamwork.

- **Research:** Start reading books, watching documentaries, and following news about space and rocketry to deepen your knowledge and interest. Resources like NASA's website and science journals can provide valuable insights.

Step 3: College and Beyond

- **Degree:** Aim to get into a university with a strong engineering or physics program. Research universities known for their aerospace engineering programs, such as MIT, Stanford, or Caltech.

- **Internships:** Seek internships or summer programs related to aerospace during college. Practical experience in the industry is invaluable and can lead to job offers after graduation.

- **Projects:** Work on research projects, join student design teams, and participate in relevant competitions. These experiences will help you build a portfolio and gain hands-on skills.

Step 4: Graduate Studies and Experience

- **Advanced Degrees:** Consider pursuing a master's or Ph.D. in aerospace engineering or a related field. Advanced degrees can open doors to specialized positions and research opportunities.

- **Experience:** Gain experience through internships, co-ops, and working on real-world projects. Networking with professionals in the field is also crucial. Attend conferences, join professional organizations like the AIAA, and connect with mentors.

Using Visualizations and Affirmations

Visualizations:

- **Imagine Success:** Regularly visualize yourself achieving your goal. Picture yourself in a lab, working on rockets, or launching a spacecraft. Visualization can help keep you motivated and focused on your goals.

- **Vision Board:** Create a vision board with images and words that represent your goals and dreams. Place it somewhere you can see it daily as a reminder of what you're working towards.

Affirmations:

- **Positive Statements:** Use affirmations to reinforce your belief in your ability to succeed. Examples include:
    - "I am capable of becoming a successful rocket scientist."
    - "I am dedicated to my studies and continually improving my skills."
    - "I will achieve my goal through hard work and perseverance."
- **Daily Practice:** Repeat these affirmations daily, especially during challenging times, to build confidence and maintain a positive mindset.

Practical Steps and Strategies

Develop Good Study Habits:

- **Consistent Schedule:** Set aside dedicated time each day for studying and homework. Consistency is key to mastering difficult subjects.

- **Active Learning:** Engage in active learning by solving problems, conducting experiments, and participating in group studies.
- **Seek Help:** Don't hesitate to ask teachers, parents, or peers for help if you find certain topics challenging.

Explore and Experiment:

- **Hands-on Projects:** Build simple rockets or model aircraft. This practical experience will help you understand the principles of aerodynamics and propulsion.
- **Science Kits:** Use science kits related to rocketry and space exploration to gain hands-on experience.

Use Online Resources:

- **Educational Websites:** Utilize websites like Khan Academy, Coursera, and edX for courses in physics, mathematics, and engineering.
- **Forums and Communities:** Join online forums and communities where you can ask questions, share knowledge, and learn from others interested in rocketry and space.

Attend Workshops and Camps:

- **STEM Camps:** Participate in STEM (Science, Technology, Engineering, Mathematics) camps or workshops to gain exposure to new concepts and technologies.
- **Space-related Events:** Attend talks, exhibitions, or events hosted by space agencies or organizations.

Build a Support Network:

- **Mentorship:** Find mentors who can guide you, such as teachers, professors, or professionals in the field.
- **Peer Group:** Surround yourself with friends who share similar interests and goals. This support network can provide motivation and collaboration opportunities.

Monitoring Progress

Set Short-Term Goals: Break your long-term goal into short-term objectives. For example, aim to excel in your upcoming math exam or complete a science project. Celebrate your achievements, no matter how small, to stay motivated.

Regular Self-Assessment: Periodically assess your progress and adjust your plans if needed. Reflect on what's working well and what could be improved. Stay flexible and be willing to adapt your strategies as you learn and grow.

Final Thoughts

Turning your dream of becoming a rocket scientist into reality is a journey that requires dedication, hard work, and strategic planning. By setting clear goals, breaking them down into manageable steps, and using visualizations and affirmations, you can stay motivated and focused on your path. Remember, the journey is as important as the destination, so enjoy the process of learning and growing along the way. Keep your curiosity alive, stay persistent, and believe in yourself—you have the potential to achieve great things!

Continuing Your Journey

Becoming a rocket scientist is a long-term commitment that will require continuous learning, adaptation, and resilience. As you progress in your academic and professional journey, it's important to stay focused, seek out opportunities for growth, and remain passionate about your goals.

Keep Up with Industry Developments:

- **Stay Informed:** Keep yourself updated with the latest developments in aerospace engineering and space exploration. Follow reputable sources like NASA, SpaceX, ESA (European Space Agency), and other space research organizations. Reading scientific journals, attending conferences, and participating in webinars can help you stay ahead in the field.

- **Subscribe to Journals and Magazines:** Publications like the "Journal of Aerospace Engineering," "AIAA Journal," and "Aviation Week & Space Technology" are excellent resources for the latest research and technological advancements in aerospace.

Build Technical Skills:

- **Advanced Software Skills:** Familiarize yourself with industry-standard software used in aerospace engineering, such as MATLAB, Simulink, SolidWorks, and ANSYS. These tools are essential for simulations, modelling, and design.

- **Coding and Programming:** Strengthen your programming skills in languages such as Python, C++, and Java. These are often used in developing control systems and simulation software for rockets.

Gain Practical Experience:

- **Internships and Co-ops:** Seek out internships with aerospace companies, government agencies, or research institutions. Practical experience is invaluable and can significantly enhance your understanding of theoretical concepts.

- **Student Projects and Competitions:** Participate in student design competitions such as NASA's University Student Launch Initiative, the Spaceport America Cup, and the

CanSat Competition. These competitions offer hands-on experience and the opportunity to apply your knowledge in real-world scenarios.

Pursue Advanced Education:

- **Graduate Programs:** Consider pursuing advanced degrees such as a master's or Ph.D. in aerospace engineering, astrophysics, or a related field. Advanced degrees can open doors to specialized roles and research opportunities.
- **Specializations:** Explore specializations within aerospace engineering, such as propulsion systems, spacecraft design, avionics, and orbital mechanics. Specializing can make you an expert in a specific area, increasing your value in the industry.

Network with Professionals:

- **Professional Organizations:** Join professional organizations like the American Institute of Aeronautics and Astronautics (AIAA), the Institute of Electrical and Electronics Engineers (IEEE), and the Society of Automotive Engineers (SAE). These organizations provide networking opportunities, professional development resources, and access to conferences and events.
- **Mentorship and Collaboration:** Find mentors in your field who can offer guidance, support, and advice. Collaborate

with peers and professionals on research projects and industry initiatives.

Stay Motivated and Persistent:

- **Setbacks and Failures:** Understand that setbacks and failures are part of the journey. Learn from your mistakes and use them as stepping stones towards success.
- **Continuous Improvement:** Always look for ways to improve your skills and knowledge. Stay curious, ask questions, and never stop learning.

Develop Soft Skills:

- **Communication Skills:** Effective communication is crucial in any engineering field. Work on your ability to explain complex concepts clearly and concisely, both in writing and verbally.
- **Teamwork and Leadership:** Cultivate your teamwork and leadership skills. Many aerospace projects require collaboration with diverse teams. Being able to lead and work well with others is essential.

Becoming a rocket scientist is a challenging yet incredibly rewarding path. It requires a blend of academic excellence, practical experience, technical skills, and personal qualities such as resilience, curiosity, and determination. By following these steps and maintaining a steadfast commitment to your goals, you can turn your dream of becoming a rocket scientist into reality.

Embrace the journey, celebrate your achievements, and continue to push the boundaries of what is possible. The sky is not the limit—it's just the beginning.

Awakening Dreams: The Fire Within

A dream is not the vision in the night,
That fades with morning's first and gentle gleam,
But that which stirs the soul with boundless light,
A burning fire that fuels each waking dream.

It whispers softly in the quiet hours,
A restless call that keeps the heart awake,
Inspires the mind with ever-growing powers,
And urges on with steps we must partake.

This dream, a beacon shining through the dark,
A force that drives us onward, bold and true,
It leaves an everlasting, vibrant mark,
And guides us to the goals we must pursue.

So, cherish dreams that wake the soul's desire,
For they are flames that set the world afire.

Chapter 12

The Thinking Process of Rocket Scientists

Scientific Method

The Foundation of Scientific Inquiry:

The path to becoming a rocket scientist isn't just about filling your head with complex equations and technical jargon. It's about cultivating a unique way of thinking, one that embraces curiosity like a compass, wields critical thinking like a scalpel, and never lets go of the responsibility that comes with such immense power. Imagine yourself joining a lineage of brilliant minds, each one a stepping stone for the next. Let's delve into the world of these scientific pioneers and see how their thought processes can ignite your own journey.

The bedrock of any scientific quest is the scientific method. Think of it as a meticulously crafted map, guiding you through the wilderness of discovery. It all starts with observation. Keenly watch the world around you, like a detective searching for clues. Then, based on what you've seen, a hypothesis forms – an educated hunch about how things might work. This isn't just a guess; it's a well-informed prediction, ready to be tested. Here's where the real magic happens – experimentation. You meticulously design a controlled environment, a playground for your hypothesis to run wild. You gather data, facts whispering their secrets, and then comes the crucial analysis. This is where you become a translator, transforming raw numbers into a coherent story. Statistical tools become your allies, helping you decipher the patterns and draw conclusions, the culmination of your scientific odyssey.

Take the legendary Sir Isaac Newton, for instance. He didn't simply glance at the sky and magically conjure up his revolutionary laws of motion and gravitation. No, he was a master of the scientific method. He meticulously observed the movements of celestial bodies, a deep curiosity gnawing at his mind. He proposed a hypothesis – a force, he reasoned, must be governing this grand celestial ballet. He then embarked on a series of experiments, meticulously collecting data. Through tireless analysis, he unraveled the secrets hidden within the numbers, forever changing our understanding of the universe. And Newton, with characteristic humility, acknowledged the giants whose shoulders he stood upon, a testament to the collaborative spirit that fuels scientific progress.

Take Marie Curie, for example. Her groundbreaking discoveries in radioactivity weren't the result of a lucky happenstance. She, too, was a master of the scientific method. Driven by a relentless curiosity about the world, she meticulously observed materials like uranium, noticing they emitted mysterious rays. She dared to hypothesize that there were elements even more potent, elements science hadn't yet encountered. Through rigorous experimentation and analysis, she not only confirmed her suspicions but unearthed two entirely new elements – radium and polonium. Her discoveries not only revolutionized science but also laid the foundation for fields like nuclear medicine. And just like Sir Isaac Newton, Curie embodied the spirit of collaboration, acknowledging the giants whose work paved the way for her own.

This is merely the first chapter of your scientific odyssey. As you delve deeper, you'll encounter countless brilliant minds, each one offering a fresh perspective, a unique way to tackle a problem. Remember, the qualities of a rocket scientist aren't confined to textbooks. They're a way of life – a constant questioning, a relentless pursuit of knowledge tempered with a deep sense of responsibility. It's about using that knowledge to not only push the boundaries of science but also to make the world a better place. So, put on your thinking cap, unleash your inner detective, and get ready to explore the universe, one scientific inquiry at a time. The cosmos awaits your insatiable curiosity!

Critical Thinking and Scepticism

As you forge your path towards becoming a rocket scientist, remember, it's not just about harnessing the raw power of equations. It's about cultivating a moral compass that guides your scientific pursuits. Every discovery, every invention, carries an inherent responsibility – a responsibility to ensure your work serves humanity and the world around you.

Think of it like building a magnificent spaceship. The intricate calculations, the groundbreaking technology – they're the engine that propels your creation forward. But without a skilled pilot, a navigator with a keen sense of ethics, that same ship could veer off course, wreaking havoc. That's the role critical thinking plays in your scientific journey. You'll learn to question assumptions, to dissect information with a discerning eye. It's like being a detective, meticulously examining every clue, every established theory, to ensure it holds water.

Take Albert Einstein, the man who revolutionized our understanding of physics. He wasn't content with simply accepting the prevailing Newtonian mechanics. His relentless curiosity, his skepticism towards the norm, fueled his groundbreaking theory of relativity. It was a paradigm shift, a testament to the power of critical thinking in science. And Einstein, ever the champion of curiosity, famously declared, "The important thing is not to stop questioning. Curiosity has its own reason for existing."

Ethical Considerations

Ethical considerations are another crucial facet of this scientific compass. As you delve deeper into your research, you'll confront moral dilemmas that demand careful navigation. Imagine yourself conducting a groundbreaking experiment – the potential for good is immense, but there's also a chance it could have unintended consequences. This is where your ethical compass comes in. You'll learn the importance of informed consent, ensuring everyone involved in your research understands the potential risks and rewards. Honesty becomes your watchword – you'll meticulously document your findings, avoiding plagiarism at all costs. And any potential conflicts of interest, any biases that could cloud your judgment, must be brought to light with transparency.

Remember, the scientific community is a collaborative effort, a vast tapestry woven by countless brilliant minds. You'll stand on the shoulders of giants like Einstein and Curie, but the future of science rests on your shoulders too. So, let your curiosity be your fuel, let critical thinking be your guide, and let a deep sense of ethical responsibility be the compass that steers your scientific journey. The universe awaits your responsible brilliance, young scientist. As you forge your path towards becoming a rocket scientist, a profound truth settles on your shoulders – immense power often walks hand-in-hand with immense responsibility. The rockets you design, the technologies you pioneer, have the potential to shape the very destiny of humanity. That's why, alongside the thrill of scientific discovery, you'll cultivate a deep awareness of the ethical considerations that intertwine with every groundbreaking innovation.

Imagine yourself standing at the precipice of a monumental discovery. Your research brims with potential, promising advancements that could propel humanity to new heights. But with such potential comes a sobering reality – the possibility of unintended consequences. This is where the ethical compass you forge becomes your guiding light. It compels you to carefully consider the potential impact of your work, not just on the scientific landscape, but on the very fabric of society and the environment we inhabit.

Take the story of J. Robert Oppenheimer, the enigmatic physicist who led the Manhattan Project. He spearheaded the creation of the atomic bomb, a weapon of unimaginable destructive power. Yet, in the face of its devastating effects, Oppenheimer grappled with a profound moral dilemma. The scientist who had unlocked the atom's destructive potential became a fervent advocate for international control of nuclear weapons. He envisioned a future where atomic energy wasn't a harbinger of destruction, but a beacon of progress, used for peaceful purposes. His haunting quote, "I am become Death, the destroyer of worlds," echoes the stark choice that science can sometimes present.

Ethical considerations permeate every aspect of your scientific journey. Informed consent becomes a cornerstone of your research. You ensure that everyone involved in your projects fully understands the potential risks and rewards, their participation a free and informed choice. Honesty becomes your guiding principle – meticulous documentation and a commitment to avoiding plagiarism are paramount. Any potential conflicts of interest, any biases that could cloud your judgment, must be brought to light with unwavering transparency.

The scientific community is a grand tapestry woven by countless brilliant minds, each one adding a thread to the ever-evolving picture of our universe. You'll stand on the shoulders of giants like Oppenheimer, learning from their triumphs and grappling with their moral quandaries. The future of science rests on your shoulders too, young scientist. Let your scientific curiosity be your fuel, critical thinking your guide, and a deep sense of ethical responsibility your compass. As you explore the cosmos, remember, the power you wield can illuminate the path or cast a long shadow. The choice, and the responsibility, are ultimately yours.

Curiosity and Lifelong Learning:

As you set your sights on becoming a rocket scientist, remember, the journey begins with a spark – a burning curiosity about the universe and the incredible mechanics that govern it. It's this very curiosity that becomes the fuel that propels you forward, a relentless thirst for knowledge that knows no bounds. It's a lifelong commitment to learning, a constant chase after that elusive "aha!" moment when a puzzle piece clicks into place and unveils a new facet of the cosmos.

Think of Richard Feynman, a pioneer in the field of quantum mechanics. His brilliance was legendary, but it was fueled by an insatiable curiosity that extended far beyond the confines of his chosen field. He wasn't content with simply unraveling the mysteries of the subatomic world; he devoured knowledge from every corner of the scientific buffet. Biology fascinated him, the intricate dance of life as captivating as the choreography of the cosmos. He even found joy in the rhythmic pulse of the bongo drums, a testament to his openness to exploring the world in all its diverse forms. Feynman's life embodied the spirit of lifelong learning, a reminder that a curious mind is a mind that constantly evolves.

And his famous quote, "I was born not knowing and have had only a little time to change that here and there," perfectly captures the essence of a scientific journey. It's a journey of perpetual discovery, a humbling acknowledgment that there's always more to learn, more secrets waiting to be unearthed in the vast expanse of the universe. So, embrace your curiosity, young scientist. Let it be your compass, guiding you through uncharted territories of knowledge. Remember, the more you learn, the more equipped you'll be to tackle the challenges that lie ahead, the closer you'll be to crafting those magnificent rockets that will one day pierce the veil of our atmosphere and propel us towards the stars.

Teamwork and Collaboration:

The road to becoming a rocket scientist isn't a solitary trek. It's a collaborative ascent, a symphony of brilliant minds working in harmonious concert. Imagine yourself standing at the launchpad, not alone, but surrounded by a team as diverse as the constellations above. Each member brings a unique perspective, a specialized expertise that adds another layer of brilliance to the mission. This collaborative spirit is the engine that propels scientific breakthroughs forward, fostering innovation at every turn.

Think back to the awe-inspiring Apollo 11 mission, the one that etched Neil Armstrong's legendary words, "That's one small step for man, one giant leap for mankind," into the annals of history. The success of that mission wasn't the work of a single genius, but a tapestry woven by thousands – scientists, engineers, technicians, all collaborating in a beautiful dance of expertise. They understood the power of teamwork, the magic that unfolds when diverse minds come together, united by a common goal.

This spirit of collaboration will be your guiding light as you navigate the complexities of rocket science. You'll learn to value the perspectives of your team members, to appreciate how their unique skillsets can elevate your own research. Together, you'll brainstorm solutions, tackle challenges from every angle, and push the boundaries of what's possible.

But the journey doesn't end there. As you delve deeper, you'll find yourself constantly learning from the giants who came before you. Their legacies serve as guideposts, their groundbreaking discoveries a testament to the power of the scientific method. You'll embrace this meticulously crafted approach, a roadmap that ensures your research is grounded in evidence and leads to replicable results. Critical thinking will become your second nature, sharpening your skepticism and demanding you to question assumptions at every turn. It's this healthy skepticism that fuels innovation, that compels you to constantly refine your theories and seek out new perspectives.

And woven into the very fabric of your scientific journey will be a deep commitment to ethical standards. You'll understand that the power you wield comes with immense responsibility. Every discovery, every invention, must be guided by a moral compass, ensuring your work serves the greater good and protects the world around you.

So, as you embark on this extraordinary adventure, young scientist, remember, it's a journey fueled by curiosity, a relentless pursuit of knowledge that knows no bounds. Embrace the power of collaboration, learn from the wisdom of the past, and never lose sight of the ethical responsibility that comes with wielding such immense power. With these qualities as your guiding stars, you'll be well on your way to achieving your goals and leaving your own indelible mark on the field of rocket science. The universe awaits your brilliance, a canvas waiting to be splashed with the colors of your discoveries.

The Complexity of Rocket Science: Landing on the Moon

The Vast Distance and High Speed. The Moon is approximately 384,400 kilometers (238,855 miles) away from Earth, a distance that dwarfs any terrestrial journey. To put this into perspective, this distance is about 30 times the diameter of the Earth.

The Moon orbits the Earth at a speed of about 3,683 kilometers per hour (2,288 miles per hour). This is significantly faster than a commercial aircraft, which typically travels at around 900 kilometers per hour (560 miles per hour).

Implications for Space Travel:

The vast distance and high speed of the Moon require precise calculations to ensure that the spacecraft's trajectory aligns perfectly with the Moon's orbit. Any miscalculation can result in the spacecraft missing the Moon entirely.

The Challenge of Precise Targeting

Launching from a Moving Platform:

The spacecraft must be aimed at a point in space where the Moon will be when the spacecraft arrives, not where it is at the time of launch. This involves predicting the Moon's position days or even weeks in advance.

The journey to the Moon takes about 10 to 15 days. During this time, the spacecraft must travel through the vacuum of space, where gravitational forces from both Earth and the Moon continuously affect its trajectory.

Precise targeting involves constant adjustments to the spacecraft's path to account for these gravitational forces and ensure it stays on course.

The Precision of Calculations

Mathematical and Computational Challenges:

Calculating the spacecraft's trajectory involves complex mathematics and physics. Scientists use principles of orbital mechanics to determine the correct path.

These calculations must account for numerous variables, including the spacecraft's velocity, the gravitational pull of the Earth and the Moon, and the effects of other celestial bodies. Rocket scientists employ a methodical and rigorous approach to problem-solving. Their thinking process is characterized by the use of the scientific method, critical thinking, and innovation. Each of these components is essential for the successful execution of complex missions, such as landing on the Moon.

The scientific method involves a structured approach to investigation, starting with observation, followed by forming a hypothesis, conducting experiments, analyzing data, and drawing conclusions. This method ensures that findings are based on evidence and can be replicated by others.

Application in Rocket Science:

For example, when planning a lunar landing mission, scientists observe celestial bodies, hypothesize optimal trajectories, and use simulations and experiments to test these hypotheses. Data from previous missions are analyzed to refine calculations and strategies.

Evaluating Information:

Rocket scientists must critically evaluate information and question assumptions to avoid biases and errors. They use critical thinking to assess the validity of data, the reliability of sources, and the feasibility of proposed solutions.

Example: Apollo 13 Mission:

During the Apollo 13 mission, an oxygen tank explosion jeopardized the mission. The NASA team used critical thinking and innovative problem-solving to devise a plan to return the astronauts safely. They evaluated all available information, questioned existing assumptions, and developed a creative solution using the spacecraft's limited resources.

> *"Failure is not an option." — Gene Kranz, Flight Director for Apollo 13*

The Precision of Calculations

Mathematical Rigor:

Calculating a spacecraft's trajectory requires advanced mathematical techniques, including differential equations and numerical analysis. These calculations must account for the gravitational pull of the Earth and Moon, the spacecraft's velocity, and other celestial forces.

Use of Technology:

Modern space missions rely on powerful computers and sophisticated software to perform these calculations. For instance, the guidance computers on the Apollo missions performed real-time calculations to adjust the spacecraft's trajectory and ensure a precise landing.

"In preparing for battle I have always found that plans are useless, but planning is indispensable." — Dwight D. Eisenhower

The Incredible Task of Lunar Landing

Multiple Stages of Landing (Continued):

Launch:

The spacecraft must be launched with precise timing and velocity to achieve the correct trajectory. Any deviation can result in mission failure.

Translunar Injection:

This maneuver involves firing the spacecraft's engines to transition from Earth's orbit to a trajectory toward the Moon. It requires precise timing and angle to ensure the spacecraft is on the correct path.

Midcourse correction

These adjustments are necessary to correct any deviations in the spacecraft's path. Small thrusters are used to make precise changes in speed and direction, ensuring the spacecraft remains on the correct trajectory.

Lunar Orbit Insertion:

Upon reaching the Moon, the spacecraft must decelerate to be captured by the Moon's gravity and enter a stable orbit. This involves precise engine burns to reduce speed and achieve the correct orbit.

Descent and Landing:

The final stage involves the spacecraft descending to the lunar surface. This requires precise control to slow the descent and land safely at the designated location. The landing sequence involves a series of maneuvers to reduce speed and navigate the terrain.

Example: Apollo 11 Landing:

> *That's one small step for man, one giant leap for mankind." — Neil Armstrong*

The Margin for Error

Extremely Small Tolerances:

The margin for error in lunar landing missions is incredibly small. Even minor miscalculations can have catastrophic consequences. Scientists and engineers must account for every possible variable and ensure that all systems operate flawlessly.

The spacecraft must carry enough fuel for mid-course corrections and the final descent. This requires careful planning and precise calculations to ensure there is sufficient fuel without adding unnecessary weight.

Example: Lunar Module Fuel:

During the Apollo 11 landing, the Lunar Module had only about 30 seconds of fuel remaining when it finally touched down. This close call highlights the critical importance of precise fuel management.

The Potential for Failure

Launch Issues: Any problem in ground systems and first stage ignition.

Trajectory Errors: Miscalculations or unforeseen forces can cause the spacecraft to deviate from its path, potentially missing the Moon.

Communication Delays: The distance between Earth and the spacecraft introduces communication delays, complicating real-time adjustments and decision-making.

Failures of various Systems onboard, like Valve leakages, Electronics component failures, and so on.

Example: Apollo 13 Mission:

The oxygen tank explosion on Apollo 13 is a prime example of how mechanical failures can threaten a mission. The crew's survival depended on the team's ability to troubleshoot and innovate under extreme pressure.

Landing on the Moon is a monumental achievement that showcases the complexity and precision of rocket science. The vast distance, high speed, precise targeting, and numerous potential points of failure underscore the immense challenges involved. The thinking process of rocket scientists, characterized by rigorous analysis, meticulous calculations, and innovative problem-solving, is crucial to overcoming these challenges and achieving such incredible accomplishments. This complexity is what makes rocket science a field of endless fascination and relentless pursuit of knowledge. As you embark on your journey to become a rocket scientist, embrace the mindset of critical thinking, meticulous planning, and relentless innovation. With these skills, you too can achieve extraordinary feats and contribute to the ever-expanding frontier of space exploration.

The First Successful Landing

The fact that NASA's Apollo 11 mission successfully landed humans on the Moon on its first attempt is a testament to the extraordinary precision and ingenuity of the scientists and engineers involved. This mission, which took place on July 20, 1969, required years of planning, testing, and the development of new technologies.

Landing on the Moon exemplifies the pinnacle of rocket science. The precision, calculations, and sheer complexity involved in such a mission are beyond ordinary comprehension. It is a testament to human ingenuity, perseverance, and the relentless pursuit of knowledge. This incredible achievement underscores the profound complexity of rocket science and the meticulous effort required to turn such an ambitious goal into reality.

Imagine the countless times the process of lunar travel and landing was envisioned in the minds of many scientists and engineers before it actually happened. The way these rocket

scientists think is fundamentally different from ordinary thinking. Let's explore this fascinating realm a bit further.

Imagine being part of an exciting journey that started on February 22, 1962. This was when the Government of India set up the Indian National Committee for Space Research (INCOSPAR). Led by Dr. Vikram Sarabhai, known as the father of the Indian space program, and Dr. Homi J. Bhabha, a respected nuclear physicist, INCOSPAR had a groundbreaking mission. Their aim was to launch India into the world of space exploration and advanced technology.

Picture this: at a time when even advanced nations like the USA and Russia were just starting their space research, with only a few small launch vehicles to their name, India dared to dream big. We didn't even have the capability to build bicycles domestically, let alone rockets. The metals needed for rocket construction were yet to be invented. Undeterred, we leaped into the cosmic void, hoping to grow wings on the way up. And miraculously, those wings did sprout!

By 1980, India had launched its first satellite into orbit. Fast forward 14 years, and we celebrated the triumph of ISRO's Workhorse PSLV. This incredible leap, achieved within a human lifespan, is often seen as a victory of technology. But it's so much more—it's a testament to the indomitable spirit and innovative mindset of rocket scientists.

To think like a rocket scientist is to view the cosmos with the eyes of a visionary. These trailblazers dream of achieving the impossible and seek to unravel the mysteries of the universe. They turn failures into learning opportunities and see limitations as stepping stones to success. For them, setbacks are not obstacles but intriguing puzzles to be solved. Driven by a blend of ambition and humility, they aim for lasting breakthroughs rather than temporary wins. They understand that the rules can be challenged, norms questioned, and new paths forged. Rocket scientists embrace the idea that boundaries are meant to be pushed and that through perseverance and innovation, they can achieve extraordinary feats.

In the vast expanse of space and time, rocket scientists navigate with a relentless curiosity and a fearless spirit. Their minds dance with equations and their hearts beat to the rhythm of discovery. They are the alchemists of modern times, turning dreams into reality, one calculation at a time. With every launch, every landing, they rewrite the story of human potential.

Embrace the Rocket Scientist Mindset

Join this exhilarating journey of thought and innovation. Embrace the mindset that transforms the impossible into the possible. Let's soar to new heights together, just as ISRO envisioned over six decades ago.

Ownership and Curiosity: When you become a rocket scientist, you'll take ownership of your life. You'll question assumptions, stereotypes, and established patterns of thinking. Where others see roadblocks, you'll see opportunities to bend reality to your will. This mindset empowers you to approach challenges with a fresh perspective and an unyielding curiosity.

Problem-Solving and Innovation: You'll approach problems rationally and generate innovative solutions that redefine the status quo. Equipped with a tool kit that enables you to spot misinformation and pseudoscience, you'll forge new paths. This ability to think critically and innovate is essential in making informed decisions and pioneering new technologies.

Leadership and Vision: As future business leaders, you'll ask the right questions and use the right set of tools to make decisions. Instead of letting the world shape your thoughts, you'll let your thoughts shape the world. You'll lead with vision, turning ideas into reality and driving progress in your field.

Resilience and Adaptability: Rocket scientists transform failures into victories and turn limitations into stepping stones. Setbacks become intriguing riddles, not barriers. Fuelled by a mix of ambition and humility, they strive for enduring breakthroughs rather than fleeting successes. This resilience is crucial in navigating the complexities of space exploration and technological advancement.

Thinking Beyond Limits: You won't just think outside the box; you'll bend the box to your will. By challenging norms and questioning the rules, you'll blaze new trails. This fearless approach to innovation ensures continuous growth and the discovery of new possibilities.

Becoming a rocket scientist is about more than just mastering technical skills. It's about adopting a mindset of curiosity, resilience, and innovation. It's about daring to dream big, questioning the impossible, and relentlessly pursuing breakthroughs that push the boundaries of human achievement. Let's embark on this journey together and redefine what's possible in the world of space exploration and beyond.

Rocket Scientists: Connoisseurs of Uncertainty and the Unknown

To many, the unknown is a vast, shadowy expanse filled with trepidation and doubt. But to you, the aspiring rocket scientist, it's a vibrant frontier, a canvas splashed with the colours of possibility! Where others see chaos and risk, you see beauty and boundless opportunity. You aren't daunted by uncertainty; you relish it, for it's the very fuel that propels your innovative spirit.

Embracing Uncertainty: Your insatiable curiosity drives you to delve into the mysteries that confound others. You're an explorer, drawn to the edge between the known and the unknown, just as physicist Alan Lightman described. There, on that precipice, exhilaration replaces fear. It's a place where groundbreaking theories are born, where the dance with the enigmatic leads to the most profound discoveries.

The Beauty of the Unknown: Historian Daniel J. Boorstin brilliantly captures this sentiment: *"The great obstacle to discovering was not ignorance but the illusion of knowledge."* This pretence of knowing stifles our curiosity and blocks out invaluable learning from all around us. When we think we know it all, we blind ourselves to our own stagnation.

Innovative Spirit: For rocket scientists, uncertainty is not a barrier but an invitation. The unknown challenges you to question, to innovate, and to explore. It's where you test the limits of what's possible and expand the boundaries of human knowledge. Each question leads to another, and each discovery opens the door to new possibilities. This relentless pursuit of knowledge and understanding is what drives progress in the field of rocket science.

Learning from Failures: In the journey of exploration, failures are inevitable, but they are not to be feared. Instead, they are valuable lessons that guide you closer to success. The willingness to fail, learn, and try again is a hallmark of a true rocket scientist. It's through this process of trial and error that the most significant breakthroughs are achieved.

Visionary Thinking: As a rocket scientist, you are not confined by the present limitations. You think beyond the current technologies and theories, envisioning future possibilities. Your visionary thinking allows you to see potential where others see obstacles, to find solutions to problems that seem insurmountable.

To think like a rocket scientist is to embrace uncertainty with enthusiasm and curiosity. It's about seeing the unknown not as a threat but as a realm of endless possibilities. By challenging the illusion of knowledge and remaining open to learning, you pave the way for groundbreaking discoveries. So, step boldly into the unknown, let your curiosity guide you, and turn uncertainty into a canvas of innovation and exploration.

Think of Albert Einstein, a man who dared to question the established order. He didn't shy away from the unknown; he embraced it, forever altering our understanding of the universe. As Lightman reminds us, the frontier of knowledge isn't a place to be feared but a realm brimming with excitement and potential. Here, the essence of scientific inquiry lies, waiting to be unravelled. *Bertrand Russell nailed it when he said, "the problem with the modern world is that the foolish are cocksure while the wise are full of doubt."*

Embracing the Rocket Scientist Mindset

You, the rocket scientist, embody the human spirit of exploration. You stare into the abyss of the unknown not with despair, but with fervent determination. Your ability to find exhilaration at the edge of the known world, to dance with the mysteries that lie just beyond, is what sets you apart. This mindset isn't just the key to remarkable scientific advancements; it's an inspiration for us all. By adopting the perspective of a rocket scientist, you can learn to greet the unknown with confidence and curiosity, transforming challenges into opportunities for growth and discovery. The universe awaits, a vast expanse teeming with possibilities. Let's embrace the unknown, together.

The Rocket Scientist's Approach

In the exhilarating world of rocket science, your mastery in embracing uncertainty unlocks boundless potential! Rather than chasing quick fixes, be driven by an insatiable curiosity. The instant you let go of the need for certainty, genuine progress takes flight. Even after winning a Nobel Prize, physicist Richard Feynman saw himself as a "confused ape," maintaining a relentless curiosity that allowed him to perceive subtleties others overlooked. He famously said, *"I think it's much more interesting to live, not knowing, than to have answers which might be wrong."*

Feynman's perspective demands an acceptance of our ignorance and a generous helping of humility. When you say those three daunting words—I don't know—your ego shrinks, your mind expands, and you become more receptive. Admitting your lack of knowledge doesn't mean ignoring facts; it involves a deliberate kind of uncertainty that makes you acutely aware of what you don't know, driving you to learn and evolve.

The Power of Curiosity and Humility

Embracing the unknown with curiosity and humility allows you to transform setbacks into stepping stones. Each failure is a lesson, each challenge an opportunity to innovate. The journey of discovery is filled with twists and turns, and it's your relentless curiosity that propels you forward. This mindset is crucial for scientific advancements, as it opens the door to new ideas and perspectives.

A Call to Action

So, let's take a page from the book of rocket scientists. Let's welcome uncertainty and view it as a realm of possibilities. Let's adopt a mindset that celebrates not knowing, that thrives on exploration and continuous learning. In doing so, we not only advance science and technology but also inspire those around us to embrace curiosity and humility.

The universe is vast and filled with unknowns, but it's also full of opportunities for growth and discovery. By embracing the mindset of a rocket scientist, we can transform challenges into opportunities and turn the impossible into the possible. Let's embark on this journey together, exploring the mysteries of the universe and pushing the boundaries of human knowledge.

Uncertainty, often seen as a barrier, is actually the birthplace of innovation. By eagerly diving into the unknown, you turn challenges into golden opportunities. The end of predictable outcomes heralds the beginning of groundbreaking discoveries.

On this thrilling scientific journey, uncertainty is not a roadblock but a powerful catalyst. It is the energy that propels your inquisitive mind beyond the familiar, sparking the flames of progress where routine fades. Embracing uncertainty leads to joy, discovery, and the realization of your true potential. It means venturing into uncharted territory and uncovering things that, for a fleeting moment, no one else has witnessed. Life becomes richer when we see uncertainty as a friend rather than a foe.

Therefore, your mission should not be to seek swift answers but to revel in the deep intrigue that uncertainty brings. In this vast, uncharted territory, the seeds of immense value are planted, waiting for pioneering spirits like yours to nurture them into revolutionary breakthroughs.

Nothing Succeeds Like Failure: How to Transform Failure into Triumph

Another critical aspect of dealing with uncertainty is the implementation of redundancies in rocket design. For instance, rockets often have two computers—one as a primary and the other as a backup, much like a spare tire for a car. This redundancy is crucial for handling unexpected situations and ensuring mission success. Safety margins are meticulously calculated and incorporated to further mitigate the impacts of uncertainty.

This approach stems from the rocket scientist's belief that failure is not welcome. At the same, time there's no such thing as a zero-risk rocket launch. You still have to compete with physics. You can plan for some mishaps, but the cosmic banana peel is always around the corner. Accidents are inevitable when you're creating a controlled explosion in a machine as complex as a rocket. If failure weren't an option, we never would have dipped our toes into the cosmic ocean. Doing anything groundbreaking requires taking risks, and taking risks means you're going to fail—at least some of the time.

Given that failure can be extremely costly and, in some cases, life-threatening, we avoid taking **unnecessary** risks. If a defect is discovered, it is thoroughly addressed and rectified before proceeding. There is no room for a casual or careless attitude in this field.

Failure is often seen as the end of the road, a setback that stymies progress and derails ambitions. However, in the world of innovation and discovery, failure is not a dead end but a stepping stone to success. Embracing failure and learning from it can transform your setbacks into triumphs. Here's how you can turn failure into a powerful tool for growth and achievement.

Most rocket scientists would recoil at a casual attitude toward failure. In rocket science, failure can mean the loss of human life and cost taxpayers hundreds of millions of dollars. It can also mean that decades of hard work go up in smoke—both literally and figuratively. The numerous explosions and mishaps during the race to the Moon were not celebrated; they were embarrassing and catastrophic, taken with the utmost seriousness.

For rocket scientists, celebrating failure can be as perilous as demonizing it. In their high-stakes field, the consequences of failure are too grave to be dismissed lightly. Each setback represents a significant investment of time, resources, and human effort. Yet, these scientists understand that failure is an inherent part of pushing the boundaries of what's possible.

Rocket scientists adopt a balanced approach to failure. They neither celebrate it nor allow it to hinder their progress. Instead, they meticulously analyze each failure to understand what went wrong and how to prevent it in the future. This rigorous process of learning from mistakes is what drives progress and innovation.

Failures are documented, scrutinized, and transformed into valuable lessons. This methodical approach ensures that each failure contributes to the advancement of knowledge and the refinement of technology. Rocket scientists use these experiences to build more robust systems, improve safety protocols, and innovate with greater precision.

In essence, rocket scientists view failure as a critical component of the learning process. **"Learn Fast; Not Fail Fast" is our philosophy**. By acknowledging and addressing failures, we pave the way for future successes. This mindset is what propels us forward, enabling us to achieve remarkable feats that once seemed impossible

The Story of SpaceX Falcon 1: From Failure to Triumph

The story of SpaceX Falcon 1 is a tale of resilience, innovation, and the relentless pursuit of success. The first three consecutive launch failures of Falcon 1 were devastating, but they ultimately paved the way for the company's triumph in the space industry. Let's dive into the details of these early challenges and how SpaceX overcame them.

First Launch: March 24, 2006

The first launch of Falcon 1 took place on March 24, 2006, from the Kwajalein Atoll in the Pacific Ocean. Excitement was high as SpaceX aimed to prove that a privately funded company could develop a reliable and cost-effective rocket. However, just 25 seconds after liftoff, disaster struck. A fuel line leak caused a fire in the engine bay, leading to the loss of control and the rocket's crash into the ocean. The failure was a significant blow, but Elon Musk and his team were undeterred. They analyzed the problem meticulously, identified the fuel line issue, and implemented design changes to prevent a recurrence.

Second Launch: March 21, 2007

Undeterred by the first failure, SpaceX prepared for their second attempt. On March 21, 2007, the Falcon 1 lifted off once again from Kwajalein Atoll. This time, the rocket successfully cleared the pad and soared into the sky. However, 301 seconds into the flight, the second stage engine shut down prematurely due to a fuel slosh issue. The rocket fell short of reaching orbit and plunged into the ocean. Despite the setback, SpaceX had made progress, and the team was determined to learn from their mistakes. They investigated the fuel slosh problem and modified the propellant tanks to improve stability during flight.

Third Launch: August 3, 2008

The third launch attempt came on August 3, 2008. Spirits were cautiously optimistic, as SpaceX had addressed the issues from the previous flights. The Falcon 1 lifted off smoothly, and the first stage performed flawlessly. However, during the stage separation, residual thrust from the first stage caused it to collide with the second stage, resulting in another failure. The rocket and its payload were lost. This third consecutive failure was a crushing blow, pushing the company to the brink of bankruptcy. Yet, Elon Musk and his team refused to give up. They made crucial adjustments to the timing and sequencing of the stage separation to prevent such collisions in future flights.

Fourth Launch: September 28, 2008

SpaceX was running out of both money and time. The fourth launch attempt on September 28, 2008, was a make-or-break moment for the company. With all eyes on them, the Falcon 1 once again took to the skies. This time, everything went according to plan. The rocket successfully reached orbit, making SpaceX the first privately funded company to achieve this milestone with a liquid-fuelled rocket. The relief and joy were palpable. Years of hard work, relentless testing, and unwavering belief had finally paid off. This success validated SpaceX's approach and marked the beginning of a new era in space exploration.

The Road to Success

Following the successful fourth launch, SpaceX secured contracts with NASA and other commercial clients, providing the financial stability needed to continue their ambitious plans. The lessons learned from the Falcon 1 failures were invaluable. They laid the foundation for the development of the Falcon 9, a more powerful and reliable rocket that would go on to become a workhorse for the company.

Falcon 9's numerous successful launches, including missions to the International Space Station (ISS) and the deployment of commercial satellites, showcased SpaceX's ability to deliver on its promises. The company's emphasis on reusability, demonstrated through the groundbreaking recovery and reuse of Falcon 9's first stage, revolutionized the industry and significantly reduced the cost of access to space.

The story of Falcon 1's early failures and subsequent success is a testament to the power of perseverance and innovation. Each failure was a stepping stone, providing crucial insights that led to improved designs and operational procedures. SpaceX's journey from near-collapse to becoming a leader in the aerospace industry is an inspiring example of how setbacks can be transformed into stepping stones for success. Today, SpaceX continues to push the boundaries of what is possible, driven by the same spirit of resilience and determination that saw them through those challenging early years.

Rocket Scientists Handle Failures Differently

In the unforgiving world of rocket science, failure isn't a four-letter word, it's a data point. Every launch, every test, is a meticulously planned experiment. The key isn't just reaching orbit, it's learning from every blip on the telemetry, every unexpected shudder of the engine. Those are the whispers we chase, the anomalies that could spell disaster if ignored.

Imagine a high-tech black box strapped to every rocket. We don't need conversations, but every sensor reading, every valve position – that's the gold mine. We build these rockets to be as tough as possible, but the data they collect after a failure, that's what's truly fireproof. It's the key to unlocking the mysteries of what went wrong.

That's the philosophy behind NASA's "Flight Rules." All Rocket Launching agencies have their own documentation called "Lessons Learned". It's a hard-won library of every hiccup, every miscalculation encountered since the first astronauts touched the stars. It's a testament to the fact that even the most spectacular failures hold valuable lessons. We don't want to reinvent the wheel with every launch. We want to stand on the shoulders of giants, learning from their mistakes so we can push the boundaries even further.

Rocket Scientists do not encourage failures, but they advertise failures. They do not ask who made the mistake, but they find out what went wrong. But these Flight rules are guideposts, not shackles. They steer us in the right direction, but they don't stifle innovation. We need to constantly challenge assumptions, dig beneath the surface of established procedures. That's how breakthroughs happen.

The truth is, we're all human. We point fingers when things go south, but the real failing is "not learning from the experience". Every engineer, every technician on a launch team – we all have a responsibility to dissect failure, to understand its root cause. As

Ed Catmull, former president of Pixar Animation Studios and Walt Disney Animation Studios says, it's about separating the fear from the fall. We can't control the inevitable hiccups, but we can control our response. **We build a culture where failure is a teacher, not a terminator.** It's the only way to keep pushing the boundaries of what's possible, one launch at a time.

NOTHING FAILS LIKE SUCCESS

The Space Shuttle Challenger disaster occurred on January 28, 1986, when NASA's Space Shuttle Challenger broke apart 73 seconds into its flight, leading to the deaths of its seven crew members. The mission, designated STS-51-L, was intended to deploy a communications satellite and conduct the first Teacher in Space Project, which included school teacher Christa McAuliffe.

Detailed Account of Challenger Disaster:

Pre-Launch Concerns:

Engineers from Morton Thiokol, the company responsible for the shuttle's solid rocket boosters (SRBs), expressed concerns about the O-rings used to seal the joints of the SRBs. The forecasted low temperatures for the launch day could compromise the O-rings' ability to seal properly.

Despite these concerns, NASA managers, under pressure to maintain the launch schedule, overruled the engineers' recommendations to delay the launch. On the morning of January 28, the temperature at Kennedy Space Centre was unusually cold, with ice forming on the launch pad. The countdown proceeded, and Challenger lifted off at 11:38 a.m. EST. The first few seconds of the flight appeared normal.

At 58 seconds into the flight, the O-ring on the right SRB failed to seal properly due to the cold temperatures, allowing hot gases to leak and burn through the SRB joint.

At 73 seconds, the external fuel tank, which contains liquid hydrogen and liquid oxygen, structurally failed, causing a catastrophic explosion.

The shuttle disintegrated, and the crew compartment was seen falling into the Atlantic Ocean. The Presidential Commission on the Space Shuttle Challenger Accident, also known as the Rogers Commission, was formed to investigate the disaster.

The commission identified the failure of the O-ring as the primary cause and highlighted organizational and communication failures within the space agencies

It was revealed that space agencies 'culture and decision-making processes, including the normalization of deviance and schedule pressure, contributed to the disaster.

Connection to Columbia Disaster:

The Columbia Space Shuttle disaster occurred on February 1, 2003, during re-entry, resulting in the deaths of all seven astronauts on board. The mission, designated STS-107, was intended as a scientific research flight.

Successes and Complacency:

In the years following the Challenger disaster, NASA implemented several safety improvements and the shuttle program continued with a series of successful missions.

However, the successes led to a gradual erosion of vigilance and a return to complacency, similar to pre-Challenger attitudes. During the launch of Columbia on January 16, 2003, a piece of foam insulation from the external fuel tank struck the left wing of the shuttle. This impact breached the thermal protection system, which was designed to protect the shuttle from the intense heat of re-entry. On February 1, as Columbia re-entered Earth's atmosphere, superheated air entered the damaged wing, leading to the shuttle's destruction.

The shuttle broke apart over Texas, killing all seven crew members, Including Indian origin Kalpana Chawla.

Investigation and Findings:

The Columbia Accident Investigation Board (CAIB) found that the foam strike was the immediate cause of the disaster.

The CAIB also identified deeper systemic issues, including a flawed safety culture, lack of effective communication, and an organizational culture that discouraged dissenting opinions.

The investigation highlighted that NASA had not fully learned from the Challenger disaster, as similar issues of normalization of deviance and organizational failures persisted.

Success is like a wolf in sheep's clothing, creating a disconnect between how things appear and how they really are. When we succeed, we convince ourselves that everything went perfectly as planned. We tend to overlook the warning signs and the need for change. Each success boosts our confidence and makes us take bigger risks. However, just because you're on a winning streak doesn't guarantee you'll keep winning. As Bill Gates puts it, success is "a lousy teacher" because it "seduces smart people into thinking they can't lose." Research backs up this idea. Success leads to overconfidence in the status quo, which in turn stifles dissent, precisely when dissent is most needed to prevent complacency.

The Challenger and Columbia disasters underscore the importance of a robust safety culture, effective communication, and the willingness to address and act upon safety concerns. Both tragedies serve as stark reminders of the risks inherent in space exploration and the critical need for constant vigilance and improvement in safety practices.

Conclusion: Embracing the Rocket Scientist's Mindset

As we conclude this chapter on the thinking process of rocket scientists, it's clear that their unique mindset is a powerful tool for innovation and exploration. Rocket scientists exemplify the human spirit of curiosity and resilience, transforming the unknown into a canvas of limitless possibilities. They teach us that embracing uncertainty, questioning assumptions, and viewing failures as learning opportunities are essential for achieving groundbreaking advancements.

By adopting this mindset, we can all learn to approach challenges with confidence and creativity, turning obstacles into opportunities for growth. The universe, with its vast and uncharted expanse, beckons us to explore and discover. Whether you're aspiring to launch rockets or pursuing dreams in any field, the principles of thinking like a rocket scientist can guide you toward remarkable achievements.

So, let's dare to dream big, embrace the unknown with curiosity and humility, and continuously strive for excellence. The journey of exploration is just beginning, and together, we can push the boundaries of what's possible

Chapter 13

Advancing as a Rocket Scientist

To become a rocket scientist and excel in your career, I have some tips. The journey of continuous improvement and striving for excellence is paramount. Here's how you can focus on these aspects:

1. Set Clear, Specific Goals:

Example: Define your ultimate goal as "Becoming a lead engineer on a Mars mission by 2035." Break this down into smaller steps:

Short-term goal: Complete a bachelor's degree in aerospace engineering with top grades.

Mid-term goal: Secure an internship at a renowned space agency or aerospace company, like NASA or SpaceX.

Long-term goal: Earn a master's degree or Ph.D. in aerospace engineering, focusing on propulsion systems or orbital mechanics.

Create a Timeline: Establish a realistic timeline to achieve each goal, keeping yourself accountable and on track.

2. Immerse Yourself in Your Passion:

Example: Dedicate time to reading influential books such as "Rocket Propulsion Elements" by George P. Sutton or "Introduction to Flight" by John D. Anderson. Watch documentaries like "Apollo 11" or series like "Cosmos: A Spacetime Odyssey."

Engage in Practical Activities: Join a local model rocketry club where you can build and launch your own rockets. Participate in science fairs or competitions like the International Rocketry Challenge.

3. Find Role Models and Mentors:

Example: Research the career paths of scientists like Dr. Robert Goddard, the father of modern rocketry, or Dr. Sally Ride, the first American woman in space. Understand the challenges they faced and how they overcame them.

Seek Mentorship: Approach professors in your university's aerospace department for guidance. Use platforms like LinkedIn to connect with professionals in the aerospace industry. Join organizations like the American Institute of Aeronautics and Astronautics (AIAA) for networking opportunities.

4. Visualize Your Success:

Example: Spend a few minutes each day visualizing yourself achieving specific milestones, such as presenting your research at a conference, working in a NASA control room, or witnessing a rocket launch you helped design.

Create a Vision Board: Include images of rockets, space missions, your dream workplace, and motivational quotes. Place it where you see it daily.

5. Develop a Study and Work Plan:

Example: Use a planner or digital tool like Trello to organize your tasks. Allocate specific time slots for studying subjects like fluid dynamics, thermodynamics, and computer programming.

Time Management: Use techniques like the Pomodoro Technique (25 minutes of focused work followed by a 5-minute break) to maintain concentration and productivity.

6. Stay Positive and Motivated:

Example: When you encounter setbacks, remind yourself of your passion for space exploration and the impact your work can have on humanity. Engage in positive self-talk to boost your morale.

Positive Influences: Listen to motivational podcasts or watch inspirational speeches by scientists and engineers. Surround yourself with peers who share your passion and positivity.

7. **Develop Self-Discipline and Consistency:**

Example: Establish a daily routine that includes time for coursework, research, and self-care. Stick to your schedule to build consistency.

Rewards System: Reward yourself for completing tasks. For instance, after finishing a challenging assignment, treat yourself to a favourite activity or snack.

8. **Build a Strong Support Network: Embrace Challenges and Learn from Failures:**

Example: When faced with a difficult problem in your coursework, view it as an opportunity to deepen your understanding. If you fail a test, analyze your mistakes, seek help from your professor, and create a study plan to improve.

9. **Continuous Improvement and Excellence**

Keeping up with the latest research and developments: In the field of rocket science, technology and methods are continually evolving. It's crucial to stay informed about the latest research, innovations, and breakthroughs. Here are some tips and strategies to help you stay on the cutting edge of developments:

Read Scientific Journals: Regularly dive into journals like the "Journal of Spacecraft and Rockets," "Aerospace Science and Technology," and "Acta Astronautica." IEEE transactions etc. These publications are treasure troves of the latest research findings and technical advancements. Make a habit of reading at least one article a day or setting aside specific times each week to catch up on recent issues.

Subscribe to Industry Newsletters: Sign up for newsletters from reputable aerospace organizations and companies. Newsletters from NASA, SpaceX, and the European Space Agency (ESA) provide timely updates on their latest projects, research, and technological advancements. These can often give you a quick overview of what's happening in the industry without the need for deep dives.

Follow Relevant Blogs and Publications: There are numerous blogs and online publications dedicated to space science and rocket technology. Websites like Space.com, The Space Review, and Ars Technica's space section offer insightful articles and analyses. Following these can provide a broader context to the scientific and technological developments in the field.

Attend Webinars and Online Courses: Many universities and institutions offer free or affordable webinars and online courses on various aspects of rocket science and aerospace engineering. Platforms like Coursera, edX, and MIT OpenCourseWare are excellent resources to deepen your knowledge and stay updated on new topics.

Join Online Communities and Forums: Engaging in online communities such as Reddit's r/space and r/rocketry, or joining professional networks on LinkedIn, can be incredibly valuable. These platforms allow you to discuss recent developments, share insights, and ask questions to a broad audience of professionals and enthusiasts.

Participate in Research Projects: Look for opportunities to collaborate on research projects, either within your organization or with external partners. This hands-on experience is invaluable and keeps you at the forefront of new discoveries and innovations.

Networking with Experts: Attend industry conferences, symposiums, and workshops to meet and learn from leading experts in the field. These events often feature presentations on cutting-edge research and provide excellent networking opportunities.

Stay Curious and Ask Questions: Never stop being curious. Ask questions, seek out mentors, and don't be afraid to explore new ideas and concepts. Curiosity drives innovation and keeps you engaged and passionate about your work.

10. Embrace Challenges:

Understand that the path to becoming a rocket scientist will have its challenges and setbacks. Each obstacle is an opportunity to learn and grow. Stay resilient and keep pushing forward.

11. **Leverage social media**:
Follow thought leaders, organizations, and influencers in aerospace on platforms like Twitter and LinkedIn. Social media can be a quick way to catch up on the latest news and trends.

12. **Set Personal Learning Goals**:
Establish personal learning goals and track your progress. Whether it's mastering a new software tool, understanding a complex engineering concept, or staying abreast of the latest mission reports, setting goals can help you stay focused and motivated.

13. **Engage in Professional Development Programs**:
Many aerospace organizations offer professional development programs. These may include workshops, certification courses, and seminars that focus on the latest tools and techniques in rocket science. Enrol in these programs to refine your skills and stay ahead of the curve.

14. **Contribute to Academic and Industry Publications**:
Writing and publishing your research in academic journals or industry magazines not only enhances your knowledge but also establishes your reputation as an expert in the field. It provides an opportunity for peer review and constructive feedback, which can further refine your understanding and approach.

15. **Utilize Advanced Simulation and Design Tools**:
Familiarize yourself with the latest software and tools used in rocket science, such as computer-aided design (CAD) software, simulation programs, and data analysis tools. Proficiency in these technologies can significantly enhance your ability to innovate and solve complex problems.

16. **Attend Live Launches and Test Flights**:

If possible, attend live rocket launches and test flights. Observing these events first-hand can provide invaluable insights into the practical aspects of rocket science and the intricacies involved in each mission phase.

17. **Engage with Cross-Disciplinary Teams**:

Working with teams from different disciplines, such as materials science, computer engineering, and astrophysics, can broaden your perspective and enhance your problem-solving skills. Cross-disciplinary collaboration often leads to innovative solutions and a more holistic understanding of complex issues.

18. **Mentorship and Networking**:

Seek out mentors who have extensive experience in the field. Their guidance can help you navigate challenges and identify opportunities for growth. Additionally, building a strong professional network can open doors to collaborations, job opportunities, and access to exclusive resources.

19. **Stay Physically and Mentally Fit**:

A career in rocket science can be demanding. Maintaining physical and mental well-being is crucial for sustained performance. Regular exercise, healthy eating, mindfulness practices, and ensuring adequate rest can keep you energized and focused.

20. **Develop Soft Skills**:
Technical expertise is essential, but soft skills such as communication, teamwork, and leadership are equally important. Attend workshops on these skills and practice them in your daily interactions. Being able to clearly convey complex ideas and work effectively with a team can significantly impact your success.

21. **Explore Emerging Trends**:

Keep an eye on emerging trends in space exploration, such as reusable rockets, interplanetary missions, and advancements in propulsion systems. Understanding these trends can help you anticipate future developments and position yourself as a forward-thinking professional.

22. **Volunteer for Challenging Projects**:
Don't shy away from challenging projects or assignments. Volunteering for these can provide hands-on experience and accelerate your learning curve. It demonstrates your commitment and willingness to go the extra mile, making you stand out to your superiors and peers.

By integrating these practices into your career, you'll cultivate a mindset of continuous improvement and excellence. This proactive approach not only enhances your capabilities but also ensures you remain a vital and dynamic part of the ever-evolving field of rocket science. Embrace every opportunity to learn, innovate, and contribute, and you'll find yourself not only keeping up with but leading the advancements in aerospace technology.

A Lifelong Journey to the Stars

The path to becoming a rocket scientist is anything but easy. It's a demanding climb, filled with late nights, complex calculations, and moments of frustration. Yet, for those with an insatiable curiosity and a burning passion for the cosmos, the rewards are immeasurable. As Wernher von Braun, the visionary engineer behind the Saturn V rocket, once said, *"To achieve the great, we must be willing to attempt the impossible."*

The journey begins with a spark, a clear vision of yourself pushing the boundaries of space exploration. This ambition was evident in the life of Katherine Johnson, one of NASA's "human computers" whose calculations played a pivotal role in the Apollo 11 moon landing. Despite facing racial and gender barriers, Johnson's unwavering dedication helped humanity take its giant leap onto the lunar surface.

Remember, the road won't be smooth. There will be setbacks, moments where equations seem to defy logic, and experiments don't yield the expected results. But as Marie Curie, the pioneering physicist, reminds us, "Nothing in life is to be feared, it is only to be understood. Now is the time to understand more, so that we may fear less." Every obstacle you face is a chance to learn, to refine your approach, and emerge stronger.

The key lies in cultivating resilience and perseverance. Look to the story of Sergei Korolev, the "Chief Designer" of the Soviet space program. Facing political pressure and limited resources, Korolev's unwavering determination propelled the USSR to launch Sputnik 1, the first artificial satellite, and Yuri Gagarin, the first human in space.

Chapter 14

Conclusion

By implementing the strategies outlined in this book – setting clear goals, immersing yourself in your passion, finding mentors, visualizing success, and developing a structured plan as outlined in this book– you can forge a path towards your dream career. Stay dedicated, fuel your curiosity with every challenge, and never stop reaching for the stars.

Think like Rocket Scientists Think. Rocket scientists don't shy away from audacious goals. They tackle problems that seem impossible, pushing the boundaries of what's achievable.

Set ambitious goals for yourself, even if they seem out of reach at first. Break them down into smaller, achievable steps and focus on the process, not just the outcome.

Rocket science is built on a foundation of curiosity. Scientists constantly ask "why" and "how" to understand the universe and make things work. Develop a questioning mind. Don't accept things at face value. Dig deeper, explore different perspectives, and constantly seek new information.

Rocket launches don't always go perfectly. Scientists analyze failures to learn and improve. Don't be afraid to fail. See setbacks as opportunities to learn and grow. Analyze what went wrong, adjust your approach, and keep moving forward.

Rocket science demands innovative solutions. Teams brainstorm, combine ideas, and build upon each other's expertise. Approach problems creatively. Don't be afraid to think outside the box. Collaborate with others, share ideas, and learn from diverse perspectives.

Rocket launches rely on precise calculations and data analysis. Scientists use evidence to make decisions and solve problems. Base your decisions on facts and information. Gather data, analyze it critically, and use it to guide your actions.

Rocket scientists meticulously plan every aspect of a launch, but they also maintain a big-picture vision. Pay close attention to detail, but don't lose sight of your overall goals. Be organized, plan effectively, and keep your ultimate vision in mind.

Rocket science is complex and demanding. Scientists face many hurdles, but they persist and find solutions. Develop grit and perseverance. Don't give up easily. When faced with obstacles, find creative solutions and keep pushing forward.

By adopting these "rocket scientist" thinking patterns, you can launch yourself towards achieving your own ambitious goals and becoming the best version of yourself. Remember, the most important thing is to think boldly, learn constantly, and never stop striving for the stars!

Your unwavering commitment and hard work will pave the way for a future where humanity's footprint extends beyond our planet, a testament to the enduring human spirit of exploration. Remember, as Neil Armstrong eloquently stated as he stepped onto the moon, "That's one small step for a man, one giant leap for mankind."

The future of space exploration rests in your hands. So, take that first step, and embark on your own incredible journey to the stars.

To a Dreaming Rocket Scientist

My dear girl, gaze at the night sky's sea,
Where stars like diamonds whisper dreams to thee.
Imagine soaring like an eagle's flight,
On wings of steel, into the endless night.

With curiosity, let your mind take flame,
A torch of wonder, in the dark proclaim.
For rockets built with passion's molten gold,
Will take you far, to worlds yet unconsoled.

In realms of science, where mysteries bloom,
Your mind, a compass, charts the cosmic room.
You'll dance among the secrets of the stars,
And sail the cosmos, breaking earthly bars.

Embrace the fire within your heart's deep core,
A roaring furnace, to the heavens soar.
Each equation, a step upon the stair,
To realms of space, your destiny laid bare.

Fear not the risks, they're dragons to be tamed,
And courage, like a knight, must be proclaimed.
A rocket scientist's heart beats bold and true,
To pierce the skies where dreams are forged anew.
In every failure, find a phoenix's rise,
From ashes, wings will span the endless skies.
For those who dare to venture and explore,
Unlock the universe, and so much more.

Remember Neil, who touched the moon's bright shore,
"One small step for a man," through space's door.
"A giant leap for mankind," he did state,
So, take your step, and let your spirit elevate.

So, my dear girl, let's journey to the stars,
With passion's flame, and curiosity's spars.
For in your hands, the universe will sing,
And dreams of space will soar on golden wings.

Annexure:

Sample Short-Term Plan for a 13-Year-Old Aspiring Rocket Scientist

Stage 1 (Age 13-14):

Education: Focus on excelling in math, science, and computer science courses.

Projects: Build simple rockets using model rocket kits.

Extracurriculars: Join a science club or start a rocketry club at school.

Reading: Read books about space, rocketry, and famous scientists.

Events: Attend local science fairs or space-related events.

Stage 2 (Age 14-15):

Education: Take advanced math and science courses if available.

Projects: Work on more complex science projects, such as creating a basic rocket propulsion system.

Competitions: Participate in science competitions and fairs.

Mentorship: Seek a mentor in the field of science or engineering.

Workshops: Attend STEM workshops or camps during the summer.

Stage 3 (Age 15-16):

Education: Continue with advanced courses, including Maths, Physics Chemistry and Computer science.

Projects: Collaborate on group projects related to aerospace or robotics.

Internships: Look for internship opportunities at local universities or research centers.

Networking: Join online forums or local groups related to aerospace engineering.

Public Speaking: Improve communication skills by participating in debate clubs or public speaking courses.

Stage 4 (Age 16-17):

Education: Prepare for college entrance exams and apply to universities with strong aerospace or other relevant and interested engineering programs.

Projects: Develop a capstone project related to rocketry or space exploration.

Experience: Secure a summer internship or research position in a related field.

Conferences: Attend conferences or lectures on aerospace technology.

Applications: Apply for scholarships and grants related to STEM fields.

Long-Term Vision

College and University:

Undergraduate Degree: Pursue a bachelor's degree in aerospace engineering, physics, or a related field. Engage in research projects and internships to gain practical experience.

Graduate Degree: Consider pursuing a master's or Ph.D. to specialize further in areas such as propulsion systems, spacecraft design, or satellite technology.

Professional Career:

Entry-Level Positions: Start your career with entry-level positions in aerospace companies, research institutions, or space agencies.

Continued Learning: Stay updated with new technologies and advancements through continuous learning and professional development.

Innovative Projects: Work on innovative projects and contribute to significant space missions, aiming to make groundbreaking contributions to the field.

Turning your dream of becoming a rocket scientist into reality is a journey filled with excitement, learning, and challenges. Remember to enjoy the process, embrace every opportunity to learn, and never stop reaching for the stars. Your passion, curiosity, and determination will pave the way to a successful career in rocket science.

Indian Institute of Space Science and Technology (IIST): A Comprehensive Overview

Introduction

The Indian Institute of Space Science and Technology (IIST) is a premier institution dedicated to the study and advancement of space science and technology. Located in Valiamala, Thiruvananthapuram, Kerala, IIST was established by the Indian Space Research Organisation (ISRO) in 2007. The institute aims to foster excellence in the field of space science and technology and to support India's space endeavours by producing highly skilled professionals.

History and Establishment

IIST was founded with the vision of providing quality education in space science and technology, promoting research and development, and addressing the need for skilled professionals in India's burgeoning space sector. The institution was officially inaugurated on September 14, 2007, by Dr. G. Madhavan Nair, the then Chairman of ISRO.

Campus and Infrastructure The IIST campus is spread over 100 acres in Valiamala, nestled amidst lush greenery and scenic landscapes. The campus is equipped with state-of-the-art facilities to support academic and research activities. Key infrastructure includes:

- **Academic Complex**: Houses classrooms, lecture halls, and laboratories equipped with advanced technology and research tools.
- **Research Centres**: Dedicated centres for research in various domains of space science and technology, including satellite communications, remote sensing, and propulsion systems.
- **Library and Information Centre**: A vast repository of books, journals, and digital resources focused on space science, engineering, and related fields.
- **Hostels and Residential Facilities**: Comfortable and well-maintained accommodation for students and faculty.
- **Recreational Facilities**: Sports complexes, gymnasiums, and cultural centres for the overall development of students.

Academic Programs

IIST offers a range of undergraduate, postgraduate, and doctoral programs tailored to meet the needs of the space industry. These programs are designed to provide a solid foundation in theoretical concepts and practical applications. Key programs include:

- **B. Tech Programs**:
  - Aerospace Engineering
  - Avionics
  - Engineering Physics
- **M.Tech Programs**:
  - Thermal and Propulsion
  - Aerodynamics and Flight Mechanics
  - Structures and Design
  - Control Systems
  - Digital Signal Processing
  - RF and Microwave Engineering
  - VLSI and Microsystems
  - Earth System Science
- **Ph.D. Programs**: Various research opportunities in specialized areas of space science, engineering, and technology.

Research and Development

IIST places a strong emphasis on research and development, encouraging students and faculty to engage in cutting-edge research projects. The institute collaborates with ISRO and other leading space organizations to undertake significant research initiatives. Key research areas include:

- **Satellite Technology**: Development and testing of small and micro-satellites for various applications.
- **Rocket Propulsion**: Research on advanced propulsion systems for launch vehicles.
- **Space Materials**: Study of materials used in spacecraft and their behaviour in space environments.
- **Remote Sensing**: Development of techniques for Earth observation and data analysis.
- **Space Physics**: Investigation of cosmic phenomena and their impact on space missions.

Collaborations and Partnerships

IIST has established strong partnerships with national and international space agencies, research institutions, and universities. These collaborations facilitate joint research projects, student exchange programs, and access to advanced research facilities. Notable collaborators include:

- Indian Space Research Organisation (ISRO)
- National Aeronautics and Space Administration (NASA)
- European Space Agency (ESA)
- Various universities and research centres worldwide

Student Life and Extracurricular Activities

IIST offers a vibrant campus life with numerous opportunities for students to engage in extracurricular activities. The institute encourages participation in sports, cultural events, and technical clubs. Some key student initiatives include:

- **Technical Clubs**: Robotics Club, Astronomy Club, Coding Club, and more, providing platforms for students to explore their interests and enhance their skills.
- **Cultural Events**: Annual cultural festival, inter-collegiate competitions, and workshops that foster creativity and talent.
- **Sports Facilities**: Extensive facilities for indoor and outdoor sports, including basketball, football, cricket, and athletics.

Placement and Career Opportunities

IIST has an excellent placement record, with graduates securing positions in ISRO, DRDO, and various aerospace and defence companies. The institute's strong industry connections and emphasis on practical training ensure that students are well-prepared for their careers.

Achievements and Contributions

IIST has made significant contributions to the field of space science and technology through its academic and research endeavours. Some notable achievements include:

1. **Successful Satellite Missions**:
   - Students and faculty of IIST have been involved in the design, development, and launch of several small satellites. These projects provide hands-on experience and contribute valuable data for scientific research.
2. **Innovative Research**:
   - Research conducted at IIST has led to the development of new technologies and methodologies in areas such as propulsion, materials science, and satellite communication. These innovations have potential applications in future space missions and commercial ventures.
3. **Publications and Conferences**:
   - IIST researchers regularly publish their findings in prestigious journals and present their work at

international conferences. This dissemination of knowledge helps to advance the global understanding of space science and technology.

4. **Awards and Recognitions**:
    - The institute and its members have received numerous awards and accolades for their contributions to space research. These recognitions underscore the high quality of work being carried out at IIST.

Future Plans and Vision

IIST is committed to expanding its horizons and achieving new milestones in the field of space science and technology. The institute's future plans include:

1. **Enhanced Research Capabilities**:
    - Establishing new research centres and laboratories to focus on emerging areas such as artificial intelligence, quantum computing, and advanced materials.
2. **International Collaborations**:
    - Strengthening ties with global space agencies and academic institutions to foster collaborative research and exchange programs.

3. **Advanced Academic Programs**:
    - Introducing new interdisciplinary programs that integrate space science with fields like data science, environmental science, and robotics.
4. **Industry Partnerships**:
    - Building stronger partnerships with industry to facilitate technology transfer, commercialization of research, and internships for students.
5. **Public Outreach and Education**:
    - Promoting space science and technology through public lectures, workshops, and educational programs aimed at inspiring the next generation of space enthusiasts.

Conclusion

The Indian Institute of Space Science and Technology (IIST) stands as a symbol of India's ambition and capability in the realm of space science and technology. With its comprehensive academic programs, cutting-edge research, and strong industry connections, IIST is not only contributing to the nation's space missions but also preparing a new generation of scientists and engineers who will lead future explorations of the cosmos. As IIST continues to grow and evolve, it remains dedicated to pushing the boundaries of human knowledge and achieving new heights in space exploration.

Conclusion

The Indian Institute of Space Science and Technology (IIST) stands as a beacon of excellence in space education and research. With its world-class infrastructure, comprehensive academic programs, and strong industry linkages, IIST continues to play a pivotal role in advancing India's space capabilities and nurturing the next generation of space scientists and engineers.

For details click the link below.

https://www.iist.ac.in

Universities in India that offer B.Tech and M.Tech programs in Space Science and Technology:

B.Tech Programs in Space Science and Technology:

1. **Indian Institute of Space Science and Technology (IIST), Thiruvananthapuram**
    - B.Tech in Aerospace Engineering
    - B.Tech in Avionics
    - B.Tech in Engineering Physics
2. **Indian Institute of Technology (IIT) Bombay**
    - B.Tech in Aerospace Engineering
3. **Indian Institute of Technology (IIT) Kanpur**
    - B.Tech in Aerospace Engineering
4. **Indian Institute of Technology (IIT) Kharagpur**
    - B.Tech in Aerospace Engineering
5. **Indian Institute of Technology (IIT) Madras**
    - B.Tech in Aerospace Engineering

M.Tech Programs in Space Science and Technology:

1. **Indian Institute of Space Science and Technology (IIST), Thiruvananthapuram**
    - M.Tech in Thermal and Propulsion
    - M.Tech in Aerodynamics and Flight Mechanics
    - M.Tech in Structures and Design
    - M.Tech in Control Systems
    - M.Tech in Digital Signal Processing
    - M.Tech in RF and Microwave Engineering
    - M.Tech in VLSI and Microsystems
    - M.Tech in Earth System Science
2. **Indian Institute of Technology (IIT) Bombay**
    - M.Tech in Aerospace Engineering
3. **Indian Institute of Technology (IIT) Kanpur**
    - M.Tech in Aerospace Engineering
4. **Indian Institute of Technology (IIT) Kharagpur**
    - M.Tech in Aerospace Engineering

5. **Indian Institute of Technology (IIT) Madras**
   - M.Tech in Aerospace Engineering
6. **Birla Institute of Technology and Science (BITS) Pilani**
   - M.E. in Aerospace Engineering

Other Institutions Offering Relevant Programs:

1. **Vellore Institute of Technology (VIT), Vellore**
   - B.Tech in Aerospace Engineering
   - M.Tech in Aerospace Engineering
2. **Amity University, Noida**
   - B.Tech in Aerospace Engineering
   - M.Tech in Aerospace Engineering
3. **Manipal Institute of Technology (MIT), Manipal**
   - B.Tech in Aerospace Engineering
   - M.Tech in Aerospace Engineering

These programs are designed to provide students with a strong foundation in space science and technology, equipping them with the knowledge and skills needed to contribute to the field of aerospace and space exploration.

About the Author

Ignatious Antony, a visionary technocrat, has embarked on an extraordinary journey of engineering brilliance! His career, deeply rooted in the prestigious Indian Space Research Organisation, saw him excel as the Deputy Director at the Vikram Sarabhai Space Centre (VSSC) in Thiruvananthapuram, Kerala. Post-retirement, his professional adventure continued as the Vice President (Technical) at a renowned Electronics System R&D organization, where he's been passionately mentoring a dynamic team of professionals, young engineers, and highly talented technocrats for the past decade.

As a highly esteemed Professional Engineer, Ignatious has led significant teams, pioneering the development and certification of avionics systems for ISRO's ambitious rocket launches. His invaluable contributions in developing mission computers, GNC systems, and other avionics systems for ISRO's launch vehicles are legendary. He also served as the Chief of the Quality Assurance Entity at Vikram Sarabhai Space Centre, ISRO, showcasing his unwavering commitment to excellence.

His life, both personal and professional, is a tapestry woven with threads of remarkable encounters—close interactions with successful professionals, engineers, rocket scientists, business executives, leaders, and senior administrative personnel, alongside highly skilled launch vehicle technicians. As a space scientist, Ignatious has gained firsthand insights into the lives of highly talented and successful individuals, as well as those whose stars have not shone as brightly.

These diverse interactions ignited a profound curiosity within him, driving Ignatious to unravel the enigma of success. His philosophy, "Excellence is everywhere. You see only what you look for. Especially search inside; you can see surprising wonders," perfectly encapsulates his approach to life and work.

Ignatious is also a prolific writer who has presented numerous technical papers at national and international conferences. His extensive travels, both within the country and abroad, have further enriched his perspectives.

Ignatious Antony resides in the serene city of Thiruvananthapuram, Kerala, with his loving wife. Together, they cherish the joy of their two children and the boundless energy of their three grandchildren.

PS: Email-Id of the author : ignatious.luck@gmail.com

Bibliography

1. Anderson, John D. *Introduction to Flight*. McGraw-Hill Education, 2016.

2. Armstrong, Neil. *First Man: The Life of Neil A. Armstrong*. Simon & Schuster, 2005.

3. Asimov, Isaac. *Understanding Physics*. Barnes & Noble, 1966.

4. Barnhart, David J., et al. *Spacecraft Systems Engineering*. Wiley, 2019.

5. Chaikin, Andrew. *A Man on the Moon: The Voyages of the Apollo Astronauts*. Penguin Books, 1994.

6. Chang-Díaz, Franklin R., and Erik Seedhouse. *To Mars and Beyond, Fast!* Springer, 2017.

7. Chirikjian, Gregory S. *Engineering Mathematics for Applied Physics*. CRC Press, 2016.

8. Covey, Stephen R. *The 7 Habits of Highly Effective People*. Free Press, 1989.

9. Cruddas, Sarah, and Lucy Hawking. *Space Explorers: 25 Extraordinary Stories of Space Exploration*. Wide Eyed Editions, 2019.

10. Dyson, Freeman J. *Imagined Worlds*. Harvard University Press, 1998.

11. Emme, Eugene M. *Aeronautics and Astronautics: An American Chronology of Science and Technology in the Exploration of Space, 1915-1960*. NASA, 1961.

12. Fisher, Roger. *Getting to Yes: Negotiating Agreement Without Giving In*. Penguin Books, 1981.

13. Garber, Stephen J. *Looking Backward, Looking Forward: Forty Years of U.S. Human Spaceflight Symposium*. NASA, 2002.

14. Gladwell, Malcolm. *Outliers: The Story of Success*. Little, Brown and Company, 2008.

15. Godwin, Robert. *Apollo 11: The NASA Mission Reports*. Apogee Books, 1999.

16. Hargrove, James L. *Engineering Principles in Everyday Life for Non-Engineers*. Wiley, 2010.

17. Hawking, Stephen. *A Brief History of Time*. Bantam Books, 1988.

18. Johnson, Steven. *Where Good Ideas Come From: The Natural History of Innovation*. Riverhead Books, 2010.

19. Kelly, Scott. *Endurance: A Year in Space, A Lifetime of Discovery*. Alfred A. Knopf, 2017.

20. Koppes, Clayton R., and Gregory D. Black. *Hollywood Goes to War: How Politics, Profits and Propaganda Shaped World War II Movies*. University of California Press, 1990.

21. Krauss, Lawrence M. *The Physics of Star Trek*. Basic Books, 1995.

22. Krugman, Paul. *The Return of Depression Economics and the Crisis of 2008*. W.W. Norton & Company, 2009.

23. Kaku, Michio. *Physics of the Future: How Science Will Shape Human Destiny and Our Daily Lives by the Year 2100*. Doubleday, 2011.

24. Launius, Roger D. *Apollo's Legacy: Perspectives on the Moon Landings*. Smithsonian Books, 2019.

25. Lemay, John G. *Rocket Propulsion Elements*. Wiley, 2002.

26. McCurdy, Howard E. *Space and the American Imagination*. Smithsonian Institution Press, 1997.

27. McInnis, Raymond E. *Engineering Your Future: A Project-Based Introduction to Engineering*. National Academies Press, 2013.

28. McKee, Robert. *Story: Substance, Structure, Style and the Principles of Screenwriting*. ReganBooks, 1997.

29. Musk, Elon. *Elon Musk: Tesla, SpaceX, and the Quest for a Fantastic Future*. HarperCollins, 2015.

30. NASA. *NASA Systems Engineering Handbook*. NASA, 2007.

31. Nye, Bill. *Unstoppable: Harnessing Science to Change the World*. St. Martin's Press, 2015.

32. O'Leary, Michael. *Rocket and Spacecraft Propulsion: Principles, Practice and New Developments*. Springer, 2009.

33. Ramo, Simon. *The Business of Science: Winning and Losing in the High-Tech Age*. Hill and Wang, 1988.

34. Reich, Robert B. *The Work of Nations: Preparing Ourselves for 21st Century Capitalism*. Alfred A. Knopf, 1991.

35. Robinson, Kim Stanley. *Red Mars*. Bantam Books, 1992.

36. Sagan, Carl. *Cosmos*. Random House, 1980.

37. Schultz, Richard. *The Physics of Space Exploration*. University Press of America, 2008.

38. Scott, David Meerman. *Marketing the Moon: The Selling of the Apollo Lunar Program*. MIT Press, 2014.

39. Shultz, Theodore W. *Investment in Human Capital: The Role of Education and of Research*. Free Press, 1971.

40. Stine, G. Harry. *Handbook of Model Rocketry*. NAR, 2004.

41. Stoker, Carol R. *Mars: Prospective Energy and Material Resources*. Springer, 2007.

42. Stone, Richard. *Smart Cities: Big Data, Civic Hackers, and the Quest for a New Utopia*. W.W. Norton & Company, 2013.

43. Tharp, Twyla. *The Creative Habit: Learn It and Use It for Life*. Simon & Schuster, 2003.

44. Tyson, Neil deGrasse. *Astrophysics for People in a Hurry*. W.W. Norton & Company, 2017.

45. Von Braun, Wernher. *The Mars Project*. University of Illinois Press, 1991.

46. Waldrop, M. Mitchell. *Complexity: The Emerging Science at the Edge of Order and Chaos*. Simon & Schuster, 1992.

47. Wallace, David Rains. *Neptune's Ark: From Ichthyosaurs to Orcas*. University of California Press, 2007.

48. Wells, H.G. *The War of the Worlds*. William Heinemann, 1898.

49. Whalen, David J. *The Rise and Fall of COMSAT: Technology, Business, and Government in Satellite Communications*. Palgrave Macmillan, 2014.

50. Zubrin, Robert. *The Case for Mars: The Plan to Settle the Red Planet and Why We Must*. Free Press, 2011.

www.ingramcontent.com/pod-product-compliance
Lightning Source LLC
LaVergne TN
LVHW021135160826
845679LV00023B/1917

* 9 7 9 8 8 9 4 4 6 7 8 1 8 *